The Sacred History of Britain

Also by Martin Palmer

The Book of Chuang Tzu
I Ching: the Shamanic Oracle
Lao Tzu's Tao Te Ching
Kuan Yin: Myths and Revelations of the Chinese Goddess of Compassion
Essential Chinese Mythology
Living Christianity
Sacred Britain
Travels Through Sacred China
Sacred Gardens
The Jesus Sutras

Martin Palmer

The Sacred History of Britain

Landscape, myth and power:
The forces that have shaped
Britain's spirituality

PIATKUS

Copyright © 2002 by Martin Palmer

First published in 2002 by
Judy Piatkus (Publishers) Limited
5 Windmill Street
London W1T 2JA
e-mail: info@piatkus.co.uk

The moral rights of the author have been asserted

A catalogue record for this book is available from the British Library

ISBN 0–7499–2199–4

Designed by Paul Saunders

Data manipulation by Phoenix Photosetting, Chatham, Kent
Printed and bound in Great Britain by
Mackays of Chatham, Chatham, Kent

CONTENTS

This book is dedicated with love and in honour of my father Derek Palmer, 1928–2002, priest, pilgrim and guide. You taught me what was truly sacred and showed us all what it means to live life faithfully. We miss you.

ACKNOWLEDGEMENTS

When I started to think about writing this book I realised I needed a lot of advice and probably some good severe criticism. So I invited a fascinatingly diverse group of people to work with me as a working group and as advisors. This group has read through many drafts; met occasionally for lengthy discussions; allowed me to visit them individually at times for deeper discussion and have ensured that I have had to justify everything I have tried to say. The best elements of this book are the results of their advice: the errors are entirely my responsibility! So a great big thank you to: Margaret Anderson, my former History teacher, for giving me roughly 8/10 for this essay despite the terrible spelling; Gill Bailey, editor, who rather touchingly always seemed to believe I really was about to finish; Gena Darwent, my colleague at ICOREC who undertook all the organising of this group; Sheila Hogbin, lecturer in History who actually seemed to enjoy all this; Professor Ronald Hutton, whose willingness to sit and wander through some 30,000 years of history was a tremendous gift; Clair Jacquiss, who brought her BBC producer's eye to bear upon this project; Eric Maddern, historic storyteller par excellence, whose feeling for narrative reminded me to keep in mind the story in history; Gordon McClennan, whose walks through ancient landscapes made them leap alive and finally, Jay Ramsay, wordsmith, poet and friend who urged me on.

My thanks also to my colleagues at ICOREC, especially Jennie Dunn who spent days working on the text and who could remember which version we were dealing with; to John Smith who heads the Sacred Land project and whose insights were invaluable. To my dear friends at Piatkus who undertook the task of licking this into shape, especially Sandra Rigby and Alan Brooke, a big thank you.

Finally to three people who through their love, care and interest have helped me not just on this book but in so many ways. To my son James Palmer a huge thank you for working on the editorial rewritings, research and for bringing his own at times wickedly quirky view of history to bear. To my mother Cecile Palmer who in the depth of mourning my father and her husband of fifty years, read through the penultimate draft but also whose storytelling since I was a child inspired a love of history in me, thank you.

In the course of writing this book I met and fell in love with Victoria Finlay who has become my companion on the journey through time and place that is our lives. She has taught me to see new worlds with fresh eyes in ways I never imagined possible. Thank you for turning my life upside down.

CHAPTER ONE

THE QUEST FOR
THE SACRED

CHILDHOOD PILGRIMAGES

I HAVE BEEN MAKING PILGRIMAGES through sacred Britain ever since I was a child. I was not always aware that this was what I was doing, but I realise that in retrospect I was a pilgrim by the time I was eleven.

I grew up on a working-class council housing estate on the outskirts of the great and ancient city of Bristol. There was nothing great or ancient about our housing estate, indeed there was nothing older than me on the whole estate – rather romantically called Hartcliffe, but with neither harts nor cliffs nearby – with the exception of one mighty oak which grew near our house. Until the early 1950s this area had been green fields.

Rising up above Hartcliffe, like a tidal wave frozen in mid-air, is the mass of Dundry Hill. Half in the city of Bristol and half in the county of Somerset, it stands sentinel over the sprawl of the city, which laps up to it but not over it. To me it was a boundary over which I could cross and find a different world.

My pilgrimage route took me through time and across the distances that an eleven-year-old could walk in a day. Admittedly this also relied upon either a bus back or an obliging, though occasionally annoyed, father coming to pick me up. It took me uphill, down into the valley on the other side of Dundry and then uphill again to cross the Mendips to the wonderful city of Wells in Somerset.

Climbing up Dundry Hill and avoiding the areas where gangs hung out, I would go first to the Wansdyke. This long, low ditch and embankment runs along the top of Dundry Hill and was built by Anglo-Saxons as a defensive ditch or trade barrier some time in the eighth century AD. The Wansdyke led me to Maes Knoll Tump. The name 'Maes' gives a hint of its antiquity, for it is a Celtic or British name dating from the time of the Romans and meaning 'open field'. The Tump itself is a huge mound that sits in the middle of an Iron Age fort. Local legend held that it was the burial mound of all those British defenders of the hill who had died when the Romans attacked in *c.* AD 46–7, capturing 'towns' across southern Britain. To us children it was a place of mad Druids, heroic warriors and wonderful tumbles down its very steep slopes.

From the Tump it was downhill to Stanton Drew in Somerset. Here I explored the lovely but simple old church, rather heavily restored by the Victorians. I also wandered amongst the stones of the Stanton Drew stone circles, wondering at their meaning and their abiding power to fascinate.

Then it was on, past a modern wonder – the reservoir lake of Chew Magna – where, when the summer was especially dry, the remains of the old village drowned by the lake in the 1950s would reappear like some huge Excalibur rising from its centre.

From the lake it was up the steep hill on to the Mendips, where I knew the Romans had mined lead, and where ancient roadways, many much older than the Romans, can still be traced. Here I would stroll past tiny hamlets and, if feeling brave, would cut across the peat bogs where, if I was not careful, I could find myself sharing a tussock of grass with an adder. Amazing how fast you can move when you need to.

The next pilgrimage site was the village of Priddy. Its beautiful, organic church still delights me. I call it organic because it seems to emerge from the very land and rocks upon which it stands like a natural growth, encouraged by generations of local farming families. From the church one is led to an astonishing ancient landscape that Priddy manages to keep secret. Here is one of the most dramatically placed of all long barrows (ancient earth-built grave-mounds) a great ancestor shrine raised over 5,000 years ago; here too are round barrows in such number that it is almost impossible to count them. This is where our ancestors buried those whom they thought were worthy of special devotion some 3,000 years or more ago.

Priddy has two further treasures to share. First of all is Ebbor Gorge. Smaller and less well known than the nearby Cheddar or Wookey Gorges, this ancient cave system was home to Palaeolithic clans who hunted here perhaps 28,000 years ago. Finally, there are the Priddy Circles: four vast, earth-rampart circles, each of them over 150 metres (500 feet) across, placed side by side. Each has a now barely discernible ditch and earthen wall, forming what is technically known as a henge. As with so many sacred sites of the henge period – roughly 4,000 to 5,000 years ago – the ditch is on the inside with the wall on the outside, so it appears that they were not created for defence. Were they some vast sacred site? Why were there four of them? To this day the faded, almost invisible Priddy Circles maintain their mystery. I would wander here as a child full of wonder and amazement, lost in echoes of a past so distant than only the faintest of hints of what might have happened could be discerned.

From the great unknown I descended into Wells, to the greatest expression of the known – my own Christian faith – that I know in Britain. Wells Cathedral is for me the most magnificent and the most homely of all our great cathedrals. I love the way that the astonishing west front, a great celebration of the stories of the Christian faith, rises up from gentle lawns; the flowing motion of the church throughout from west front to east window, broken by the very strange strainer arches, which I am told should have pushed the cathedral apart hundreds of years ago but have instead held it up; the worn steps to the chapter house, which through their curves created by countless footfalls through time tell of the business of this great place; and the way that the last great buttress, which props up the east wall, ends in a garden and has roses growing up it.

This was the end of my pilgrimage. Here I stood and drew strength in ways both similar and different from the way I drew strength from the stone circles, the long barrows and the henges. I needed to do this for the simple reason that where I lived, the sacred, religion and faith were not taken very seriously. In the 1950s and 1960s, religion was unfashionable; secularism seemed dominant. The interest in 'spiritual' issues was yet to come. To be religious or spiritual or interested in the sacred was to be seen as being a bit odd, or weird. Religion or the sacred were useful for rites of passage and at times of crises, but not for everyday life. On our housing estate we had three churches: Anglican, Methodist and Catholic. However, I would guess that no more than five per cent of the population went to church.

OLD QUESTIONS

In an atmosphere of agnosticism, the desire to explore whether the material world was just one world amongst many and to ask why life existed or what happened after death was to ask questions few wished to explore. But every site I visited en route to Wells was a testimony to me that the religious quest, the search for the sacred, was valid and had been valid in this land since time immemorial. As I stood beside the long barrow or climbed up the embankment of the great henges of Priddy or wandered amongst the overgrown stones of Stanton Drew, these were, and indeed still are, as sacred to me as my own church or the cathedral at Wells. For they told me that for thousands of years people had sought to wrestle meaning from the very land and from death; had sought to create special places where they could gather to celebrate or mourn; had taken what was given and had made something new. When I touched the worn stones of a stone circle, stood on an Iron Age burial mound on Dundry Hill or wondered about what the hunters who lived in Ebbor Gorge thought, I found myself held in a stream of awareness that this world is not all that there is, but that there is a sacred dimension to life. What is more the struggle to make sense of it and thus of life itself is one that my ancestors have undertaken for untold millennia. These great sites told me I was not alone, and nor was my quest one that I needed to take alone.

At Wells, I found my faith honoured and elevated. As I strolled around the cathedral that is one of the great Christian buildings in the world, surpassed in my opinion only by Hagia Sophia in Istanbul, I would come upon the tombs of bishops dating from 500 or 600 years ago, who were also Chancellors of England or Lord Chamberlains, and friends and colleagues of the kings and queens. At one level Wells Cathedral could not be more different than my experience of St

Andrew's Church of England church on Hartcliffe. That church is a simple 1950s building of virtually no architectural interest whatsoever, with no tombs of the mighty and no antiquity. The church and its facilities for local people, such as a youth club and coffee bar, had been regularly vandalised, robbed and mocked. But in another way it was not so very different from Wells; here in this church, Sunday after Sunday, a small but faithful group gathered. Here came those who had nowhere else to turn when in trouble, knowing they would be accepted, even those who did not regularly attend church.

I recall the church being full on the day of the Aberfan disaster in 1966, when a coal slag heap in South Wales, swollen by rain, poured down in a deadly slurry and buried alive over a hundred young children in their primary school. There were no answers that day, but there was a need to come together and to ask why. It was in this church that ordinary people, for whom being a Christian brought no status, came to celebrate marriages and births and to mourn those who had died. It was in the journey between this simple church and the glories of Wells, and through these experiences of the sacred down through time, that my love and fascination for history, religion, sacred places and the experience of faith were kindled. This book is one outcome of the exploration and journey that I am still making.

Many years later I had the great joy of making a special Sunday morning service for BBC Radio 4 with a pagan colleague and friend, Gordon MacClennan. Together we explored the sacred in the landscape of the Dorset Cursus and Knowlton Henges. Christian and pagan, we walked that land and talked about what it meant to us, sharing prayers, readings, insights and even silence together. For me, it was as natural as conducting a service in a church, for this landscape of burial mounds and sacred circles is a part of my sacred heritage, like the pilgrimage route of my childhood. In many ways the ancient sacred landscape has made me a Christian as much as have the Gospels or the traditions of the Church itself. But walking it with Gordon made me aware of currents of thought, explorations and ideas that made me reflect deeply. To us the environment and the sense of the sacred and time that it conveyed posed great issues and questions; we valued each other's insights in our attempts to find answers or responses, but were left more with a sense of the validity of our questions than with any firm answers.

We had expected that this service, broadcast when normally an act of Christian worship takes place, would provoke major criticism and hundreds of letters of protest. It turned out to be quite the reverse. We had over 500 letters, from Christians, pagans and people of no fixed belief, all of whom, save three, spoke of how the service had helped the writers reconnect to the land, to the sacred and to the past and had given them hope for the future.

THE IMPORTANCE OF THE SACRED

It is experiences such as this that have prompted me to write this book. Across Britain can be found remains, hints and suggestions of different ways of understanding the sacred. Our very landscape has been formed by these understandings and relationships. The forces of history have been shaped not only by burial mounds and churches but also by the shapes of fields and the layouts of villages, towns and cities, and even the creation of national parks and motorway routes. And one of the greatest, oldest, most powerful and yet most ignored and neglected today is the force of the sacred within and upon history.

Until recent decades, no major action was undertaken in Britain except by people who believed that God, the gods, the ancestors, or whoever, was guiding their actions, or that their actions were for the greater glory of whatever power they believed in. It is impossible to understand why people acted as they did unless you understand the vision and relationship to the sacred that underpins it. Yet we seem to have lost the ability to read not just our history but also our landscape as adventures in the sacred. I think we are also frightened of reconnecting with the sacred, for a host of different reasons. It has become embarrassing and we do not quite know what to do with it. It is my belief, though, that the sacred is one of the most powerful forces in history; that the roots of our troubles and opportunities today lie in the sacred past, and that to understand ourselves, we need to draw near to, and perhaps even touch this force in certain places, a force which has carried us to where we stand today, whether we acknowledge it or not.

This book, therefore, is a journey into the sacred history of Britain. As we make this journey, we will discover that the demise of formal religion, today manifested by our currently emptying churches, mosques, temples, synagogues and shrines, is not a new phenomenon. We have been this way before, a number of times, indeed at least four times in the last 5,000 years. Sacred history illuminates the crises of dying faiths, environments, and ways of life that we face today. In the very shape of the landscape, in the stories bequeathed us, and the ruins that such crises have left us, the past shows that these problems have been confronted before and that we have survived by radically rethinking the nature of our relationship with the sacred and thus with creation.

A sacred history is not just the story of the physical manifestations of a faith in a different place, whether Britain, China, Israel/Palestine or India, for example. It is telling history through the psychological, mythic, narrative, determinative and value perspective of the sense of the sacred, usually but not exclusively manifested through religion, which coloured and gave meaning to almost every action that shaped what we now call 'history'. Given that for around 100 years the notion that economics determined history was held to be true, it is perhaps time to point out that the reductionist view of history which that sad perspective represented needs to be broadened to remind people that life is actually more than just money. A sacred history is one way of reminding ourselves that we cannot be reduced to simplistic formulas and that the reasons for and experience of life are multifaceted, however complicated this might make the past.

We will discover that the rise of secularism as a force that separates the sacred from the ordinary has its roots in the very system that built the great cathedrals 1,000 years ago. We will find that the need for community and a place to share the joys and tribulations of life underlies the long barrow of some 6,000 years ago as much as it does the church on my housing estate. Nor is the issue of the environment, and the crisis that confronts us with changes beyond our compre-hension, unique to the age in which we live. Indeed, every time a religion died or changed radically in Britain in the last 5,000 years, it was at least in part because we had abused the natural environment. It is also the case that much of the compassionate structure of our culture has been built by faith, honouring the sacred within all. In this way schools and hospitals are as much an expression of the sacred as the stone circle or the church – indeed, perhaps more so.

Economics is often seen as the determining force of history, but human relationships, shaped by understanding our place in the world and cosmos, have always had a more powerful influence than anything else and continue to do so to this day. The relationship between humanity and our world is ultimately about the sacred. It is religious faith, of whatever kind, that has given us a story within which we can find meaning and significance for our reason for being, our community and our place not only in history but also within an otherwise meaningless universe which threatens to crush us by its sheer infinity.

Since my early pilgrimages as an eleven-year-old through the sacred landscape and history of my own land, I have had the great fortune to travel professionally on similar explorations of other sacred landscapes and histories from China to Mexico, from Canada to India and many places in between. In my roles as Director of the International Consultancy on Religion, Education and Culture and more recently as Secretary General of the Alliance of Religions and Conservation, I have been the guest of many different faith communities in almost fifty countries around the world. I have walked pilgrimage routes with Taoist monks in China, helped Hindu high priests restore sacred forests in India, advised on Islamic structures for environmental restoration in Indonesia and so on.

In former communist Mongolia my colleagues and I work with the Buddhist communities in recreating sacred protected zones ensuring the survival of some of the world's most endangered species and habitats. The reason we do this is that wherever religion is found it constitutes the longest surviving human institution of all. The sacred has helped protect more of the world's endangered landscapes than any government scheme, such as the creation of national parks, has ever done – and the sacred has been doing this for centuries or even millennia. For example, the Shinto sacred forest of Ise, Japan, has a record of sustainable management by the priests of the Grand Shrines that stretches back unbroken to 4 BC; the churchyards of Britain – 6,000 of which are run as mini eco-systems by the churches and local communities – contain more endangered species of plant, insect, and animal than the National Park of the Peak District.

THE MEANING OF THE SACRED

Wherever you are in the world, if you scratch below the surface you will find the sacred all around you. But what do I mean by the sacred? Let me start by defining sacred places.

The first kind of sacred place is one where the forces of nature combine in such dramatic or wondrous combinations as to make even the most jaded person stop and stare. Such places are, to put it poetically, where the veil between heaven and earth is gossamer thin. Here the sacred breaks through into the natural in ways that defy words. These tend to be immensely personal places, where associations, feelings and emotions combine with the actual view or scenery in ways which only make sense within the personal experience of whoever is apprehending them, whether an individual, a pair of lovers, a family or anyone else. For me the Quantock hills in Somerset and the mountains at dusk around Ulaan Baator, Mongolia are such personal sacred places.

The second kind of sacred place is one that has been touched by a great life, a wonderful event or a tragedy, a place where you can touch history and the personality that made history there. For me such a place is somewhere such as St Ninian's cave, Whithorn, Dumfries and Galloway in Scotland, which has a holiness because of its association with St Ninian that is fused with the splendour of the natural environment. I also feel it at the cave of Chang Tao Ling on Qingqing Shan Mountain in Sichuan province, China, where the founder of Taoism received his vision in the second century AD.

I have also felt the sacred at Masada in Israel, where Jewish defenders committed mass suicide rather than fall into the hands of the Romans; I have felt it at Clifford's Tower in York, where the Jews in the twelfth century committed mass suicide rather than fall into the hands of the English mob, and I feel it every time I look at a First World War memorial in some little village.

Finally, in the incomparable words of T.S. Eliot, there are those places that are 'Where prayer has been valid'. Many of these are great and ordinary places that we have erected, created, loved, forgotten, ignored and occasionally rediscovered over time: stone circles, burial mounds, churches, temples, synagogues and chapels that cover this land. Places unbounded by walls have also become places where prayer has been valid. Some are very temporary, such as the wayside 'shrines' of flowers where a young person died in a road accident. Most of these places will be deeply personal and intensely local. In the whole of Bristol where I grew up, there are many fine churches but only two have places where I feel this special kind of sacred aura: the Lady Chapel in St Andrew's, Hartcliffe, and a small side chapel in Bristol

Cathedral. Elsewhere I have found this most especially at the seventh-century Christian site of Da Qin in China and at Iona in Scotland. You too will have such places; some may be formal places of worship; others may be ancient places or just a special garden or spot where you are confronted by the need for prayer.

The fact is that we can create this third category of sacred place wherever we wish, and ultimately the sacred pervades all. In special places all we do is recognise it and call it forth by name. To anyone who believes in a loving creator, the entire world is sacred; for some, the notion of such a creator may not be theirs, but nevertheless, a sense of a purpose, a meaning greater than just the sum total of all that exists, is one that most people experience and can partially identify with. We should always remember that such places are but signposts to the sacred nature of all life.

There is much more to the sacred than just place, however. Worldwide, for the last 6,000 years at least, the main force motivating human activity, building, thinking and planning has been awareness of the sacred. Sacred forces have largely created the landscapes of China, India, Syria, Egypt, El Salvador, indeed anywhere you can name. Pilgrimage routes, sacred cities, shrines, tombs, taboo areas, sacred mountains, holy rivers, divine forests dedicated to deities, gardens created for the glory of temples and churches, farms run by religious orders of one faith or another are all manifestations of the quest to grapple with, encounter and even contain the sacred. However, it is one of the saddest inheritances of secularism that this awareness of the sacred has frequently been ignored, ridiculed or lost.

Every land has its own sacred history and each is both similar and yet also distinctive. Britain is no more sacred than anywhere else. It is also no less sacred than the Holy Land of the Middle East or the sacred rivers of India. There is much in our sacred history that holds true for almost every other land. Yet there are also distinctive elements that have shaped this land and its peoples in ways that have not shaped other lands and peoples. For example, the British have a strange aversion to sacred art. We underwent the longest known period of an absence of religious activity in any recorded culture. We had a cultural revolution in the sixteenth century, which nearly destroyed us, and yet from which we built a vision of the sacred which took us to the ends of the world. From our understanding of the sacred came our concepts of the welfare state and of modern democracy, both of which have had immense impacts upon the rest of the world.

The sacred dies when it becomes locked into unchanging tradition. It dies when the environment it has sought to create and sustain breaks down. It dies when the reason for its being has been lost through corruption, abuse or ignorance. It dies when it is privatised and seen as a purely individual activity. Yet the sacred is also the main drive for change. It is the vision that fires the imagination and takes us beyond the here and now to ask why and where are we going. It is the force that makes ordinary individuals risk all to uphold a truth or to defend those weaker than themselves. It can become the most reactionary force and it can be the only thing to break such forces. Ultimately the sacred is incredibly dangerous for it can make people either the greatest of saints, or the most terrible and righteous tyrants.

What we cannot do is ignore the sacred. It is the force that has shaped our land, our history and our humanity. And it is just possible that it can put us in touch with truths so vast that all we ever see is one corner of the edge of its glory; that it shows us that there may be, as Hamlet says to Horatio: 'More things in heaven and earth, Horatio, than are dreamt of in your philosophy.' That is the excitement and risk of seeking to encounter the sacred.

CHAPTER TWO

IN THE BEGINNING

NO WORDS, NO SACRED BOOKS have come down to us from the earliest peoples of Britain. I must ask you instead to come with me and to walk the very land to catch a glimpse of what life, what the sacred might have meant to them. We have to hunt for clues, hints literally scattered across and within the landscape. The origins of the sacred existed long before the first written histories and the first constructions of specifically sacred sites. Perhaps the first stirrings of the human consciousness of the sacred or response to the sacred in Europe can be seen in the amazing art in France and Spain of the Palaeolithic period (c. 38,000 to 8000 BC), where animals and people were painted in ochre colours on cave walls with incredible vitality. To imagine the role of the sacred in Britain during this period, however, we have to work from tiny scraps of evidence, as we have virtually no art from that time, and certainly nothing to compare with the astonishing cave art of France and Spain. All we have at the moment are just a few fragments of carved work, but not a single painting.

Let us look at those fragments. In one of the most charged of sacred landscapes, the hills of the Peak District in Derbyshire, three pieces of prehistoric art have been found. Three bone carvings from a cave in the Cresswell Crags indicate how little British art has changed since those ancient days. The first is a beautiful, almost mystic carving of a horse's head on a deer's rib. The second piece is engraved with a similarly fine picture of a reindeer, which was probably the main animal hunted by the early people who lived in those caves. The third carving is of a little man with a huge penis. From the sublime to the pornographic; from animals to naughty pictures. Not much appears to have changed in British tastes over the millennia. This little statue of a man is usually described as a deity or a fertility symbol. Until we come down to 'history' – that is when we have written records to refer to – archaeologists tend to assume that any depiction of naked people or bits of genitalia, male or female, must be sacred. Well, possibly. It is also just as likely to be a joke – a piece of adolescent fun on a boring evening in at the cave with the family. For if art is one of the great revolutions of ideas, a conceptual revolution along the lines of making tools, both of which are traditionally described as gifts of the deities, then with the creation of art probably came humour and fun. A society that can afford the time for art can probably afford the time for games and enjoyment, as well as ritual and 'high art'. The reason for thinking that the depiction of genitalia is not necessarily sacred is really quite simple: people love naughty bits! Such art could be compared with the craze for half-naked women from classical mythology that the most respectable of English nineteenth-century gentry had on the walls of their homes. They did not believe these deities existed but they liked a bit of classy breast. For these reasons, I am very cautious about assuming that naked people or 'naughty bits' are automatically sacred. Fun, humour and sex are probably stronger reasons for their creation than religion. I find this idea rather embarrasses archaeologists.

For example, take the case of Roman Samian ware. This famous Gaulish red-glazed pottery was the first choice of the discerning Roman family everywhere in the Roman Empire for nearly 500 years. Visit any museum with a Roman collection and you will see examples of it; I have personally dug up bucket loads from sites all around the old Roman Empire. There are two volumes at the British Museum that record in detail with illustrations the main styles and designs. Volume one is of moderate size and contains all the non-pornographic designs. It is these that you will find proudly displayed in museums worldwide. Volume two, which is twice the size or more, contains all the pornographic designs. Why do we not find these on display?

In that cave in Derbyshire, the sacred found expression through the ability to depict the world through a new medium. Reality could now be captured, frozen, re-expressed and distorted. Perhaps the horse's head and the reindeer were good-luck charms for hunting or totem animals, or just beautiful and worthy of capturing in art. Likewise, the little man may have been made for ritual, charm or fun. For whatever reasons the carvings were made, they took reality and changed it for a purpose beyond mere existence, hunting or basic living. In them, perhaps, we witness the first expressions of the sacred in Britain; the first hint that our forebears were beginning to do more than just exist. They were beginning to make the world their own, to capture and redefine it through, amongst other things, art. This is what the notion of sacred does. Not all art is sacred, but the sacred and art both represent humanity's ability to create and transform reality.

A SIMPLE BURIAL: LIFE AND DEATH IN MICROCOSM

As with most prehistoric cultures, it is the treatment of the dead that gives us the best idea of what the sacred meant to them, though we have to remember that the lack of almost any evidence of the sacred in ordinary life doesn't mean it did not exist. It was probably much more important than the rituals of the dead – but buried things tend to survive better.

Although we know almost nothing of the culture of the people who inhabited Britain in earliest times, we can draw some conclusions or, at least, informed speculations, from the nature of the sites they built. At the extreme west end of the Gower Peninsula in Wales, in a magnificent landscape of cliffs washed by the waves, can be found what may be the first sacred site in Britain to date. In a cave known as Goat Hole Cavern, at Paviland, a young man was ritually buried, perhaps as long as 27,000 years ago, his body laid out as though sleeping, or perhaps in a foetal position. Red ochre (earth coloured by iron) was scattered over him.[1]

This is our earliest religious site, our earliest burial for what seems to be ritual reasons. It is simple and touching in its concern for the dead man and for the potential future that awaits him beyond death. Recent newspaper reports of the discovery of body-painting materials from over 40,000 years ago raises the possibility that the red ochre was body paint, perhaps painted on him in death as in life. Others see this red ochre as an attempt to make the body more lifelike – to appear more alive, even in death. Either way, in purely practical terms it is an unnecessary action, and therefore must be expressive of some concept beyond the simple disposal of a corpse. So too is the dramatic setting of the site. It seems possible that someone had buried this man with care, not just for this world, but also for the next.

This burial, then, was a deliberate and thoughtful act. It is the earliest evidence in Britain of some belief in the power of life to overcome death and of the possibility of some life beyond this one. This, the idea that life and death are significant in themselves, and that the dead needed to be buried in a way both respectful of death and expressive of life, is, in its way, a conceptual revolution as significant as art and one of the major expressions of the sacred.

THE MISSING OTHERWORLD

This burial is all the more interesting because it appears to be uncharacteristic of the age. The Palaeolithic period tends to be depicted in popular culture, and even in many scholarly works, as an intensely spiritual age, where humanity was constantly conscious of a spirit world beyond the physical one. But if we look at the great artwork of the Palaeolithic era, the marvellous cave paintings, there is no evidence of any belief in anything beyond the raw power of certain animals such as the bear and the antelope. For example, in the recently discovered Chauvet Cave in France, there is evidence that suggests that in the innermost cave there was a shrine of sorts to the cave bear, where offerings of worship or appeasement were made to this ferocious creature.[2] This echoes the later shamanic cult of the sacrificed bear, which is found throughout Siberia and China, the homelands of traditional shamanism, where very early songs (from 1500 to 400 BC) relating to the bear cult were recorded. In these earliest texts, the bear is portrayed in mythology and song as a fearsome entity whose role is to embody pure animal strength; he has no benign function.[3] The iconic use of the prehistoric bear here may be not as a divine symbol, but as a symbol of the raw power of nature. Its association with the spiritual world and forces could well be a later development from the late Palaeolithic or even the Mesolithic periods.

The only other possible religious aspect of Palaeolithic art is that symbolised by, for example, the figure rather imaginatively known as the Sorcerer, found on the walls of a cave in Lascaux, France. This appears to show a human figure dressed in deerskin and antlers, perhaps as part of some kind of ritual. However there is considerable debate about the nature of this figure and others like it, and, whatever else it may be, it is certainly another example of animal-power religion – supernatural but not divine; possibly the worship of the most vital food supply rather than anything more transcendent.[4]

Palaeolithic artwork depicts only this world. There is virtually no sense of a world beyond this one either physically, in terms of the stars, or mythically, in terms of imaginary beings.[5] It shows no creature that cannot be seen today, or whose remains cannot be found in a major museum. The focus of the artists was on the existing, living, physical world they inhabited – a world very much of this world, for almost no depictions of stars, let alone of the sun or moon, have been found amongst the thousands of depictions of animals, birds and human beings.

The Gower Peninsula burial, in its signs of a belief in a transcendent or other world, appears to be unusual for its age. And even this tomb is simple and understated, as if those who buried the young man were on the edge of something, but were not sure what it was. Substantial signs of a belief in a possible otherworldly existence are a long way off in the burial mounds of the Neolithic period, some 20,000 years or more later.

THE LEGENDS OF WAYLAND SMITHY

For anybody who has walked in the British countryside, the long barrows that hump out of the landscape are a familiar shape. One of the most impressive and well-known is that of Wayland Smithy, which lies on the Lambourn Downs in Oxfordshire. For centuries legends claimed that the God Wayland, a great smith, dwelt within the mound, and that any traveller passing by should leave his or her horse tied up overnight by it. They should also leave money – a silver sixpence was normal in the late nineteenth century.[6] In the morning, the horse would have a complete set of new horseshoes that lasted far longer than ordinary ones. Woe betide anyone who tried to see the god at work, however. Those who hid there overnight, hoping to learn the smith's secrets, were found the next day, dead or mad.

The approach to the site is dramatic. To reach the burial mound, you travel up from the ancient Vale of the White Horse, dominated by the skyline of the downs and the stunning and enigmatic chalk-carved white horse that snakes its way along one hillside. Once you reach the top of the downs, you begin to walk along one of the oldest roads in Britain, the Ridgeway, which has wound its way from Avebury to near Wallingford, snaking along the Marlborough and Lambourn Downs for perhaps as long as 6,000 to 7,000 years.

It is the rooks that first warn you that you are approaching something rather special. Wheeling out from the tall trees that dominate the landscape, they herald your approach to one of the most powerful of Neolithic burial sites in England. Its power stems not least from the sense of awe that the site has even today, which has long outlasted those who built and maintained it, some 5,500 years ago. Turning aside from the Ridgeway, you follow a short path through the fields to the tree-shrouded arena that is Wayland Smithy. From the path you can already see the huge stones that flank, or perhaps seal in, the tomb.

I always find as I enter the shade of the trees and come into the rough circle that they form around the mound that I am a little apprehensive. Quite why I cannot say, but it is as if I sense that this is a place in which you either should take off your shoes and walk carefully, for you walk on holy ground, or a place you should shun.

The long mound itself is very impressive, but even more so are the great stones that stand as sentinels before the small entrance into the tombs. Once past them, you enter a world that appears ridiculously small, given the scale of everything else about this site. The tombs themselves are a fraction of the overall long barrow. A damp, low corridor of just 9–12 metres (30–40 feet) leads to a chamber at the end, with a couple of side tombs lying just off it. Whatever this was, it was not a mass grave; only the very special seem to have been entombed here. When the site was fully excavated, bones of only a few score individuals were found, yet the tomb appears to have been in use for perhaps 1,000 years. The most likely theory is that the tombs housed the skulls and bones of the tribal ancestors of those who worked the hilltop fields and ran the small farms. They were buried here so that as ancestors, and those responsible for originally working and creating the land, they could watch over their descendants from their graves.

Perhaps the name Smithy and the legends about it are dim memories of a community that grew wealthy by servicing the needs of travellers along the Ridgeway. Certainly the rest of the name indicates how powerful and mysterious a site this has been down the millennia, for Wayland was a Scandinavian god who had nothing whatsoever to do with the people who built this mound. Wayland is the god of iron working, but the people who built Wayland Smithy some 5,500 years ago never saw iron in their lives. Stone was their raw material, especially flint, and to this day you can find examples of their flint working all around the Ridgeway. Wayland arrived after Christianity was well established; when there were already chapels in the valley and Christian pilgrims were walking the Ridgeway. Those who worshipped Wayland arrived in Britain at the earliest 4,000 years or more after the mound was built, either during the expansion of the Anglo-Saxons in the 450s onwards, or through the terrible Viking invasions that devastated England and Scotland from the 790s onwards. But it is likely that the worship of Wayland came to this site only around the time of Alfred the Great, when the Danes briefly overran the area – c. 870 onwards.

In Norse folk legends, as in many cultures, smiths were magical, and in some way in league with powerful, and sometimes sinister, forces. There are numerous stories associated with smiths, especially those who worked on the edges of forests. Although the legend of horseshoeing at Wayland Smithy probably dates from only the eighteenth century, or possibly a little earlier, it captures something of the special feel of this place. Of the site's original name we have no idea, and of its original inhabitants only fragments have been found. Wayland Smithy sums up many of the ways in which the sacred features of the land have been worked and reworked in Britain, adapted to fit each new time and culture, yet still based around the same feelings of awe, respect and fear.

From other well-named long barrows comes a fairly consistent picture of what the sacred meant to those who built them. These vast constructions – Wayland Smithy is 36 metres (120 feet) long – housed only a small number of skulls and bones, probably those of the most prominent former members of the community. At Belas Knap in Gloucestershire, for instance, archaeologists have reconstructed the cobbled courtyard in front of the long barrow. Historians such as Ronald Hutton and Aubrey Burl conjecture that the local people held their festivals, marriages and birth ceremonies in these areas.[7]

They speculate that at these barrows, for perhaps as long as 1,000 years, the farming and trading communities that had settled the uplands across Britain came to mourn and celebrate, joined by the skulls – the physical presence of their ancestors. Maybe they took out the skulls on special occasions, rather as great-granny's tea service is used in certain families for major occasions today; the skulls were certainly separated from the rest of the bones, and show signs of having been frequently moved. If so, then there seems to have been a rather friendly relationship with the ancestors. They were, literally, guests at the feast.

THE MESOLITHIC ECO-CRISIS

To understand why farming ancestors who had created the very means and land for agriculture would have been the focus of such devotion, we need to step back in time to the virtually forgotten and neglected time before the New Stone Age – the Neolithic age. In between the Palaeolithic era and the burial mounds of the Neolithic era some 5,000 to 6,000 years ago, and crucial to an understanding of the role of the sacred in Neolithic Britain, lies the almost always forgotten Mesolithic era, roughly between 10,000 and 5000 BC.

The Mesolithic period produced no great artwork. Indeed, in a way it produced retrogressive art of a quality far lower than that of the Palaeolithic. It saw none of the great explosion of agriculture and building that is the hallmark of the Neolithic age. The Mesolithic peoples are largely notable for what they did not do, achieve or create. If there was a sense of the sacred, we have no sense of it during this strange era. It seems, though, that these people were dangerously irresponsible in their relationship with the natural world. As the last great Ice Age ended around 8000 BC, humans began to hunt the burgeoning wildlife to an extent far above what was needed for simple survival; almost, it seems, revelling in their power to destroy. Worldwide, from around 10,000 BC onwards we see the loss of major species after major species. In Australia, for example, all the giant mammals were wiped out during this period, while evidence of over-hunting has come from a giant elk's bones found in Yorkshire which show that this one animal had been hunted – unsuccessfully on at least two occasions – a number of times. Indeed the species died out soon after, hunted to extinction.[8] By 7000 BC, the effects had come back to haunt the peoples of the Mesolithic times, and with many of the species they had relied upon for food now extinct, such as the Irish elk, the woolly mammoth, and the woolly rhinoceros, the human population declined steeply.

It looks as if the Mesolithic peoples, then, were responsible for the first humanly created ecological crisis. It is not impossible that the first religion of which we have clear evidence in Britain – that of the builders of the long barrows in the Neolithic era that followed – arose at least in part as a response to irresponsible overuse of the natural environment. The new religions were clearly connected with agriculture, which was probably developed in the so-called 'Fertile Crescent' of the Middle East and spread with astonishing speed from *c.* 6000 BC, reaching Britain *c.* 5000 BC. With it came the first clearly religious cultures, such as those of Egypt, China, Mesopotamia, and Britain. But why? Why should agriculture spread so fast, and why should it be associated with religion?

The answer, I believe, is that agriculture addressed a pressing need: it granted the ability to manage nature. This ability is described in so many cultures as a gift from the gods precisely because it seemed to show that there was a deity or deities who, if they were invoked and their instructions followed, could help humanity survive; deities who could make the world blossom, bring forth fruits and crops regularly, and provide domestic animals which never died out, making life just that little bit easier.

The first signs of a belief in any form of benign deity appear with the coming of the discovery of agriculture and a more fertile environment. The uncertain, dangerous world of the hunter was replaced with the more settled, reliable world of the farmer, and with this new security came a belief in a power that had provided it, a benign power. The discovery of agriculture was a gift from the gods, and they needed to be thanked for this gift. Here we see the possibility of a world of the dead and of spirits, of ancestors and gods who were seen as having protective powers and benign intentions; powers that make life in this world easier, just as agriculture did.

THE DEAD AND THE LIVING

In the West Kennet long barrow, the remains of over forty people were found in the five chambers, consisting primarily of skulls or fragments of skulls. Some have a family resemblance, which strengthens the idea of a community tomb for the ancestors. To see these as simply burial places, however, is to miss the point. After all, if you looked at an old church today, knowing nothing about Christianity, you could see it, surrounded by its burial ground, with its crypts underneath and its memorials on the walls, as nothing more than a huge monument to the dead. This, though, would be to completely miss the point of the Christian faith, which sees no break in community between the dead and the living; all are part of the communion of saints. As the Apostle's Creed says, Christ shall come 'to judge the quick [the living] and the dead' together. It is only in this context that the burial of the dead within the parish church makes sense. That this is also a site for baptisms, marriages, prayers, tears, joy, and silence would be invisible to any archaeologist who did not know of the Creed or the nature of Christian life and belief.

So it is with the long barrows, and indeed with all prehistoric sites. We have virtually nothing of the crucial bits of information about their theological, emotional, mythic and communal contexts which would enable us to really understand their world. We must remember, too, that these sites grew organically, just like a parish church. Think of the usual map by the door of an old church. It will probably show the outline of where the original small wooden Saxon church stood, which was then replaced by a single-aisled Norman church in stone, in turn enlarged by chantry chapels and side aisles during the medieval period. The tower was probably enlarged and rebuilt over a number of centuries, and then the whole place was 'restored' by earnest Victorians. The long barrows grew to their extraordinary sizes in a similar way. For example, Wayland Smithy had three distinct stages of development. First the land was cleared and sarsen-stone paving laid. Tombs were created from lined stones, and a rough circle of wooden posts was placed before these tombs, creating a courtyard of sorts. At some later date, perhaps as much as 500 years later, this was covered by a small mound, ditches were dug east and west of the mound, and a forecourt was created with flanking stones. Finally, perhaps 500 years or so later in around 3500 BC, the small mound was covered by a long barrow, enclosing the former sites and creating a new tomb site to the south of the old tomb.

The challenge for any history is to try and enter the minds of those who created it. For a sacred history, this becomes even more important. Yet, until the last few centuries BC, we have no written accounts to work from. All we have are the archaeological remains, such as the long barrows. These alone can offer us some insight into the thought patterns of the people for whom such places were important. This is why we need to understand the organic nature of their growth; the role of the dead; the communal aspects of the site. Yet we also have to acknowledge how little we know and will ever know unless one day the very stones talk to us of what they have seen and heard. Small and insufficient as they are, the faint hints of why the long barrows were built and how they expanded are amongst the only clues we have about this section of our sacred history.

All we know for certain is that these long barrows were both community centres and places of burial. The ancestors who had carved out the community's land from the forests, who had defended it and expanded it, seem to have been revered here, as we saw earlier. These communities were quite small: often you will find six or more long barrows within a short radius, each perhaps the focus of a hamlet or small farmstead community. Indeed, there are fifteen long barrows within a 5-kilometre (3-mile) radius of where, a millennium later, Stonehenge was to rise. It is of course possible that barrows in close proximity mark the same community moving from area to area, as it exhausted the land and had to farm on new, virgin territory.

We can say very little else about the long barrows. We have no artwork that gives us any clue as to what went on in these places. Indeed, astonishingly, in mainland Britain we have virtually no artwork at all for the whole of the Neolithic period (c. 5000 BC to c. 1800 BC), and certainly nothing to compare with the decorated stones in the long barrows of Ireland so close by. Just as we have only pitiful odds and ends from earlier periods, so we have only one or two very odd bits from the Neolithic era. It is possible that the people of that time worked in perishable materials, but, unless that was the case, from the lack of carvings on rocks or stone statues, we have to conclude that art was not a significant factor in British culture. In the rest of Europe, however, Neolithic artwork is plentiful. Should this alert us to a distinctive British issue? Perhaps there was a certain reticence in Britain about what the spiritual actually was? The absence of art seems to me not just an accident, or simply a fascinating oddity of British ancient culture: it is an issue which raises very interesting questions about the nature of the sacred as perceived in Britain throughout the Neolithic age.

It is customary for the relationship between the sacred and art to be treated in one of two ways: exuberantly, as in Christian, Hindu, or Taoist art, or sparingly – shunning the depiction of living creatures – as in strict Jewish or Islamic art. Nowhere else in the world during the Neolithic era do we find a culture apparently adopting this second stance. It is one of the most fascinating mysteries of sacred Britain. Was the lack of art a theological decision, comparable to the belief in Judaism and Islam that only the Creator can make such images? Was it a sign of a higher form of spirituality that rejected images as unworthy? Or did it signify ambivalence towards the sacred, perhaps even a degree of agnosticism? The struggle to understand this absence, so far barely commented upon by historians, could open whole new ways of understanding our prehistory, for this pattern continues right down to the last few centuries BC.

A CRISIS OF FAITH?

One day, some 5,000 years or more ago, Wayland Smithy was closed. Vast stones were dragged into place and the entrance sealed off. The skulls of the ancestors were left to rot, no longer invited to witness the rituals and events of their descendants' lives. What had happened?

Whatever it was, it happened all across the land, and at roughly the same time. The phenomenon can be found, for instance, at the equally spectacular but less atmospheric West Kennet Long Barrow, Wiltshire. This is a long barrow set on a rise with a clear and unrivalled view of the nearby Silbury Hill. Huge stones close its front and the entrances to the small tomb chambers. Some time around 3200 BC, this ancient long-used tomb was sealed shut and never opened again until the advent of archaeology. At Belas Knap in Gloucestershire the forecourt fell silent, the feasts ceased and the entrances were closed. Within virtually all the long barrows the skulls of the ancestors were shut behind walls of huge stones, as if a people had turned their backs on their ancestors and had no further use for them. Or was it something more disturbing than this, something more profound?

The long barrows were magnificent constructions, as we have seen. So why did they die? Why were these vast works of community effort deliberately closed, perhaps even deliberately buried under vast tonnes of chalk, wood and stone?

The answer probably lies in the humanly created ecological crisis that began to bite around 3200–3000 BC, as a result of early Neolithic agricultural practice. We know of the Neolithic deforestation and destruction of the ancient forests by fire from strong traces of ash and soot left in the ice cores of the Arctic. The transition of land from forest and grassland to intensive agriculture maintained over a long period put a previously unknown strain on delicate ecosystems. The historian Clive Ponting describes the effects of such overuse:

> The creation of artificial environments to grow food and the rise of communities not only concentrated the environmental impact of human activities but also meant that it was far more difficult for human societies to escape the consequences of their actions. In particularly sensitive ecosystems and where the impact of human modifications to the environment was particularly concentrated in its effects, the foundations of society could be so damaged as to cause its collapse.[9]

The possibility, which I raised earlier, that the succession of long barrows in the area indicates a community moving after exhausting their soil further suggests that the people were not very good at sustaining their land. Certainly it seems likely that as a consequence of overuse, perhaps combined with climate changes, by 3200 BC the upland ecology was breaking down, probably leading to crop failures and starvation. There is an interesting indication of the scale of the collapse that took place: pollen analysis shows that the number of elms fell dramatically at this time, indicating a major shift in the nature of the environment. It is clear that many settlements on the uplands, such as Windmill Hill in Wiltshire, were abandoned during this time, and there appears to have been a dip in the population. As the landscape changed dramatically, so old established patterns of settlement and agriculture collapsed or were abandoned.[10]

Let us imagine what this meant. For centuries, you and your ancestors have worshipped the skulls and spirits of your ancestors, who carved this land from the forest. You have assumed that if the correct rites and rituals are performed, the ancestors will continue to be benevolent and your land will be fertile, ensuring you a (for this era in history) secure and relatively comfortable life (the evidence from the tombs is that those buried there – who were relatively important and rich individuals – generally lived short, diseased lives).

Then the crops start failing, the climate changes, settlements can no longer survive where they are. Your people start dying, whole families are wiped out by starvation, and perhaps violence – there is evidence of increased warfare during this time at settlements such as Windmill Hill, and from the fortification of previously undefended areas. In other words the settled, workable world you thought you knew and had some control over is collapsing. So where does this leave your belief in your benign, benevolent ancestors, your gods, and your shrines?

It seems as though the ecological collapse brought about the first discernible crisis of faith in Britain. The people and the fields seemed to have lost their protection. So the question arose: have we failed the ancestors and gods? Or more profoundly disturbingly, have the ancestors and gods failed us? Either way, the old religion which, for 2,000 years or so, had sustained this way of life, appears to have been deliberately and firmly finished off. The skulls were put back inside the ancestral tomb centres for the last time. The tombs were sealed, once and for all. The dead were left to their shadows and dust, and the people turned their backs on their past, their faith, and their sacred places. They abandoned not just their settlements on the uplands, but even the tombs in the lowlands. The faith failed, and thus died.

The closing of the long barrows is the first evidence we have of the failure of a faith in Britain, the first part of a pattern that repeats itself many times. Britain had entered its first discernible period of agnosticism. Doubtless all sorts of beliefs arose, but it was to be some time before a new overarching belief system emerged to replace that of ancestor worship and the building of long barrows as community centres.

CHAPTER THREE

THE AGE OF THE STONES

STAPELEY HILL: A NEOLITHIC FACTORY

S TAPELEY HILL IS A GENTLE SLOPE, rising slowly and then rolling back down to the Shropshire countryside, softer than the crags and dark shadows of the hills and forests near it on the Welsh borders. To wander on the ancient pathway that runs along it is a delight. As you rise up, the view is one of unfolding hills, fields, trees and woods, with barely a house in sight. Walking this peaceful and quiet hill, you are in one of the most rural and unspoilt areas of Britain. I love to come here, to gather my thoughts and, as someone who spends much of my working life overseas, to ground myself in my own land, history, and mythology.

But the present-day quiet belies a past that was very different. A hundred years ago you would have been walking alongside miners and quarrymen, who were blasting the rocks or mining for lead. Huge wagons rumbled up and down the ancient trackway, and the raucous communities of miners and quarrymen often caused problems in the area. For example, they liked to set off gunpowder charges in the hollows of the ancient stones on the hill, particularly during festivals or at weddings, disturbing the peace of the neighbourhood, and blowing up by accident many of the standing stones. Go back to the Middle

Ages, and the stream of people crossing the hill and visiting the now almost completely destroyed holy well of Our Lady Mary was so great that it was said to rival the great pilgrims' way to Canterbury. Indeed, so considerable was the trade that the local priory at Chirbury had its own equipment for making pilgrim badges of St Mary's well. The badge mould was found during the nineteenth century in the churchyard of the old priory church, now the parish church of Chirbury, and can still be seen there on request.

The track over Stapeley Hill roughly 5,000 years ago was, in some ways, an equivalent to the M6 of today. This was no rural stroll, but a major trackway to one of the largest industrial sites of the late Neolithic era. Just beyond the southern end of Stapeley Hill lies the site of Cwm Mawr, where, from around 2500 BC onwards, beautiful stone axes were made from picrite, a dark grey-green stone that can be highly polished. These axes were traded extensively across Britain, and were probably never used as weapons or tools, but as symbols of wealth and authority. There are also signs that the hill itself was mined during this period.

Perhaps the fact that this was a busy area 4,500 years ago is why, on this modest but lovely hill, there are three stone circles. Right across Britain at this time, Neolithic communities, having moved from the unsustainable uplands, were clearing the lowlands of forest and scrub, burning down huge areas of forest to create farmlands, building stone walls for their fields, mining, trading and generally creating the basic layout of the landscape we see today: cultivated fields set between small clumps of trees, with scattered communities farming them. Britain housed a series of busy and developing cultures, which had an impact upon the environment. One of their most enduring and endearing traces is the creation of stone circles, such as the three on Stapeley Hill.

The most impressive today, Mitchell's Fold, lying right beside the ancient trackway, is very typical of most stone circles. Our image of stone circles is naturally shaped by the gigantic sites such as Avebury and Stonehenge, but the vast majority of them are like Mitchell's Fold: small, modest and made of local stone simply rolled, pushed and heaved into place. Mitchell's Fold has little magic about it. It seems a very practical and functional space. Indeed, so unawesome is it that in the Middle Ages the local farmer ploughed straight across it, seemingly oblivious to its existence.

Originally there may have been some thirty stones, none very large.

Today, less than half survive. The largest, quite impressive in its way, is 1.9 metres (6¼ feet) high, but the majority are less than a 1 metre (3 feet) high, with the smallest being 0.3 metres (1 foot). This entire stone circle could probably have been built in one long weekend by a gang of lads keen to display their strength. To my mind, more impressive and atmospheric is the almost square stone slab and desecrated burial mound some 70 metres (230 feet) to the south-east.

To the north-east of Mitchell's Fold, 2.5 kilometres (1½ miles) away, lies the second of Stapeley Hill's three stone circles. Hoarstones is a very mundane stone circle, being only small local stones placed in a far from regular circle. If Mitchell's Fold took a long weekend, Hoarstones could well have been made in a day and a half, if not less. Of the third circle, Whetstones, virtually nothing is left. It lies just under 0.75 kilometres (½ mile) east of Mitchell's Fold and, as I know to my own cost, can take a very long time to find. Whetstones was one of the most popular sites for the miners to blast, and by the 1860s it was reduced to the rather sad bits and pieces that you can just about find today.

SACRED OR SECULAR?

At Stapeley Hill the natural questions are: why would there need to be three stone circles in such a small area, and what did people use them for? The possible answers shed a considerable light on the hundreds of other stone circles in Britain.

At this time, Britain was criss-crossed by trade paths, of which many have survived to this day, such as the Ridgeway and the track across Stapeley Hill that Mitchell's Fold lies beside. Indeed, while one trackway still survives on Stapeley Hill today, it is likely that two to three routes converged on the area and that each stone circle lies on one of the routes. There was a veritable motorway system of tracks, which serviced the growing populations and demands of the communities in Britain, and even visitors trading from abroad. The stone circle lies beside the trackway over Stapeley Hill like a motorway service station, and perhaps a service station was what it was. It was designed to be close to the trackway in order that people would use it, just as churches were built beside market-places or alongside major roads.

Its use, though, I think is unlikely to have been purely religious, even though our normal view of stone circles is that they were religious sites. For over 200 years or so the host of romantics who rightly found such places both stirring and absorbing, have fed us with images of Druids making blood sacrifices at stone circles – or in these more eco-conscious days, Druids performing environmentally sensitive rituals to ensure the harmony of the world. These are dramatic images, usually with full moons or rising summer suns, strange headgears and glistening knives, and rituals aplenty.

Sadly, this is probably all nonsense, with perhaps one or two exceptions. To begin with, as we shall see in Chapter 4, the stone circles had been abandoned, shunned, and ignored for hundreds of years before any Druid appeared in Britain. Furthermore, it is highly unlikely that the vast majority of the stone circles ever witnessed anything more extraordinary than mundane rituals to do with rites of passage – 'baptisms', marriages, funerals – or trading agreements, with the odd party thrown in. As Ronald Hutton has observed, it is likely that the vast majority of 'sacred sites' such as henges and stone circles 'had various functions, so that some may not have been sacred sites at all'.[1] The assumption that they were all 'religious' is almost certainly wrong. Moreover, although people have gone to great lengths to attribute astronomical significance to them, the fact is that if you stand anywhere in a circle, you will naturally find something pointing towards the sun at the solstice, the moon at its fullest, the Dog Star, the place where Uncle George lives or anything else you want to see as the focal point of the site. No signs of astrological calculations or a calendrical system of belief have ever been found: no notations, no scratches and no notched sticks.

To see the stones as built in harmony with nature is, I believe, another mistake, for I see no evidence that the circles were for the celebration of natural power or beauty. Rather, their presence, often at crucial sites of the Neolithic exploitation of the natural environment – places where the forests had been stripped for wood or hills quarried for stone, like Stapeley Hill – seems to demonstrate that they were, perhaps, symbols of power, trade and industry. In this way they showed human dominance over nature, as if they are crying out 'Look at what we can do!' They were designed to stand out from the landscape, not to blend in with it. Five thousand years of British weather has made them appear 'natural' and mellow. The stone circles were permanent marks upon the landscape, as dramatic and blatant a mark by humanity as for example the towers of power stations are today: powerful symbols of a human society that appears in the scale and degree of its exploitation and reshaping of nature to be set apart from the rest of the natural world.

My belief is that whatever purpose the stone circles were created for, this activity took place inside them rather than being focused on some astrological phenomena, and that the people using the trackway over Stapeley Hill probably used the circle there as an agreed trading place, almost a shop front. As we know, few industries actually sell you their products on site, and the axe factory at Cwm Mawr is unlikely to have been an exception. The dust, noise, industrial secrets, protected piles of raw materials and so forth would have been good reasons for keeping traders at a distance. The three stone circles, each on a different trackway, were probably trading places for the factory – and were also as a result sacred places.

To appreciate this, think of traditional British market towns, such as Devizes, Wiltshire or Sandbach, Cheshire, where the heart of the town is the market-place. What were these market-places but open spaces (now surrounded by buildings), where people came to trade? You can still see the tradition of stones marking important communal sites. At Sandbach, for example, two magnificent Anglo-Saxon crosses, set up some time between the eighth and ninth centuries AD, dominate the market-place.

Most of the stone circles probably fulfilled a similar function to the medieval market-place: as marked spaces where deals could be struck in public, and where oaths and promises made were binding, witnessed both by an attending audience, and perhaps also invoking spirits, ancestors and deities – a common practice in Neolithic Britain as, for example, in Egypt and Sumeria. Much trading in various cultures continues to combine the two in a similar way. For example, Islamic deals to this day are finalised by invoking God as witness.

Another example is the Bristol Nails in Corn Street, the main trading place of old Bristol. These are bronze pillars, erected in the late sixteenth and early seventeenth century. They are shaped like large tables and inscribed with religious inscriptions dedicating them and the trade that took place on them to aspects of the Trinity. Here deals were struck in public by word and not by written deed. Once a deal was struck, money was placed on top of a Nail (so called because the Nails look like old-fashioned nails) – hence the phrase 'paying on the nail'. Indeed, the invocations to the Godhead on the Bristol Nails may be an indirect echo of the invocations at stone circles which brought the binding awesome power of the sacred to ensure their role as trustworthy trading places.

The Rollright Stones, a circle in Oxfordshire, stand beside an even older trackway than the one at Mitchell's Fold. It is a site I know well, having been involved, with the author Terry Pratchett, in trying to help a local group purchase and protect this strange site. Yet it is not a place of any great spiritual or mystical power for me. It is certainly ancient. The Oxfordshire trackway may even date from Mesolithic times, around 8000 BC, when the site of the future Rollright Stones was already cleared and occupied. Certainly it was a major track then, running through some of the most agriculturally productive lands in Britain; it was also already a burial area – the remains of two burial mounds can still be seen near the Stones. Today the trackway is a minor tarmac road with the Rollright Stones lying just to its side. I believe that we have here, once again, a sacred trading place. Aubrey Burl agrees, considering this site to have been primarily a trading place, 'a depot from which Cumbrian stone axes were exchanged'.[2] Its strangeness comes more from its worn, wormeaten stones than from any mystical spirituality. This was a place of importance because it was a place of meeting and trade, sanctioned by the sacred. A sort of holy B&Q.

Axe buying at Mitchell Fold may well have been charged with the sacred. After all, these axes seem never to have been used for everyday purposes, but instead to have had a ritual significance. Axes have always been associated with authority, from the *labrys*, the axes that were the symbol of the ancient Cretan kings based at Knossos, and which give us the term 'labyrinth' in the story of the Minotaur, to the axes wielded by the executioners of the medieval European kings. The authority of the axe as a symbol can perhaps be glimpsed on many neo-Classical buildings of Britain to this day. In the neo-Classical style of the nineteenth and early twentieth centuries, a popular decorative feature, especially favoured by banks, law courts, and other such authorities, was the fasces. This was a bundle of sticks, bound together at the middle, enclosing an axe with its blade turned outwards; it originated around 200 BC as the symbol of the authority of the lictors, the consular bodyguards of Rome. Mussolini used the fasces as a symbol of the authority of his new party – hence the term 'fascists'. I would argue that the authority resident in the fasces takes us indirectly back to the ritual role of the polished axes traded at the circles of Stapeley Hill. It is also worth noting that axes are among the very few artefacts ever found within stone circles, such as the unfinished one found at Castlerigg in Cumbria. Additionally, the only carvings on the stones at Stonehenge that have been clearly identified are those depicting axes and daggers, with axes being most common.

Activity at stone circles, I believe, was both sacred and secular, though that is a distinction the people themselves are highly unlikely to have made. The people inhabited a sacred world and whatever powers they believed in were invoked at the circles for very pragmatic reasons. It was through these actions that these very places became charged with a powerful numinous significance, which still draws us to them.

A NEW RELIGION

One of my favourite stone circles is Arbor Low in the Derbyshire hills. These hills abound with burial mounds, stone circles, megaliths, mystical chasms, sacred wells and hill forts. But of all the sacred sites in this area Arbor Low is the most dramatic. There can be few places in the world where you wander through a working farmyard, drop your entrance fee into a bucket, dodge the slurry, and then climb over the farmyard wall to a major archaeological site. I rather like this, and I hope it never achieves the status of Avebury or Stonehenge, where the tourism has destroyed a lot of the atmosphere, and made it difficult to approach the site as a pilgrim in an open and receptive mood.

As you approach the site the ground rises steeply in front of you, then you wander to the left towards an obvious opening in this rise. The site that greets you is astonishing. It is as if you have walked into a theatre and are staring at the stage. There is a flat, elliptically circular area covered by huge stones lying prone upon the ground, surrounded by an embankment and a ditch. Where the encircling earth embankment has its two openings, there is an earth bridge leading to the platform. The site is tremendously awe-inspiring and, because not many people go there, one is often able to wander, slack-jawed, around it.

Dated *c.* 3200 BC, it is one of the earliest stone circles. It may contain within it a hint of the transition from long-barrow ancestor worship to a new religion that emerged into the vacuum created by the death of the ancestor cults. The hearts of the long barrows were the tombs, where the basic design was three or four huge stones to form the walls of the tomb chamber, and one vast stone lying across them to form the roof. Near to Arbor Low at Minning Low it is possible to see a number of these, exposed to the air. The tomb was then covered by soil and made into the familiar shapes of the mounds and barrows. British weather seems to have quite swiftly denuded many of the tombs of their coating of soil, exposing the megalithic stones in the centre.

Clearly, the sight of these stones came to be the symbol for a tomb. When the old religion died, there was a sentimental attachment to the idea of the ancestors and their tombs, even if they were no longer the centre or even the purpose of sacred sites and functions. So, at many of the earliest stone circles, mock tombs were erected: tombs which appear to have been rarely if at all used for a real burial. This is what happened at Arbor Low. At the heart of the platform area is what is known as a cove. This is an archaeological term for what is essentially the earliest example of the British love of pastiche and of pseudo-architecture of the past. A cove is sort of nostalgic nod in the direction of old values, for it is essentially a mock Neolithic tomb. I would compare this to the rash of pseudo-farm buildings dating from the late 1980s to the present day, which house supermarkets on the edges of town, and which make it just that little bit easier to feel that these places are not ultimately destroying the values, lifestyle and architecture of traditional farms, upon whose lands these temples to commerce are so often erected.

Those early stone circles of significant size and stature often seem to have had coves, as can be seen at the north and south circles at Avebury (*c.* 2800 BC) or the stones of Stenness, Orkney, as well as at Arbor Low (*c.* 3200 BC). It seems likely that having a cove represented a sense of continuity with the past religion and the ancestors, although it does not appear that any skulls were transferred from the old tombs to these new sites. But then it is also the case that mock farm buildings housing supermarkets today don't tend to have piles of manure in the corner or pitchforks resting beside the door!

The earth platform at Arbor Low is some 52 metres (170 feet) by 40 metres (130 feet), made more dramatic by two deep ditches that run like a segmented moat around it. It contains not only the cove but also forty-six substantial stones, which once perhaps formed a standing circle. However, there has been much academic discussion about whether they were ever erected. They are impressive stones, all local and thus probably representing a good day or two's work in fetching each of them and manoeuvring them into position.

Surrounding the whole site is the henge – that is to say the two deep ditches and a wall of earth. In defensive sites, the ditch is of course on the outside with the wall rising up on the inside, but in most sacred sites, the ditch is inside and the wall outside. It has been suggested that this shows that whatever force was inside was so powerful that people wanted to prevent it from escaping. However, such henges always have exits – Arbor Low has two – so this hypothesis seems unlikely unless the 'forces' within were rather thick and couldn't work out how to use exits. But these are substantial defences, and if they were not built to keep some supernatural force inside, then what on earth were they for?

I believe the answer is simple, and Arbor Low is where it first became clear to me. Mundane as it may seem, at Arbor Low we are looking at a particularly beautiful theatre and the henge is the seating. Whatever went on in the central space was possibly largely symbolic – hence the cove. The inclusion, even at a purely symbolic level, of a tomb and an echo of the old religion, indicates that this was not just a theatre, but also a place of sacred ritual and drama – though again this division of secular and religious would not have made much sense. After all, in all ancient cultures where we have written records, such as those of ancient Greece (*c.* 600 BC) or Zhou China (*c.* 1100 BC), drama originated with religious festivals and rituals. I think we should see Arbor Low as a sacred drama site.[3]

Such a link between henge and theatre is to be seen even more clearly at Dorchester in Dorset. Just beside the main Weymouth–London railway line, no more than a hundred yards from the end of Dorchester South railway station, is Maumbury Rings. The Romans turned this compact and dramatic Neolithic henge, created somewhere around 2800 BC, into an actual amphitheatre.

A wonderful thing about so much of our prehistory is that it indicates the sacred origins of other, relatively recent features of our landscape. The graveyard-cum-parish church is, for instance, the long barrow reincarnated. Medieval markets, with their sacred stones and crosses, are ancient stone circle trading sites recreated, and the theatres of today are perhaps pale memories of the sacred dramas that caused places such as Arbor Low and Maumbury Rings to be built.

Arbor Low is especially fascinating because of its discernible impact on the sacred geography of the area. Close by are eight chambered tombs, centres for the veneration of the ancestors. These fell into disuse with the rise of Arbor Low, or possibly Arbor Low rose because they were no longer used. Either way, the sacred power invested in them and the community energy expended on them found a new focus at Arbor Low, which itself then became a magnet for later burial mounds. The sacred power having transferred to the henge and stones, the later burial mounds clustered near the numinous power of the henge and stone in order to share in the sacred. In this one small area, we have the story of the death of one faith and the transfer of the sacred to another, newer faith.

However, we have no idea what the sacred drama was that the henges were made for. Britain, uniquely in contemporary and neighbouring cultures, has hardly any art to give us clues. Not a picture on a pot, few carvings on stones (some circles on an outlying stone at Long Meg and her Daughters in Cumbria and the axe heads found carved on some stones at Stonehenge). No statues or rock carvings and just a couple of controversial wooden statues. Whatever the reason for the non-art tradition in Britain, it survived the collapse of the old religion and appears to have been maintained just as rigidly by those who followed the new one.

WOOD CIRCLES

Stone, being more durable and impressive than wood, has tended to be the focus of attention at prehistoric sites, but a remarkable discovery at Stanton Drew in Somerset has raised fascinating new questions. I grew up near these stones and have loved them for many years. I know all the legends and songs associated with them: one tradition describes them as dancers at a wedding, who did not stop when the Sabbath came. The devil came to play for them, and then turned them into stone.

Today, Stanton Drew is a quietly impressive set of stones, set in the midst of a field, but their quietness hides an interesting story. Some time around 3000 BC, this site housed not stone circles, but a vast wooden construction. Evidence of up to 900 wooden pillars, set in concentric circles with some form of burial at the centre, has recently come to light through the work of Bristol University. As yet no one has any clear idea what the site was for, but it probably had some symbolic purpose. It is completely unlike the burial mounds that went before and which lie in such profusion in the surrounding areas. Apart from its use of a circle, it is also unlike the stone circles which seem to have been built about 300 years later. Its central space seems too small for ritual drama, and the spacing between the wooden pillars is too narrow for ritual processions.

Other such wood henges, as they have been called, have been found with increasing frequency in the last few years. For example, there was a huge one at Avebury and another near Stonehenge. At Stanton Drew, the wooden constructions are much more sophisticated than the later stone circles, even though the wooden constructions came before the stone circles – most such wood henges are from *c.* 3000 BC. As yet there is no clear idea as to what they were used for or why the somewhat technologically inferior stone circles replaced them. Whether or not they tell us anything about the nature of the sacred in Britain remains to be discovered. What is intriguing is that when the builders came to construct Stonehenge's main feature – that of stones laid across the top of other stones forming a huge wall – they carved the stones to fit together as if they were pieces of wood.

To understand what might have been going on I want you to come with me to two of the most significant of the stone circles – the cathedrals or possibly also stock exchanges and power centres of their time.

AVEBURY AND STONEHENGE

Over a period of at least 1,000 years at Avebury in Wiltshire, wood henges, circles, avenues, Silbury Hill and much else were erected. Vast effort was poured into what was clearly a major pilgrimage centre, drawing upon a considerable labour force in order to create a site that was, at that time, of unparalleled magnificence in England. Callanish, on the Isle of Lewis in Scotland, was a similar achievement. Perhaps around this time the hills and valleys of both areas were denuded of trees and turned into the bare landscape we know today. The demands for fuel, building materials and equipment in making these centres would have been a severe strain on the local environment.

It seems that Avebury was the place to be seen in and buried at. The burial mounds built at the peak of the popularity of Avebury – c. 2800 to 1800 BC – are impressively wealthy ones, homes for the noble dead. The great avenues were designed to take huge processions, and seem to have been used regularly. So much so that the areas along the sides of the avenues where presumably ordinary people walked – only the most special people being allowed to walk inside the rows of stones – were pressed down hard by the weight of the devout over the centuries and the compaction is still discernible in the soil to this day.

Avebury was clearly a trading centre for the Wiltshire Downs providing some of the best trading flint in Europe; a liturgical sacred drama centre, as shown by the henge; and a pilgrimage centre, as seen in the avenues, which were used for ritual procession-cum-pilgrimages as the varying soil compactness along the avenues shows. It was also probably much more. The artificially created Silbury Hill is an enigma that confounds all who try to explain Avebury. The Egyptian Pyramids, the ziggurats of Babylon, and the tombs of the early Emperors of China are probably the only constructions that equal Silbury Hill's scale and length of construction time. Despite excavations and explorations, its purpose remains hidden. All that can be said is that this was a mighty communal place, probably combining the modern functions of Trafalgar Square, the Houses of Parliament, the Stock Exchange and Westminster Abbey, a public assembly for decision making, trade and worship, for it is only in recent centuries that they have been divided into separate spheres.

What is clear is that the old ancestor religion had really died. Under the worship of local ancestors associated with a specific people and their bit of land, the creation of a huge site, such as Stanton Drew, Avebury or Stonehenge, would have been inconceivable and unnecessary. Whatever else Avebury tells us its size indicates that the community structures of this period were becoming larger and stronger, and that almost certainly there were now local leaders who controlled large swathes of land and people. Avebury was not the outcome of the mentality that built the nearby and much smaller West Kennet long barrow 1,000 years before, but the work over time of an increasingly large community of people. Yet, perhaps the most astonishing fact about Avebury is that by c. 1400 BC, some ordinary farmer was so unimpressed by the site that he or she simply ploughed right across the main sacred avenue. This fact clearly indicates that by that time no one walked there any longer and the site was little more than a farmyard or field with some rather large stones.

This is fascinating because it suggests that the sacred moved and, indeed, was quite capable of leaving a site. By 1500 BC or thereabouts, this site was no longer sacred, no longer drawing the wealthy crowds or devout pilgrims. It was still used by some, but they were but a pale shadow of the communities and powers which once held this as the centre of their world.

Whatever it was that powered this site, it was not permanent. That power and sacredness had been deliberately drained away to the greatest powerhouse of prehistoric Britain: Stonehenge. The tombs that were built in the area around Avebury after c. 1600 BC are poor tombs, those of essentially unimportant people. To find the great tombs of that period, you have to travel to Stonehenge, to which, it appears, the sacred power of Avebury had gone.

The growth of Stonehenge's power can be dated by the decline of all other sacred sites within an ever-increasing radius of the site. Sites as far as 240 kilometres (150 miles) away seem to have been destroyed or simply abandoned by those for whom Stonehenge became the only sacred place of real significance.

Yet there is nothing inherently 'sacred' about the site. It is not one of those dramatic natural environments such as a great mountain or river gorge. It is on a flat and undistinguished plain, not raised high on a hill or secreted in a valley. Indeed, for many centuries this was just one amongst a number of henges and stone circles in the area. It was not until some time between 2200 and 2000 BC that Stonehenge began to take off in terms of scale, grandeur and expense, and that the distinctive shape of Stonehenge that we have to this day was created. It is not without significance that the way in which the stones were grooved in order for the top stones to lie across the uprights is entirely based upon woodworking, perhaps based upon the very skills which had earlier created Woodhenge a few miles east of Stonehenge. This phenomenon of building in stone as if with wood is found in many ancient cultures. For example, early Buddhist sites in India such as Sanchi, near Bhopal have vast stone railings and pillars carved, grooved and fitted as if these massives of stone were wood turned on a lathe.[4]

We know that Stonehenge took centuries to build and rebuild. The stone was hauled from great distances and the sheer effort and inventiveness necessary to create this site was beyond comparison with anything else yet undertaken in Britain.

As with Avebury, we have no idea what happened here. Stonehenge has an astronomical significance. The well-known alignment of the stones with midsummer sunrise certainly seems deliberate, but I would argue that it is a mistake to attach too much importance to this fact. One issue is whether, given the shifting axis of the world, the sun is still in the same place it was 4,000 years ago on midsummer. And why would the rising sun be of such importance? After all, the people who created Stonehenge were a basic, if well-armed, culture of farmers, who had little need to know exactly when the midsummer sun rose. It is far more likely that it was used as a spotlight for dramatic effect on a ritual drama that took place within the sacred space. Again, the lack of any signs of calendrical measurements, records or marks raises questions about the supposed mathematical needs of these people. If we remember that the henges may have been theatres where people viewed dramas, we see the same perspective at work at Stonehenge. What could be more dramatic than a sunrise celebration which had the midsummer sun as a spotlight?

What happened here was certainly nothing to do with the Druids, for they did not yet exist. Again, apart from the carving of axe heads and daggers on a few of the stones, dated to about 1600 BC, no artwork or artefacts exist to enlighten us and there is nothing to show us what happened here. All that seems clear is that Stonehenge became so powerful that by the end it dominated the sacred landscape and life of its world for tens, if not hundreds, of miles. Thus, when it fell, everything fell with it.

And fall it did.

THE COLLAPSE OF THE CIRCLES

Around 1100 BC an extension of the avenue at Stonehenge was begun, curving down to the River Avon. It was never completed. By *c.* 1000 BC, it seems that Stonehenge was abandoned, and its sacred walkways became silent, its stone circles ignored, even shunned.

Across Britain the other stone circles also became dormant. There is not a single one that shows any activity after roughly 1000 BC. Many had already been silenced by Stonehenge, but others, beyond its reach, died at about the same time. Arbor Low fell silent, its stones left to weather in the wind and rain. Avebury, already fallen to a subservient position, was now left to the elements. For some unknown reason the people deserted these places, which they had used for a variety of purposes for some 2,000 years.

The reason seems to have been the same as that which led to the sealing of the great tombs some 2,000 years or so earlier. The religion behind, around and within these places had died. It had failed the people, or perhaps, yet again, the people thought they had failed the powers of these places. Environmental collapse and with it societal collapse, starvation and chaos seem to have descended with startling speed upon the land.

There is little doubt that the population had grown rapidly, as indicated by the sheer size of Avebury and Stonehenge. The forests had been cleared in many areas, the soil was overworked, and farming was struggling. Natural forces exacerbated all this. Around 1150 BC a huge volcano off Iceland exploded, completely blocking out the sun through the sheer quantity of volcanic ash it threw into the atmosphere. Across the northern part of Europe, vegetation died, crops withered and trees perished through the lack of sunlight. In some places, such as much of western Ireland, all life died out and the settlements and farms that had existed since early Neolithic times perished and disappeared under rotting vegetation, which has now become peat. It was not until the coming of the Christian monks in the fourth to sixth centuries that these areas were reinhabited.

In Britain, the destruction of the traditional farming way of life was almost as dramatic. Under peat bogs across Britain can be found the old Neolithic and Bronze Age field systems. A way of life perhaps two or even three millennia old ended, possibly within a matter of a decade or so. It seems likely that the psychological shock that this caused led to the death of the religion of the stone circles and henges. Once again, the people of Britain abandoned a way of life and a sacred view of the world, as the stone circles fell silent and their faith died with them.

There now began an astonishing time in British history. The collapse of the faith in and around the stone circles was apparently so devastating that for some 500 to 600 years there is no clear sign of any belief system, sacred sites or even burial rituals in Britain. As Hutton says:

> In the British Isles, the late Bronze Age, from *c*. 1100 to *c*. 600 BC is a period apparently entirely destitute of ceremonial monuments and almost without burials of any kind … It seems that the British and Irish had simply turned their backs upon the old sacred monuments, and perhaps upon the old sacred ways.[5]

For nearly 600 years, Britain appears to have been without any kind of corporate belief system, without any overarching sense of the sacred that manifested itself in any outward display, building or action.

Why? Perhaps the scale of the collapse of the faith was so vast and so horrific that people talked of it for centuries and feared putting their trust in anything new. Perhaps the ancient aversion to art, so distinctive in Britain, meant that there were no symbolic and mythic resources to fall back on once the old sites had been abandoned. All this is speculation. What is clear, unless some very dramatic archaeology yet to be undertaken proves otherwise, is that Britain lost its sense of the sacred, and even its confidence in burial ritual, for hundreds of years. I know of no other culture, anywhere in the world, where such a break in the sacred can be found. When the sacred did return, it did so quietly and unostentatiously, and it shunned the building of stone shrines and edifices as if they were cursed.

The 5,000-year-old Neolithic Cove at Stanton Drew was made to resemble a burial chamber but never contained a body. The Neolithic stones of Stanton Drew and the parish church both testify to the timeless quest for answers to the search for the sacred. (*Martin Palmer/Circa Photo Library*)

ABOVE The giant stones closing the 6,000-year-old long barrow of Waylands Smithy, the Ridgeway, entombed the remains of the venerated ancestors. Erected *c.* 3200 BC, the stones sealed the end of ancestor veneration as a result of the collapse of Britain's first distinct religion. (*John Smith/Circa Photo Library*)

RIGHT The dramatic length of a long barrow is stunningly illustrated in this photograph of West Kennett Long Barrow, Wiltshire. The long barrows grew in length over some 1,500 years. (*Skyscan Balloon Photography/English Heritage Photo Library*)

ABOVE The stone circle of Avebury is one of the most important ancient sites of Britain. Begun in *c.* 2800 BC, it lost power to Stonehenge *c.* 1800 BC. In its day with stone avenues, stone circles and the as yet unexplained Silbury Hill, it was the major ritual site of Southern England. (*Victoria Finlay/Circa Photo Library*)

RIGHT The stone circle *c.* 3000 BC of Castlerigg, Cumbria is unusual in being dramatically situated on wind and snow swept moors above the lakes. (*Martin Palmer/Circa Photo Library*)

The drama of sunset at Stonehenge highlights the theatrical nature of this, the most important and ultimately most destructive of the great stone circle ritual centres. (*English Heritage Photo library*)

CHAPTER FOUR

THE RETURN OF THE SACRED

THE RIVER-GODDESS

B UXTON, IN THE DERBYSHIRE HILLS, was one of the great hot-spring centres of both British and then Romano-British culture. Contained in its Roman name for Buxton is an original British name that tells us a great deal about its sacred nature. The Romans called it Aquae Arnemetiae, meaning the Waters of Arnemetiae. The first part of the word Arnemetiae is the name of a goddess closely associated with the waters in the Celtic world. Her name is variously spelt as Ane, Anu, Ana and Danu, and she is linked to many cultures and continents; hers is an interesting and curious story.

Some time around 1600 BC, a group of tribes burst out of central Asia: the forerunners of the people whom the Romans and the Greeks knew as Celts. As so often happened in central Asia, the population had built up to such a point that it became imperative for the people to migrate. And, as also so often happened, the tribes dispersed in different directions. One group began a slow march towards Europe across central Asia and southern Russia, while another group made its way south to India. Both spoke roughly the same language and had broadly the same beliefs, deities and sense of the sacred. The group that migrated towards India appeared in its ancient world as a destructive military force that swept away much of the older culture and imposed itself upon the people. It brought with it its stories and deities and, encountering writing for the first time, began to transcribe its stories and beliefs. These writings are the Vedas: the foundation of Indian sacred traditions to this day. Indeed, the various Indian religious traditions are often referred to as Vedic beliefs, for they all share the beautiful, haunting texts of the Vedas, written some 3,000 years ago, as their original source of inspiration.

One of these writings, the Rig Veda, mentions a goddess of terrifying powers, Danu, mother to demons, especially the demon Vrtra, renowned for his ability to contain floodwaters.[1] Danu is thus seen as a goddess related to water and, in later sections of the Rig Veda, she is identified with the waters of heaven, the formless primordial waters of the universe. She is particularly a deity of the primal power of water, for both good and bad.

The group that went towards Europe also took Danu's legends with it. As it travelled through central Asia and on into Russia and then into central Europe, it settled and gave names to the natural forces around it. Thus the name of Danu came to be linked to the mighty River Don, which flows through Central Russia, and to the River Danube, which scores a line across Central Europe to the Black Sea. In each name we hear an echo of the belief in Danu, goddess of the primal, terrifying, uncontrollable waters.

By the time the Celtic influence had reached Britain, the goddess had become more benign. She was still linked to waters, especially to primal sources of water, such as springs and holy wells. In Britain, the hot waters of Buxton were dedicated to her and probably set within a holy wood, for the second part of the Roman name for Buxton, Arnemetiae, means a sacred grove or wood.

But the story of Danu does not stop there. Two breast-like hills in the south-west of Ireland are called the Paps of Anu – made even more breastlike by probably humorous Bronze Age locals who put a rounded burial mound on each hill! In this name her motherly role has come to the fore. In Celtic mythology she is the mother of the Tuatha de Danann – the clan or children of Danu. In the legends, they appear either from the north or the southern islands, or even descend from the sky. In the collection of ancient Welsh romances, the *Mabinogion*, the Children of Dan appear again, Dan now being a male figure.[2]

Later it seems that Danu, or Anu, became connected with a Christian saint. When the Christian faith developed, it too saw many springs as sacred and dedicated them to the figure of a mother and a protector of sacred waters. By far the commonest dedication for holy wells and sacred springs in Britain, Ireland, and France is to St Anne, the mother of the Virgin Mary, and, indeed, the well at Buxton bears her name. Anu to Anne – the sacred flows on.

Through the origins of its Roman name, Buxton reminds us that the sacred often goes beyond any one particular faith, and that certain aspects of the sacred in Britain, such as the sanctity of living waters, have remained constant through at least 2,000 years.

DID THE CELTS COME TO BRITAIN?

For many interested in Britain's ancient sacred past, the coming of the Celts is a central feature of their beliefs and mythology. But is it good history? The Celts are one of the great arguments of history at present. The debates range from 'Did they ever exist?' through 'Who were they?' to 'When, if at all, did they invade?' The layperson needs to tread carefully through a minefield of conflicting accounts, none of which is particularly helped by the growth of a vast sentimental tourism market of 'Celtic' arts, ideas and so on.

In essence, the debate concerns whether the Celts existed as a distinct people. If they did, then did they invade or migrate into Britain around 500 BC, or was the Celtic 'invasion' more of an artistic, cultural, and conceptual movement, which spread by being imitated by local peoples, reaching Britain around 500 BC.[3] I am happy to sit on the fence on this. What is clear is that, either by the physical entrance of the Celts or the influence of Celtic ideas, British society began to change around 500 BC. This laid the foundations for the creation of the sacred landscape of Buxton, the emergence of huge fortified hilltops such as the great one at Maiden Castle in Dorset and so many other places in Britain, and reintroduced notions of the sacred. Therefore, to fudge the issue, I will use the term 'the British' as an umbrella term for the various diverse peoples who lived in Britain from *c.* 1000 BC to the conquest by the Romans in the mid-first century AD. When it is appropriate to refer to trends, artistic styles or peoples actually recorded as Celts by contemporary historians and writers, I will use the term Celt or Celtic.

Although I refer to the sacred as being reintroduced at this time, we cannot say for certain that it ever left. What had happened after the disastrous failure of the stone circles belief system was that the people appear to have become chary of any of the old sacred sites, for there is no evidence that the vast majority of them were used during this period. What little use there was is fleeting, rather than the reoccupation or reuse of the site. The desire to change the landscape through the creation of sacred sites had apparently gone.

THE ROMANTIC CELTS

Today there is a great romanticism about the early British, and about the Celts in general. They are seen as being more environmentally and religiously sensitive than just about any other peoples in the history of Europe, and especially of Britain. There is probably some truth in that, as with the beginning of the Celtic influence in Britain, from 500 BC onwards, sacred sites began to reappear, but gone were the great stone structures of tombs or circles, or the huge earthworks of the henges. In their place were humble huts in forests, small shrines in woods, and simple shelters at springs. This revival of the sacred in Britain is focused around natural features. This was a new aspect of the sacred, for there is no evidence that either the old religion of ancestor-worship or the religion of the stone circles had any special reverence for rivers, streams, woods or forests, even though these were exploited for their natural resources in order to construct the great tombs and circles.

It is possible that the collapse of the grandiose sacred centres and concomitant centralised power, as manifested by Stonehenge, led to a collapse of the society that built them. Given the absence of any significant buildings for the period c. 1000 BC to c. 200 BC, the demands upon the natural environment would have been considerably less than they were in the time of the megalomaniac stone circle creators' final days. As a result, Britain may have recovered environmentally, with woods and forests spreading on land that had been abandoned and wasteland with scrub cover on the peat bogs emerging from the collapsed agriculture.

It appears that, apart from the sunless years caused by the volcanic eruption off Iceland around 1150 BC that killed so much of the agriculture, the period from *c.* 1000 BC to *c.* 700 BC was one of a drop in the overall temperature, which has sometimes been called a mini-Ice Age. This meant longer winters and shorter summers, and thus a truncated growing season, which lead to further farmlands being abandoned. Nature would have taken back these deserted fields, clothing them again in woods, forests or grassland.

Perhaps, then, when the new Celtic sense of the sacred arose, it did so in a land where nature was more visible than it had been for many centuries, even millennia. However, this was not to last. Despite the supposed Celtic love of the forests, land, waters and hills, by the time the Romans arrived in AD 43, much of Britain was as intensively farmed and as exploited as it had been at any other time in prehistory. The main feature of the Celtic landscape is the hundreds of hillforts, a testimony to a very aggressive society which, although it may have had a good relationship with nature, seemed also to have problems with other human beings. Nevertheless, an element of overt nature veneration entered the psyche of Britain around 500 BC that has never quite departed.

ISLAND OF THE SACRED

With the advent of the Celtic era we no longer need to rely upon only the physical remains of the culture to try to understand what the sacred meant to people. From this period onwards, we have written accounts from a variety of sources, and these reveal a fascinating but strange story.

I have chosen to stick primarily to the contemporary foreign sources and archaeological evidence rather than, as many writers have done, extrapolating backwards from the Celtic myths, such as the Welsh *Mabinogion* or the Irish *Book of the Dun Cow*. While these stories are full of rich detail, heroic adventure and strange gods, they were all compiled well after the Celtic cultures in question had been Christianised, and it is almost impossible to tell which of them represent authentic ancient folktales and which were newly invented. It seems almost certain, for instance, that the tales in the *Mabinogion* were created by Welsh bards in the ninth century as part of a new Welsh culture and literature, and, indeed, late-Georgian and Victorian collectors of the tales were not averse to making up new ones themselves. Basing accounts of pre-Christian British culture and religion upon such tales, therefore, is rather like researching the Middle Ages through modern fantasy novels.

It is clear from the paucity of British/Celtic temples – less than fifty have so far been found – and from the accounts of Greek and Roman writers, that the British found the sacred in nature, not in great edifices such as Stonehenge. Very few temples have been found, and they are so modest that we can almost ignore them. However it might be of interest to passengers using Heathrow Airport to know that beneath them lay the remains of one such modest, rural, quiet British temple. The classical writers depict a people for whom the forests and streams were the focus of their sense of the sacred. For example, Lucan, in his 'Pharsalia', states (in my rather old and florid Victorian translation):

> While you, ye Druids, when the war was done,
> To mysteries strange and hateful rites returned:
> To you alone 'tis given the gods and stars
> To know or not to know; secluded groves
> Your dwelling-place, and forests far remote. (I, 506–511)

Most famously, Caesar claimed that Britain was considered a holy island both by the British and the Gauls, where the Druids, who were the high priests of Celtic religion, similar to the Brahmins in India, trained their priests. Britain was known to the classical writers of the Roman Empire as the heart of the sacred world of the Gauls and Britons. Within Britain, the isle of Mona (now Anglesey), off the north coast of Wales, was supposed to be the most sacred place, a sort of vast Druidic training college. Written sources tell us of a hierarchical world within which trained religious leaders, the Druids, had a powerful role. We learn of rituals and ceremonies, and that most of these took place in woods and forests. Britain, it appears, was now a holy place, a place where spirituality was strong. What was going on?

It is possible that the classical writers were projecting onto Britain the fantasies of 'civilised' countries about the purer, more natural and more sacred nature of less 'civilised' countries. This 'Noble Savage' myth can be seen in European writing about countries and cultures as varied as China and Native America in the last few centuries. Certainly the Romans often idealised some aspects of 'barbarian' cultures, as in the famous statue of a dying Gaulish warrior, noble in his death, much copied in ancient Rome.

However, it may be that there is something deeper here. Is it possible that the apparent reticence in prehistoric Britain to depict the divine in art, combined with the experience of the collapse of two belief systems, created an awareness and relationship with the sacred, especially apparently through natural sites, that was distinctive and noteworthy? Had the period of apparent agnosticism led to the shedding of otherwise dominant traditional beliefs and allowed a more imaginative, a more innovative way of relating to the sacred to emerge? Frankly, we shall never know, though I believe we have the right to speculate, for Britain certainly has had its own unique sacred history to this point. Even with the written accounts, quite what was believed, by whom and about what remains unclear. We have only glimpses of the history of the sacred, as though through a thick mist which, in the writings and scant archaeological evidence, parts briefly. Centuries of nonsense written by latter-day aficionados, who project desires for everything from spacemen to the priests of Atlantis onto poor Stonehenge and the Druids, only obscures our view.

SACRED WARFARE

What we do know is that the British were not a peaceful people. The British lifestyle embraced cattle raids, duels and outright warfare, as witnessed by the hundreds of hillforts and the archaeological evidence of warfare and bloodshed. Ironically, we can begin to understand more about the sacred through the evidence of warfare than we can from the handful of identified pre-Roman British shrines. Once again, we have but a handful of statues, and once again we are confronted by the reticence regarding representational art, which is such a feature of England in particular, and thus a lack of evidence. However, art, often of an astonishingly abstract nature, or infused with animal motifs, finds its first major expressions in the magnificent worked bronzes and irons of this age, but most of these are on weapons and armour. Warfare seems to have become by this stage a major part of British life, and any consideration of the sacred in later Iron Age Britain must consider its central role.

The heavily fortified Maiden Castle illustrates the importance of warfare well. Its triple banks and multilayered defensive gates demonstrate immense skills, and considerable central power and authority. The technological advances of the day are also clear. Many of the hillforts now classed as Iron Age were originally Neolithic or Bronze Age – as with Maiden Castle, which has worn-down Neolithic ramparts and low ditches within its great walls. These earlier walls were usually defended by just one ditch and bank, from which spears could be thrown and arrows fired. However, around 200 BC the slingshot was invented. Using a strip of leather and usually a piece of chalk or flint, a strong person could fire a potentially lethal slingshot uphill, considerably further than a bow could fire an arrow or a spear could be thrown. Thousands of slingshots can still be found littering these sites to this day. As the slingshots got better, so more defensive rings of ditch and rampart were added to the hillforts, keeping the attackers as far away for as long as possible and keeping the defenders out of slingshot reach.

Maiden Castle is probably the supreme example of this defensive system. By c. 50 BC there was a considerable town within it with streets, residential areas, cattle pens, and so forth. This is a supremely military world. Thus far no sacred site has been found within the precincts of Maiden Castle other than a much later – third to fourth century AD – Roman shrine. There would probably have been a shrine or temple, but it would almost certainly have been located in the woods nearby, or down by the source of the river. The reticence about the sacred seems to still be in evidence. It is a feature of all the hillforts that they were without any religious centres as such. Is it possible that warfare itself was seen as sacred and thus a hillfort was both a military and a holy site? Whatever the case, the distinct 'shrines' lie off in the woods or down in the valleys beside streams and rivers.

Perhaps the earliest indication of the sacred significance of natural features comes, ironically, from their use as a dump. At Llyn Cerrig Bach, Anglesey, a bog excavated during the Second World War proved to contain a considerable collection of Iron Age weaponry, which appears to have been deliberately thrown into the bog from a stone spur jutting out over the site. Likewise, the magnificent Battersea and Wandsworth shields, dredged from the River Thames and now to be seen in the British Museum, appear to be part of ritually or ceremonially dumped weapons in that all of them were apparently deliberately slighted. That they were thrown into water is significant, for if water was seen as sacred, especially, as is indicated in many Christian Celtic stories, as a doorway to the underworld, then throwing the weapons of your foes into such places was tantamount to making an offering.

It seems to me that taking their foes' weapons, upon which, as it is clear from the workmanship, the British lavished considerable fortunes, and throwing them away was the final insult, the ritual humiliation of a defeated enemy. I am reminded of the Serpent Column created in 479 BC by the victorious thirty-one Greek cities that defeated the Persian invasion. The magnificent curled serpents that rise some 4.5 metres (15 feet) were made from the melted shields of the defeated Persians, and the column was raised as a thanksgiving and final triumph. Much battered, it can still be seen in the Hippodrome at Istanbul, where it was brought in the fourth century AD.[4]

THE DREADED ISLE: ANGLESEY AND THE FALL OF THE DRUIDS

Today the Menai Strait, the thin, narrow strip of water that separates Anglesey from mainland Britain, is a place of gentle seaside resorts, cottages, and scenic views, topped and bottomed by the two old towns of Bangor to the north and Caernarfon to the south. On a warm summer's day the coastline of Anglesey viewed from the Welsh mainland side is a picture of tranquillity and gentle country beauty, but on a windy winter day, with low dark clouds and rain lashing down, it presents a very different face. On such a day it is possible to imagine the terrifying sight graphically described by the Roman writer, Tacitus. We catch a glimpse of the British in full flow both militarily and sacredly: 'The enemy lined the shore in a dense armed mass. Among them were black-robed women with dishevelled hair like Furies, brandishing torches. Close by stood Druids, raising their hands to heaven and screaming dreadful curses.'[5] Leading up to this day in AD 60 was the decision by the Romans to conquer Anglesey once and for all, having been thwarted in their earlier attempts. It was a hotbed of resistance to the Roman invasion and a refuge for those who had resisted the Romans, and it was thickly populated.

Equally significant was the fact that the Druid religion was one of only three religions that Rome openly and steadfastly persecuted. The other two were Christianity up until the beginning of the fourth century AD, which they saw as atheistic and undermining the role of civic religion in Roman culture and Judaism, which refused to accommodate Roman beliefs – which the Romans inferred as being a rejection of Roman culture *per se*. The Romans waged war against the Druids because the Romans had banned human sacrifice in 197 BC, and enforced this wherever they went. The Druids would not comply and thus were placed outside the pale of acceptable religions. Some modern writers on the Druids claim rather dubiously that these sacrifices were voluntary, but the evidence for this is scant.

The Romans, Tacitus says, were terrified by the sight of the enemy on the shore of Anglesey, and were not too keen to advance. However, the Batavian auxiliaries (essentially mercenary troops from tribes in present-day Germany/Netherlands) were less worried and, using their formidable marine skills, swam their way across the Strait. The Romans triumphed, overcoming the Druids, who then disappeared from history in Britain, though they were encountered in Ireland by St Patrick 400 years later. The absence of any mention or evidence of the action of Druids in Britain after AD 60 seems to indicate that they were either destroyed or brought to heel and tamed.

According to the fullsome claims of their significance by some classical writers, and many modern ones, the eclipse or suppression of the Druids should have led to the collapse of British culture for, according to them, the Druids were the spiritual and intellectual heart of British culture, both lawgivers and judges. As Ronald Hutton has noted, the further away from actually meeting or encountering the Druids a classical writer is, the more benign they appear. Conversely, as he also points out, the nearer the writers got to the Druids, the more they vilified them.[6]

Interestingly, however, the Druids' demise or taming had no discernible effect on the ordinary practice of religion in Britain by the British. Far from collapsing, the traditional culture seems to have found it quite possible to merge British deities and ideas with Roman ones. Indeed, one might argue that the fusion brought new life and vigour to a rather staid tradition, given the remarkable number of post-invasion shrines, statues and religious artwork in comparison to the pre-43 AD material, and the number of British gods who were jointly worshipped, according to the archaeological evidence, with Roman deities.

This raises interesting questions about what exactly the role of the Druids was. We can perhaps locate them in sacred groves and forests of which there is strong evidence in both classical writers and in place names to this day.[7] Roman writers depict them as stern lawgivers and judges who combined, as was usual at that time, the role of judge with that of priest. We know that the training to become a Druid was a lengthy one – up to 25 years – but perhaps by seeing them as essentially 'priestly' figures we have missed the point. They appear to have combined the roles of priests, judges and perhaps even been executioners. They were clearly somewhat feared by the ordinary people, and there is no evidence that their passing was particularly lamented. In fact one rather gets the sense that many ordinary Britons may have been unconcerned at seeing them go, and simply got on with finding a *modus vivendi* with the new power of Rome, which supported their basic religious life, offered perhaps a better legal structure, brought many creature comforts and ensured that order was the norm. Given the links between Celtic culture and Vedic India, perhaps we should see the Druids as the Brahmin caste of their world. To this day the Brahmins adopt a highly superior attitude to others in India, and are not much loved as a result. Gandhi tried to overturn their power by elevating the lowest of the lowest caste to the status of 'Children of God' but this has had little effect on Indian culture. The removal of the Druids may have been quite a liberating experience for the ordinary British serf or farmer.

Sadly, we can say very little with certainty about the Druids. They appear to have been of passing significance to the sacred life of Britain, for their going leaves not a ripple on the surface of archaeology, shrines, worship or even mythology of the period. It is as if they were the District Commissioners of Imperial India who ruled without question, but once they and their lifestyle and the Raj went, they disappeared, leaving only a faint trace.

ROMAN BRITAIN AND THE COMING OF A NEW SACRED BRITAIN

Already strongly influenced by Roman culture through cross-Channel trade, British society slowly became thoroughly Romanised. The

Roman contribution to the sacred in Britain was to strengthen and make explicit much of the British sense of the sacred and to introduce Christianity (see Chapter 5), which, in common with all forms of Christianity at that time, took on the local colour of the culture into which it moved. The Romans were always happy with the pantheons of other cultures, willing to accept new gods and often fusing them with their own to create joint deities. They were magpies in religion themselves having taken most of their models for the gods and goddesses and for religion itself from either a romanticised vision of their own agricultural past – hence the Vestal Virgins tended a fire in a straw thatched hut in the centre of marbled and imperial Rome, pretending to be simple village girls, or they borrowed them lock, stock and thunderbolt from Greece and later Egypt. In other words, Rome did not contribute anything of its own sense of the sacred but acted either as an amplifier of what already existed or later as a conveyor of another tradition, Christianity.

One of the best examples of this fusion is to be found in a Roman villa, tucked away along a maze of country lanes near Cirencester in Gloustershire. Chedworth Villa lies in a thickly wooded area, giving one a sense of travelling back in time, which adds greatly to the atmosphere of the site. Chedworth was a grand Roman villa. Windowpanes, statues and jewellery, combined with the sheer scale of the villa and its baths, indicate that a wealthy Romano-British family lived there. There was clearly a family shrine containing statues of the normal Roman deities associated with such shrines, and there was also a sacred spring and pool from which water for the baths was drawn. Here one can see a fusion of the British with the Roman, for it looks as if native deities of the waters were worshipped alongside classical nymphs, as the scale of the sacred pool and the shrine is considerably larger than would be expected in a villa in Italy. This suggests that water, and the spring in particular, was significant beyond just a supply for daily needs. Here a British perspective of the sacred in nature combines with a Roman delight in hot baths in a triumphant merging of the spiritual and physical. Appropriately, the site remained a holy one after the coming of Christianity, and was even used as a baptismal font.

Lydney, on the River Severn, offers another example of the fusion of the British with the Roman. Here, just above the river, was a magnificent Romano-British sacred centre dedicated to the healing powers of the river and the spring, and to the local British deity, Nodens. Here statues of other healing and water deities from the Roman world found a home, and Nodens was worshipped in combined form with the Roman goddess Minerva. It is a late shrine, expanded to its fullest glory in the mid-fourth century, when Christianity was already an established religion in the Empire.

Lucan writes of the Celtic regard for waters:

> *There was a grove, immemorially inviolate,*
> *Hidden from the air above*
> *by interlacing branches . . .*
> *There fell fountain streams,*
> *there gloomy images of gods*
> *Stood guard, jutting, human-carven*
> *in tree-trunk shape . . .*[8]

Bath and Buxton, the two most significant Romano-British sacred centres, perhaps best attest the sacredness the British attached to water. Both centre upon sacred and healing waters, both took up and honoured British deities yet also incorporated Roman deities, and both went on to continue their sacred role within a Christian context.

At Bath, you can literally see the layers of sacred history in Britain. Standing down below the present ground level on the floor of the Baths, you are above an Iron Age causeway that led worshippers, often in need of healing, to the spring. Looking around, you can see the magnificence of the Roman baths, while above you can glimpse the façade of Bath Abbey, one of the finest medieval churches in Britain. Even the Georgian buildings of the city reflect a continued fascination with the sacred, for they were designed to reflect the order and symphony or harmony of the universe as understood by post-Newtonian British architects and intellectuals (see Chapter 13).

At Bath, the British had worshipped and sought healing for perhaps 300 to 400 years before the Romans came. When the Romans developed the site, they dedicated it to the goddess Minerva, one of the most popular Roman deities, and to the local deity Sulis, the goddess of the hot springs in British mythology, so continuing the sacred nature and role of this site, as occurred in a more rural way at Chedworth.

The Neolithic burial mounds and Bronze Age stone circles are far more dramatic places to visit and thus far more visible than the British/Celtic influences. Yet the break with the faiths associated with them was so complete, that they have contributed little directly to the sacred tradition in Britain today other than as vehicles for the reflections of romantics and persistent reminders of the human quest for meaning. These reflections may have contributed to later ideas of the sacred, but have almost nothing to do with these sites' original purpose. On the other hand, it can be argued that the British tradition of the veneration of nature, secluded retreats for places of worship and of reverence for water, have persisted to this day. It is with the emergence of British/Celtic spirituality and sense of the sacred that trends still pertinent to today first arise. The Romantic movement, the National Trust, the huge interest in gardening, equating it with 'being nearer to God', are all expressions of this and contribute towards a sacred understanding of Britain.

For the first time, we can touch a sense of the sacred of which we know something, not just because we have written accounts, but also because we can recognise elements of our own sacred psychology in the world views tantalisingly glimpsed in texts and sites from the Romano-British period. It took, however, the coming of Britain's first engagement with one of the newly emerging mission faiths to take this to the next level – one which is still the dominant sense of the sacred today and which also spawned the first attempts at creating a sacred history of Britain.

CHAPTER FIVE

THE ADVENT OF CHRISTIANITY

THE RISE OF THE MISSION FAITHS

A S FAR AS WE ARE AWARE, no Roman priest of Jupiter ever felt called to lead a mission to try to convert the British to Jupiter worship; nor did any Druid ever launch a missionary movement to convert the people of Rome to Druidry. There is no evidence that the stone-circle religion ever sought to convert others, or that the builders of the long barrows sent missionaries to other countries. The only other possible example of a 'mission' is the spread of standard designs for stone circles and for megatombs, but this is perhaps like the spread of the dome design of Hagia Sophia in Constantinople into the Islamic architecture of the Ottoman Empire – the imitation of great art. Faiths were local; they had a world view essentially focused on a given place or people, and people appear not to have felt called to convert others to their views and practices.

All this began to change with the rise of the mission faiths. The first of these was Buddhism. Originally it was a place faith – its place being northern India – until the conversion of the Emperor Ashoka in the mid-third century BC which led to the first recorded missionary movement. Ashoka sent pairs of missionaries in all directions, even to Egypt and Greece, to tell people of the faith of Buddhism and the teachings of the Buddha. This is the first known case of a faith believing that what it had to teach was not just for its own people, but also for the whole world.

Not long afterwards, as Jews were absorbed into first the Greek sphere of influence and then the Roman Empire, Judaism began to have a missionary drive, which opened doors to both a common language, Greek, and ease of travel. This shift of Judaism from a localised religion to a universal one can be detected in the Hebrew Bible (Old Testament). The earlier texts all see God as the God of Israel, the god of that piece of land. For example, the story of the healing of Naaman the foreigner by Elisha in 2 Kings 5, set in the ninth century BC, includes Naaman's request to take some soil from Israel to worship on when he returns to his own country, so as to be in touch with the God of Israel. The exile of the Jews to Babylon in the sixth century BC, after the Babylonians razed the Temple at Jerusalem, raised profound questions about whether God could be the god of neighbouring lands as well, captured in the mournful Psalm 137, which asks 'How shall we sing the Lord's songs in a strange land?' By the second century BC, however, we begin to see texts such as the Book of Daniel and the later part of Isaiah, which have a more missionary content.

Christianity, arising from Judaism, shared this missionary vision. While Christianity has its sacred places, such as the Holy Land, it is not a faith of that land or about that land. It is a faith which believes that what it has had revealed to it and has discovered is of relevance to all. Along with Islam, which emerged in the seventh century AD, Buddhism, Judaism and Christianity totally altered what it meant to be religious; it created a notion of the sacred that became, for the first time, truly universal in significance.

The cosmological universality of the mission faiths meant that they were better prepared to succeed in the increasingly urban world that emerged from the first to the second centuries AD onwards in the great empires of China, Rome and India. They had the power to motivate across continents, across cultures and across races, and make the sacred common to all. The story of world religion for the last 2,000 years or so is the story of the inexorable spread of these four mission faiths, the adaptation of older indigenous faiths into universal belief systems – for example Hinduism and Taoism – and the shrinking of the older, traditional place-based faiths. Thus Buddhism has pushed the

Bon religion of Tibet to the edge of extinction, has squeezed Shamanism, the indigenous religion of China and Mongolia into a corner and has reduced the traditional religion of Sri Lanka to but a pale shadow of its former self. Christianity has done the same to the traditional religions of Europe, America and Africa. Islam has a similar story to tell.

Not all that had existed beforehand was lost. Most cultural religious practice, and much of the role of the sacred, remains the same regardless of the external form of belief. It deals with the rites of passage, it gives a structure of meaning that makes ordinary life bearable, it offers a community spirit and it provides a place of reflection in a busy world. The mundane sacred – the blessing of everyday life – lies at the heart of the need for religion and the experience of the sacred for most people. The missionary faiths have always absorbed this fact, often taking on wholesale much of the everyday beliefs and practices of the former or local religions. This does not mean that paganism survived as a hidden subculture in Christianity, as some modern pagans believe. Rather, it means that the same questions, worries, concerns and needs that drove a Romano-British citizen to make an offering at the shrine at Bath or to his or her local well were, after the coming of Christianity, served by lighting candles before saints' pictures or making a pilgrimage to a holy well dedicated to St Anne or the Virgin.

In Britain, Christianity initially thrived outside the official centres of Roman power. This can be seen through one very simple example. Scattered around Britain are places called Eccles, Ecclesfield, Eccleston or Eccleshall. The names derive from the Latin for the Church, reflected in the contemporary English word ecclesiastical, meaning the hierarchical structure of the Church. Thus a name containing 'eccles' reflects a Latin-named – that is Roman – site which contained a known church building and perhaps also an ecclesiastical structure of bishops or similar. The majority of these sites have proved to be Roman-era church sites that lay just far enough away from the main Roman towns to not be troubled too much by the authorities in the periodic outbreaks of official persecution of early Christianity. Thus for example Eccles in Greater Manchester lay as a Roman site some 10 miles from the Roman city at Manchester: Eccles, Kent lay some 6 miles south of the Roman city at Rochester while Eccleshall, Staffordshire lay some

12 miles northwest of the Roman city of Pennocrucium, now the site of Stretton village, Staffordshire.[1]

With the coming of Christianity to the Middle East and especially the Roman Empire, religion had become international, and people's sacred sites were now not only local, but also thousands of miles away in Palestine or Egypt, Rome or France. While Romano-British Christianity worked within local traditions, it also maintained a sense of itself as being part of something bigger, something more profound and coherent, and something that pertained beyond just these islands.

THE BRITISH CHURCH

Christianity was a force in Britain long before the Emperor Constantine made it the leading authorised, permitted religion of the Roman Empire in the early fourth century. Christianity was emerging in Britain from at least the second century AD, and possibly earlier. It arrived with the trade and military forces of Rome itself. Christian converts were to be found by the end of the first century throughout Roman society. Merchants and slaves, traders and soldiers, wives of Imperial commissioners and wandering scholars were all as likely to be Christians as not. We have no idea who first brought Christianity to Britain, but the reality is that thousands of people in hundreds of different ways will have done so, and slowly a local Church or Churches emerged from this uncoordinated but persistent arrival of the faith in Christ into Britain. There is, curiously enough, an old tradition that Claudia and Pudens – the couple mentioned in the New Testament (2 Timothy 4:21) and who gave support to the early Church – were the daughter and son-in-law of either Caractacus, one of the last defiant rulers of Britain to be captured by the initial Roman invasion of the AD 40s, or the more collaborative British King Cogidubnus.[2]

Certainly by AD 180 Christianity was established within Britain, albeit secretly, as writing on a pottery shard found in a rubbish dump of c. AD 180 on the site of Roman Manchester has proved. It looks like a simple poem, but contains the Lord's Prayer in acrostic form. Other early Christian sites, which await much more archaeological exploration, include Bangor-is-y-coed, Wales, where it has been claimed a Christian community existed from AD 180 onwards, and where Pelagius (see page 63) is supposed to have been a student during the late fourth century. Wroxeter is another example, where the outline of a possible basilica fourth-century church has been detected.

Several villas, such as Lullingstone in Kent, have yielded early chapels and Christian art. Many churches of great antiquity, which lie just outside Roman towns, may mark the burial sites of local Roman-era saints, as Roman cemeteries always lay outside the city walls: for example St Martin's in Canterbury, All Saints in Great Chesterford, Essex, just outside the walls of the Roman city at Great Chesterford, and St Andrew's in Northover, Somerset, just north of the Roman city at Ilchester.[3]

It has become fashionable recently to reject the notion that there was ever such a distinct thing as the British Church – often called the Celtic Church – in the period *c.* AD 180–600. In part this is an understandable reaction to the sentimental and romantic outpourings of 'Celtic' materials that have often done little to help us see the tougher, more dogmatic aspects of the British Church. There is also a polemical dimension to the argument, based on the fact that interest in it was reawakened during the sixteenth century when Protestant England wanted to justify its stand against Catholic Europe.[4] The claim that, far from being a modern heresy, the English Church was as old as Rome but had been subverted, helped bolster a sense of continuity and legitimacy in the stand against Rome. This attitude is indeed to be found amongst British Protestant Christians. I recall that when colleagues and I were preparing a historical chart of the various Christian traditions and denominations we asked the media office of the British Baptist Church whether they could give us a date in the late sixteenth or early seventeenth century for the founding of the first Baptist Church. The reply came back that the Baptist Church *per se* was founded by Jesus Christ *c.* AD 33.

I feel, however, that those who use the revival of interest in the British Church in the sixteenth century as an argument for dismissing its existence are mistaken. Their mistake, ironically, is to take too literally the claims of the other side, the Catholic Church, for the existence of one Church from the time of the Roman Empire. This was itself a myth perpetuated by the Roman Catholic Church at the expense not just of smaller, older Churches such as the British one, but also of major surviving churches such as the Coptic, Syrian and Orthodox churches. There was a distinct British Church in Roman and post-Roman times.

Similarly, there was a distinct church in most cultures around the Mediterranean until the versions of the Church based upon Rome's urban Church, Constantinople's variety of Christianity and that of the Egyptian culture of Alexandrian Christianity emerged in the fifth century as the three leading claimants to be the true Church.

The early Church is often spoken of as if it were one monolithic institution. In reality, however, the Church grew in different ways and as the result of diverse forces incorporating aspects of local cultures, language and values. The early Church was in fact the early churches, of which the British Church was one. These churches experimented with incorporating local beliefs, mythologies and practices according to the areas in which they took root. Gradually, versions of the Christ story that shared common elements coalesced and were defined into what a major Church tradition considered standard Christian teaching. Those that were too radical or heretical were banished or resisted. The ideal of one Church is a historical invention of the fourth and fifth centuries AD, after the Western Church had become the faith of the Roman Empire.

Locally, Christianity, be it in Britain, Egypt or China, took a shape and form which built upon the existing traditions of the sacred and infused them with the vision of a Christ whose role depended upon the existential needs of that culture and tradition. Thus, for example, early Christianity in China (c. 635 onwards) took seriously the existential crisis of belief in reincarnation and karma and offered Christ as a solution to that dilemma whilst using Buddhist and Taoist imagery and language to describe him.[5] The same happened in Britain. One of the treasures of the British Museum is a wonderful mosaic floor found at Hinton St Mary in Dorset. Dating from the first half of the fourth century, it shows a young, beardless Christ in the centre, with scenes of the pagan deities and myths of Bellerophon and Pegasus fighting the three-headed monster, Chimaera, around the edge. This fusion between Christian and pagan mythology and symbols is to be found throughout early Christian art and sites, and the fact that Christ is beardless shows that the tradition of what he looked like was also fluid at this time – today he is usually portrayed as bearded.

From the fourth century, church historians and teachers presented a view of the early church as a single ship ploughing its way steadily through the tempestuous seas of the pagan world, buffeted by the winds and storms of heresy but nevertheless always finding the true path. Perhaps a better analogy would be to see the early churches as a series of small boats, setting off from different places, using different designs, but all under the sail of the personality and teachings of Jesus. Gradually, those boats that were out-manned, out-manoeuvred or simply not interested in the race faltered and disappeared. Yet clusters of boats survived and decided to sail together rather than separately. The clusters retained their distinct identities and only on the most extraordinary of occasions actually sailed as one fleet.

A unity of sorts was created by the claims of Rome over parts of Europe, while other parts fell under the authority of Constantinople. Outside the old Roman Empire was the Church of the East, a confederation of independent churches, each of which developed within its own culture – as, for example, in China in the seventh to the eleventh centuries, or Tibet from the sixth to the thirteenth centuries. Britain fell eventually within the domain of the Roman Church, but it is no accident that the Venerable Bede's famous book, which he wrote as a good son of Rome in the late seventh and early eighth centuries, is called *A History of the English Church and People*.

Bede has often been called the first historian of Britain, for this remarkable monk, who never seems to have travelled far from his birthplace and home in Northumbria, collected accounts from all known sources and wove them together into his great narrative. Loved by all he met, his passing in the year AD 735 was mourned across Europe as the passing of a great intellectual. St Boniface described him as 'a light of the church, lit by the Holy Spirit'. At heart, though, he was the greatest advocate of the divine purpose of the Anglo-Saxons, and thus set the tone for most of the sacred reading of British history that followed in the next 1,000 years. He was aware of the fact that the English Church was distinctive and he was also aware that the earlier British Church was even more distinctive in its traditions, beliefs and culture, indeed he often criticised it as such.

PELAGIUS: A BRITISH 'HERETIC'

A peculiarly British form of Christianity was that espoused by Pelagius, a Romano-British theologian of the fourth century. He is a fascinating character, notorious for being the main opponent of St Augustine of Hippo, the great Church father who, to all intents and purposes, defined Catholic theology until the end of the twentieth century, and who is perhaps still the single greatest theological influence on many aspects of the teaching of Christian churches today.

We know more about Pelagius than about any other British Roman of the time, which means almost nothing! He was probably born in AD 350 and died a little after AD 418. His opponents called him a Brito, Britto, Britannicus or Britanus, meaning someone from Britain.[6] It is possible that he was originally trained as a lawyer; he certainly had a thorough grounding in the classics and the works of the Church Fathers, which he used to good purpose in debates in Rome and Palestine later in his life. He was never ordained, nor was he a full monk, rather he was a lay brother or what would be called today a tertiary member of a religious community who lived an ascetic life, much of the time associated with a church or religious community, but never formally entering it.

At some time in the late fourth century AD, Pelagius left Britain for Rome to continue his education. He was certainly in Rome by the time of Pope Anastasias (AD 399–401). Pelagius was part of a group of Christians who were exploring the as yet ill-defined areas of the nature of being human within the grace of God. Pelagius taught 'if one wished, one could do what God required – for God does not command the impossible – and that, with a fresh beginning in baptism and with the teaching and example of Christ, the Christian could and should avoid all sin'. When he was finally condemned in AD 411–12 at a Council in Milan, these were the teachings which were judged by the emerging authorities of the Church to be the most perverse:

1. That Adam would have died, even if he had not sinned;
2. That the sin of Adam injured himself alone and not the whole human race;
3. That new-born children are in the same condition as Adam was before he fell;
4. That the whole human race does not die because of Adam's death or sin, nor will it rise again because of Christ's resurrection;
5. That the law as well as the Gospel offers entrance to heaven;
6. That even before the Coming of Christ there were men wholly without sin.

The strikingly modern tone of much of this debunking of certain dogmas of the traditional Church view of history and humanity is one reason for my own sense of pride that it was a British theologian who put forward such a compassionate view of humanity and God. Yet for centuries this, now widely accepted understanding of the Christian faith, was declared heretical. This attitude was rather delightfully echoed in a cartoon in the *Spectator* in 2001, which showed a vicar in his pulpit praying 'And now a prayer for those poor souls who were damned for sins that are soft-pedalled now.'

The main reason why Pelagius became so famous is that he challenged Augustine on the subject of human nature – his name subsequently became used as a title for heretics, who were labelled as Pelagians, for the next 100 years or more. Augustine (AD 354–430) began his religious life as the child of a pagan father and a Christian mother, but seems to have been indifferent to both. At the age of sixteen he became associated with the Manicheans, who were a major religious force in Roman society at the time. Their religion, a fusion of Jewish, Christian and Zoroastrian teachings and cosmology, taught that this physical world was the evil creation of an equally evil demigod. The spiritual world was seen as existing in a perpetual struggle with the physical world, all of which was to be rejected, especially sex. Augustine was involved with the Manicheans until he was twenty-eight, when he was converted to Christianity. It is doubtful, though, whether he ever really threw off the influence of Manicheism, as much of his theology reflects a sense of a dualism between the physical and the spiritual, and a resulting sense that the physical human being was worthless, evil and corrupt. In order to stress the helplessness of humanity and the grace of God, Augustine portrayed humanity as a fallen spiritual form now wrapped in sinful flesh, a state caused by the sin and the Fall of Adam. Pelagius, on the other hand, stressing the goodness of creation and the possibility of the godliness of human creation, saw humanity as flawed but essentially capable of good and understood the incarnation of Christ as a shining example of the possibilities of humanity.

Augustine, being ferociously intelligent and a better writer, won. He was also writing at a time when the Roman Empire was collapsing – it was during his life that Rome was first sacked by barbarians, and he died during a seige of his own North African city of Hippo, by barbarians. His mood of desolation and hopelessness for humanity captured the mood of the times. His views became the defining force of Western theology, and Pelagius was thought to be so dangerous that his teachings were banned. To this day it is difficult to be entirely sure what Pelagius taught because many of his writings were destroyed and only fragments have survived. However, in Bede's *A History of the English Church and People*, written in the early eighth century, Pelagius is seen as the enemy of true theology and the real Church:

> In the year of our Lord 394, Arcadius ... became joint-Emperor with his brother Honorius, and ruled for 13 years. In his time, the Briton Pelagius spread far and wide his noxious and abominable teaching that man had no need of God's grace, and in this he was supported by Julian of Campania, a deposed bishop eager to recover his bishopric. Saint Augustine and other orthodox fathers quoted many thousand Catholic authorities against them, but they refused to abandon their folly; on the contrary, their obstinacy was hardened by contradiction, and they refused to return to the true faith. Prosper the rhetorician has aptly expressed this in heroic verse:
>
> > Against the great Augustine see him crawl,
> > This wretched scribbler with his pen of gall!
> > In what black caverns was this snakeling bred
> > That from the dirt presumes to rear its head?
> > Its food is grain that wave-washed Britain yields,
> > Or the rank pasture of Campanian fields.[7]

Despite the opposition to him, many in Britain took up Pelagius' teachings, and there is even a hint that Pelagian communities appointed their own bishops. Bede says, speaking of the period *c.* AD 429: 'The Pelagian heresy introduced by Agricola, son of Severianus, a Pelagian prelate, had seriously infected the faith of the British Church.'[8]

So serious a threat had the Pelagians become to the British Church that in AD 429, St Germanus of Auxerre was sent to Britain by the Pope to put down the heresy. It seems to have been especially strong in the areas near Bangor-is-y-coed, for it was here that Germanus spent much of his time and that the traces of his missionary journeys to combat Pelagianism can still be found. In Welsh, his name is translated as Gammon, and there is near Bangor a village named Llangammon, meaning church of St Gammon.

The final showdown, as related by Bede, who is far from unbiased concerning Pelagius, is dramatic. Bede claims that the teachings of Germanus and his companions 'preached daily not only in the churches, but in streets and fields' soon brought most of the British back to what Bede calls 'Catholic' teachings. The leaders of the Pelagian Church retreated into the remoter areas of Britain or went into hiding. Then they issued a challenge:

> At length, after due deliberation, they dared to challenge the saints and appeared with rich ornaments and magnificent robes, supported by crowds of flattering followers ... but the contestants were greatly dissimilar in bearing. On one side human presumption, on the other divine faith; on the one side pride, on the other piety; on the one side Pelagius, on the other Christ.[9]

The Pelagians spoke first at great length, complains Bede. They were then roundly refuted by the venerable bishops. The end result can be predicted: 'The conceit of the Pelagians was pricked, their lies exposed, and unable to defend any of their arguments, they admitted their errors.'[10]

Personally, I strongly believe in Pelagius' teachings. It seems to me that Augustine's obsessive focus on sin and damnation has done untold damage to Christianity and created for many a culture of guilt. This is particularly apparent in the horrific doctrine of substitutionary atonement, whereby Christ is seen as having died in order to appease an angry God and expunge the sin of Adam, which tainted the entire human race. Pelagius offers us a more positive model, one that sees humanity as blessed by God, not damned. I think it is time that we turned away from the notion that we are innately evil, and looked instead at the alternative offered by Pelagius: that we all have the possibility of being good.

WHITHORN: AN EARLY MONASTERY

The most important early British Christian site is at Whithorn in Scotland. Here St Ninian is believed to have founded a monastery in AD 398, the earliest confirmed monastic site in Britain.[11] Whithorn sits on its own peninsula, jutting out into the Solway Firth. The site of the monastery has been wonderfully excavated and the finds displayed in Whithorn's museum; they are the earliest known British Christian inscriptions and tombstones yet found. The community settled in a hollow 5 kilometres (3 miles) inland from the sea, as if not wanting to draw too much attention to itself. It is possible that it did so because it was a Pelagian community that moved beyond the jurisdiction of the Roman Church and characters such as St Germanus in order to pursue its understanding of the faith. It is a fascinating possibility and one that is still being explored.

The oldest carved Christian stone, dated to before AD 450, was found at Whithorn, with an inscription beginning 'We praise you O God'. It was here that Ninian and his successors began to rebuild their world – a world of failing Roman power and ecological collapse brought on by Roman agro-business and its destruction of the environment. Here the Church began the slow process of developing new sustainable communities, and of creating farming models which have shaped Europe to this day and whose passing is deeply mourned by those who care for the environment and for human community.[12] Here a new vision, a sort of post-apocalyptic understanding of Christi-anity, emerged, much as it did in the devastated lands of the French and Italian parts of the old Roman Empire. For it was monastic Christianity that resuscitated the land, replanted the forests and woods, restored the water tables, brought back to life the streams and rivers, and reconstituted the very soil which Roman overexploitation had wrecked. Its vision was that work and prayer, environment and God were intimately linked and the one without the other was pointless.

THE FALL OF ROME

While Christianity was emerging, the Roman Empire was slowly crumbling and, environmentally, digging its own grave. Roman farming and industry was far from environmentally friendly. The creation of the northern area of the Sahara desert from what was once the grain-basket of the Empire is well known. Essentially, overexploitation of the soil, because of the unrelenting demands of feeding Rome, caused the soil to break down and turn into dust. Roman agriculture did the same to much of southern Britain. Already well advanced, deforestation was taken to the limit, and many areas of Britain have probably never regained the tree cover they had before the onslaught of Iron Age and Roman forestry and industry. For example, the extraordinary landscape of Pen Pits, Somerset is the result of Iron Age and Roman quarrying for querns. Rising up a hillside from a small stream, still strewn with fragments of worked flint and stone, are hundreds of pits and 2,000-year-old spoil heaps. Even with the passing of time and the growth of a dense wood, rich with moss and almost rainforest-like in its dankness, the landscape looks like a Yorkshire coal mine. This was a very large and heavily worked site that shows that Iron Age and Roman industrial workings were as thorough in their impact as any nineteenth-century mine.[13]

By the end of the fourth century AD, many of the traditional farmlands of the Roman Empire, from Egypt to southern Britain, were reaching a state of exhaustion, and the soil was breaking up and blowing away. Invasion by barbarian tribes, escalating devaluation of the currency, and the growth of agro-business were destroying the traditional small-farmer/market-town culture of much of the Empire. Deforestation and industrial output as a result of increased warfare with the invading tribes was so high that its traces can be easily discerned as a black layer in the ice cores from the Arctic. Indeed, no such discernible layer is found again until the height of the industrial revolution in the late eighteenth and early nineteenth centuries. The fertility of the land was disappearing, and with it the land's ability to produce food to sustain the great cities. As agriculture died, so did the cities and the villas. As scrubland spread, making the land difficult to clear, yet not providing the space for the proper regeneration of woods, so the water levels fell and the streams and rivers dried up.

The dramatic collapse of Romano-British culture is well illustrated by two inscriptions, both now to be seen in the visitor's centre at the Roman site of the Old Work at the village of Wroxeter in Shropshire, site of one of the largest Roman cities of Britain. Between them lie some 400 years – and the destruction of an entire way of life. The first inscription is one of the finest examples of a Roman carved inscription in Britain. It was erected during the reign of Hadrian, probably in AD 129, to celebrate the dedication of the forum, and although badly damaged, it is still splendid in its imperial glory. Strongly carved, it is the embodiment of the pride, strength and order of Rome, and was created to honour a city that was a model of the integration of British peoples with Roman civilisation, for Wroxeter was very specifically a Roman city, created to accommodate the local tribes. Across the aisle is the second inscription. Far from being magnificent and elegant, it looks like a joke. Crudely carved upon this lump of stone, battered and irregular, is a bastard Latin inscription, telling us that it honours a chieftain whose name, Cunorix, seems to mean 'the lord of the hounds'. This inscription was probably set up in the dying embers of the city, around AD 500 or so. By this time the city was still functioning, possibly as a bishop's seat, but the baths had ceased working and the town had shrunk and, if the inscription is anything to go by, was in a pretty poor state. What is poignantly significant is that even in its decline, it still clung to Latin as if hoping that some of its former glory might still persist.

As a child I could never understand why the Angles, Saxons and Danes who overran the Roman Empire in Britain from the fifth century AD onwards did not like plumbing. I used to look at history-book pictures of the hot baths, drainage, and well-built, warm buildings of Roman Britain, and marvel; and I knew from my travels to Roman villas that central heating and constant running hot water had been basic facts of life in this country some 2,000 years ago. But seeing pictures of the invaders living in crude shelters in the ruins of Roman villas or towns, I could not understand why they had failed to maintain the cities and villas. It seemed so sad and unnecessary that we had had to wait so long before we reinvented all the facilities of a civilised town.

It was years later that I discovered that it was not an aversion to plumbing but the collapse of the agricultural ecology, and thus of the economics and culture of Roman Britain, which made the cities uninhabitable and led to the decline of urban civilisation. This fact, combined with the usual tendency of invaders to sack first and look later, means that it is no surprise that all that remains of Roman Wroxeter is a wall fragment.

Just as the last great faith collapse – that of the stone circles – was essentially the result of a collapse of the environment and a sense of the loss of the trust in the deities, so the death of Roman 'Pagan' Britain was caused in part by environmental factors and led to the decline or absorption of one religious tradition and the growth of another. When it fell, Romano-British 'Pagan' Britain took with it virtually all the overt traditions of the British religion which it had so successfully fused. There is some evidence of deliberate destruction of Roman non-Christian sites, perhaps as a desperate reaction against the perception that the 'sinfulness' of the times was leading to divine punishment. However, it is impossible to tell whether this was by Christians or by the 'pagan' invaders such as the Angles. Most sites seem to have just declined and died, in much the same way as the stone circles did. Once again, religion in its traditional forms had failed to sustain society. This time, it had to compete with a more coherent and composite missionary faith, and failing, it died.[14]

There really is very little, if anything, other than Christianity, that can be seen as having survived the death of the Empire and the collapse of its collaborative native religion in Britain. The debate as to whether pagan culture survived to be a serious alternative movement against or flowing under Christianity has now been settled firmly: it did not.[15] The only place where there is some continuity, but with a new significance or interpretation, is within what is often dismissively called folk Christianity. For example, the springs at Buxton, as we have seen, continued the sacred association with the pagan goddess by associating the name Anu with the name St Anne, to whom the springs were dedicated, but those who came to the spring sought the Christian aid of St Anne. Karen Louise Jolly documents the continuation of pagan charms against elves within a Christian context:

> The Anglo-Saxon charms reveal the creativity involved in allowing tradi-
> tions to do what they must to stay alive – adapt. That adaptation was not
> passive, imposed from outside by a monolithic church; rather, the adapta-
> tions that made Christianity a viable religion in Anglo-Saxon culture were
> initiated from within, in the daily lives of ordinary people.[16]

THE ANGLO-SAXON INVASIONS

Back in Shropshire again and just to the east of Stapeley Hill, which we visited in Chapter 3, are the Stiperstones, a craggy outcrop hill. Here we can see a strange scene unfold in the drama of Christianity in Britain at the end of the Roman period. The Stiperstones are dramatic, standing like ragged teeth on the brow of the hill, eerie and strange. They are the focus of many legends, including one that this is where the Devil sits when the storm's thunder resounds.[17] To this day there are men and women who shun these stones at the best of times, and certainly never go near them at night or in stormy weather. But there is another story attached to these craggy outcrops. As well as the Devil's Seat, they are also known as the Bishop's Seat. For here, in or around AD 450, the Bishop of London fled and established his seat. For perhaps 50 years, this hill was the cathedral – meaning seat – of the Bishop of London, a rural St Paul's if you like. He fled here from the invading Saxons who were invited to Britain by the last of the Roman rulers, Vortigern.

To the Christians, writers such as Gildas (sixth century), Bede (eight century), Nennius (late eighth to early ninth century) and Geoffrey of Monmouth (twelfth century), who created models of a sacred history of Britain, Vortigern is in effect the British anti-Christ. As Geoffrey of Monmouth puts it, 'Satan entered his heart', because he lusted after a pagan princess. Although a Christian ruler, Vortigern allowed the pagan Saxons, led by Hengist and Horsa, to come to Britain in AD 450 in order to aid him in what were, in effect, civil wars with other Romano-British leaders. In exchange he allowed them to settle in Kent. To put this in context we need to recall that for over 150 years, the Romans had built defences explicitly to keep these marauding tribes out along the east and south coasts, such as the late-fourth-century Roman fort at Othona in Essex. Geoffrey sums up the hostile feelings of many against Vortigern in the words of Ambrosius, the epic figure who rallies Romano-British Britain in a last stand against the invaders:

> See now, my Lord Duke, if the fortifications and the walls of this place can protect Vortigern, and stop me burying the point of my sword in his entrails! He has earned a violent death, and I imagine that you yourself must be fully aware of how much he deserves it. Of all men he is surely the most villainous.[18]

By inviting the Saxons in and granting them land, Vortigern sounded the death knell of Roman Britain, traditional Celtic/British religion, and Roman Christianity in most of England. The British began to lose their lands to the Saxons and then to the Angles, who were followed by yet more tribes from the areas of the modern-day Netherlands and

Germany. Bede interprets this as punishment by God for the laxity of the Britons' faith:

> In short, the fires kindled by the pagans [the invaders] proved to be God's just punishment on the sins of the nation, just as the fires once kindled by the Chaldeans destroyed the walls and buildings of Jerusalem. For, as the just Judge ordained, these heathen conquerors devastated the surrounding cities and countryside, extending the conflagration from the eastern to the western shores without opposition and established a stranglehold over nearly all the doomed island. Public and private places were razed; priests slain at the altar, bishops and people alike, regardless of rank, were destroyed with fire and sword, and none remained to bury those who had suffered such a cruel death.[19]

The flight of the Bishop of London, a Roman citizen of great learning, is symptomatic of the huge changes that swept through Britain as the Roman world fell in upon itself and the barbarians invaded. Prior to that, it is likely that by AD 450, much of Britain south of Scotland was Christian. The churches co-existed with the older traditions but these were fading fast. However, the dominance of Christianity did not survive the invasions, and by AD 500 Christianity was in full retreat. However, unlike the localised pagan traditions, Christianity was able to migrate with its people and refashion itself in the safety of the fastnessess of the mountains of the Welsh Borders and Wales itself.

When the Bishop of London set up his cathedral at the Stiperstones, he was setting a pattern. Over the next 50 years or so, the Romano-British culture of Britain either died in the ruins of its cities and villas as plague, ecological collapse and invasion claimed them, or fled to the Welsh borderlands. By AD 500, the only places in Britain that were still Christian and retained Latin and other vestiges of Roman culture were in the hills and valleys of Wales and its border terrain such as Wroxeter, Cumbria, Dumfries and Galloway (around Whithorn), one small area of the Pennines, known as the kingdom of Elmet, and remote parts of Cornwall. In Scotland, the tribes that had defied the Romans either defied the new invaders in turn or made common cause with them. Only in Wales did the flickering light of old British Christianity hang on. It was fed not from Rome, nor from England, but from the vibrant Christianity of Ireland (where there had never been a

Roman presence of any significance) created by Patrick and by the model of monasticism.

I am always astonished by Wales. No matter how often I go there, I still find it surprises me. In England to find a stone carved with a Christian inscription or sign of the fifth, sixth or seventh century is to find a treasure. In Wales, you can see seven or eight in one afternoon of church hopping. In England, to find a church that dates from before the Saxon period you have perhaps a choice of ten sites. In Wales, to find a church that is not from that period is a surprise. When the Romano-British left England they transported to Wales a deeply Christian culture that transformed the sacred landscape of Wales. Here, where previously Rome had had difficulty establishing itself except by military force, the fleeing Romano-British Christians found a welcome and established the foundations of a strange form of Christianity. For this was perhaps the last time in the history of Christianity in the West that a form of Christianity evolved which was entirely indigenous; native to such a degree that it saw itself as having nothing to do with the wider world, Christian or otherwise. It saw the faith as being the birthright of those born of a certain lineage – Roman and born in Romano-British Wales and the other scattered Christian princedoms. It set the scene for a struggle between two very different forms of Christianity, both of which have shaped the sacred in Britain to this day.

CHAPTER SIX

THE GOLDEN AGE
OF THE SAINTS

SAINTS AND SINNERS

JUST AS TRADITION AVERS THAT the first known British theologian, Pelagius, was trained at the great monastery of Bangor-is-y-coed, so we know from the very first History of Britain that another great figure in British sacred history lived here as well. Today the site is a charming village with a fine medieval church and ancient bridge crossing the River Dee. Here traces of a Roman villa have been found, fine fragments of mosaic. Here possibly, a Roman villa was built whose owner became a Christian in the second century and from this grew a Christian community. Far enough away from Chester not to be troubled, it may well have become a formal monastery in the mid-fourth century as so many villas did, which is why monasteries look like Roman villas with their covered walkways, central courtyards and farming facilities.

By the time of our next British sacred history figure, Gildas, the old Roman monastery had fallen into disuse as had so much of Roman Britain, and the site had been rebuilt at some point in the sixth century by Romano-British Christians from Wales as a sort of spearhead into the emerging world of Anglo-Saxon kingdoms. It was here where so many worlds met and where decay, struggle, chaos, invasion and ultimately terrible outrage took place that the strange figure of Gildas, melancholic monk, writer, polemicist and historian of sorts lived and tried to interpret his world in biblical terms. With the retreat of the British into Wales, we come to the first history of Britain that interprets events in sacred terms. The monastery disappeared from history in AD 609 when, according to Bede, its 2,001 monks were massacred after the fateful Battle of Chester when the invading Saxons crushed the local British king. Gildas wrote his history in the sixth century, amidst the rubble – literally and metaphorically – of the old Romano-British civilisation, at the dawn of the new models of Christian monasticism and community which were then only just beginning to develop.

Gildas saw the Anglo-Saxon invasion as God's punishment of a faithless Church and people. He watched in horror as the invasion was followed by natural disaster and economic and ecological collapse, and he saw much that seemed to indicate an almost apocalyptic divine hand at work. In particular, he reported the greatest invasion of plague to hit the West until the Black Death in the fourteenth century: the Yellow Plague, an outbreak of horrific scale. The most dramatic recorded effects of the plague were felt further east in Constantinople. According to contemporary chronicles, up to two-fifths of the population were killed and the overall effect on the Byzantine Empire was catastrophic.[1] Bede mentions the impact of the plague on Constantinople, and notes that the plague and the consequential famine also affected Britain: 'Meanwhile the famine, which left a lasting memory of its horrors to posterity, distressed the Britons more and more. Many were compelled to surrender to the invaders.'[2]

If the mighty Byzantine Empire was severely weakened by the plague, imagine the impact on a land already weakened by ecological collapse, invasion and infighting. Quite simply, Britain was unable to cope. The medieval *Life of St Teilo* contains a vivid picture of the plague:

It was called the Yellow Pestilence, because it occasioned all persons who were seized by it, to be yellow and without blood and it appeared to men a column of watery cloud, having one end trailing along the ground, and the other above, proceeding in the air, and passing through the whole country like a shower going through the bottoms of the valleys. Whatever living creatures it touched with its pestiferous blast, either immediately died or sickened for death. If anyone endeavoured to apply a remedy to the sick person, not only had the medicines no effect but the dreadful disorder brought the physician, together with the sick person, to death. For it seized Maelgwn, king of North Wales and destroyed his country; and so greatly did the aforesaid destruction rage throughout the nation, that it caused the country to be nearly deserted.[3]

Geoffrey of Monmouth, writing 600 years after the event, reports the same phenomena and sense of horror. This was a trauma exceeding perhaps even that of the Black Death. When the Black Death came it dealt a huge blow to the model of religion that the medieval church had developed. However, the Black Death happened to a relatively stable society. When the Yellow Plague hit mid-sixth-century Britain, the country was already at its lowest ebb for centuries.

To make matters worse it seems that there was a meteor strike c. AD 530–5 so ferocious that it lit up the whole of Britain for weeks, giving the land the appearance of being on fire from end to end. Just as a volcanic eruption put paid to millennia of agriculture in Britain at the end of the stone-circle era, so the resulting fallout from this massive meteor strike may have been part of the reason for the famine that followed the cloud of pestilence. Indeed, it is even possible that the cloud itself was part of the fallout, and that the winds and the disruption that came from this new 'nuclear winter' were further consequences of this disaster.

Added to the natural disasters was the fact that the priests seem to have been telling the demoralised British people that these awful events were punishment for their sins – as Gildas had done. The average Romano-British citizen must have simply given up. By the mid-sixth century, huge areas of Roman Britain had been depopulated, either as a direct result of deaths from the Yellow Pestilence and the famine, or because fear had driven people for the last 100 years or so to seek the security of remote places. The Anglo-Saxons were able to occupy much of the prime farmland of England because there was no one left to seriously resist them.

These catastrophes not only destroyed Romano-British culture, but also seem to have killed traditional religion and most Roman forms of Christianity. After the flight of the Roman Bishop of London c. AD 450, we hear no more of bishoprics in the classic Roman mould until the end of the sixth century; nor do we hear anything more of British religious sites other than those based around Christian monks or hermits, such as the Llan (the Welsh for church) sites of Wales.

THE BRITISH CHURCH

In Wales, the mid-sixth century was a golden age of the Christian saints. Here, in the remote and defendable security of what had been an outpost region of Roman Britain, the British rebuilt their new, Christian religion. They did so by creating a new sense of the sacred, rooted in the older British traditions of nature, learning and locality, but rooted too in Christianity.[4]

They created an indigenous Christianity that was, in many ways, a Christian version of previous British beliefs. It was fundamentally and deeply Christian, but it saw itself as being for the British, and the British alone. Consequently, the great figures of this era, such as Dewi (St David), Teilo, Dyfrig (also known as Dubricius), Illtud, Cadog and many others, led missions to convert the British wherever they could be found, but with a few exceptions seem not to have considered it their responsibility to try and convert the pagan invaders who now controlled most of England. St David (Dewi) is the most famous, being the patron saint of Wales. He is credited in medieval saints' lives with travelling across the length and breadth of Wales and Southern England and of having gone on pilgrimage to Jerusalem. Historical evidence – churches named after and associated with him – shows him to have been very active in South Wales and especially the south-west region of Pembrokeshire. He is also associated historically with churches in Devon, Cornwall and Brittany, and was renowned for his asceticism and austerity.

St Teilo is similarly somewhat buried in medieval propaganda (for reasons explored in Chapter 9). He also lived in the sixth century. Traditionally regarded as a close friend of David, he was active in the same areas. St Dyfrig (Dubricius) was probably a scion of a major Romano-British family – hence the Latin name. Although active in the sixth century, he was especially popular in medieval Arthurian legends as the 'Archbishop' who crowned Arthur. One of his great centres was the monastic island of Caldey in the Bristol Channel, though he was buried on the Holy Island of Bardsey, situated off the north-west coast of Wales, only to undergo a most extraordinary transformation in the twelfth century as we shall see in Chapter 9.

In turning native, the British Church cut itself off from the wider Christian world; it seems to have become grimly 'ethnic', forgetting the international, universal dimension of Christianity. On the other hand, the British Church undoubtedly developed as a humbler, more local, and in some ways more tolerant church than was developing elsewhere in Europe. It evolved along the lines of Irish Christianity, which differed in a number of significant ways from Roman Christianity. Working in a world of tiny settlements, the Irish Christians had no use for a system modelled around urban bishoprics, but instead developed a structure based around agrarian and scholarly, artistic monasteries. A monastery would be founded, often at a site already made holy by a hermit saint, and a small settlement would then gather around the monastery. The role of nunneries and monasteries was immense, acting as centres of justice, faith, learning, and technology. The abbots and abbesses of these mighty establishments effectively ruled their local areas, appointing bishops as and when they thought necessary. This model of Christianity, with which the British strongly identified, was not the urban and urbane Christianity of formal legal councils, hierarchical bishoprics, and increasingly wealthy city priests. It was a simpler, tougher model that dealt with unlettered peoples in a harsh farming world.

British Christianity kept alive the knowledge of better times; it preserved Latin, learning and faith when most of Britain was under the rule of initially aggressive, pagan, illiterate invaders.[5] It also kept alive a version of what Christianity was really about and who and what Christ was that was very different from the narrowing understanding of Christ in the emerging Roman Church, largely defined by Greek philosophy and language. The British Christ was not the Caesar-type figure of Roman Christianity, defined so precisely in the Nicene Creed as sitting, like a co-ruling Caesar, 'on the right hand of God' – a phrase taken straight from imperial imagery and etiquette. The British Church's Christ, in contrast, is modelled on the high kings of Ireland, who were judges, warriors and rulers all in one. This is captured in one of my favourite hymns, 'Be thou my vision' which, originally written in Irish Gaelic, uses traditional Irish descriptions of kingship and warfare to describe God:

High King of Heaven
Thou heaven's bright sun!
Oh grant me thy joys
After victory is won!
Great heart of my own heart
Whatever befall
Still be thou my vision,
Oh ruler of all.

At the same time that the Roman Church was developing precise definitions of Christianity in the creeds of the fifth and sixth centuries, Britain produced Patrick. He was a faithful son of the Roman Church, but also a man of his own people, the British, and his adopted people, the Irish. Patrick (*c.* AD 383–461) is a fascinating link between worlds. He tells us in his autobiographical account – the first that we have for any Briton – that he grew up in a Roman-style family villa in the countryside of Britain. The family even had a summer house by the sea thought to be either on the Solway Firth or the Bristol Channel, from which he was captured in a slaving raid by pirates from Ireland. As a slave, he remained faithful to Christ, and when he eventually escaped he trained as a priest and returned to Ireland. His life is full of astonishing adventures, mystical experiences and even an incident of shape changing, when he was turned through prayer into a deer in order to escape the pirates who were trying to recapture him. His understanding of his faith could not be more different in emphasis from the almost legalistic creeds that still dominate the Church today. His creed is as follows:

There is no other God except God the Father, nor has there ever been in times past, nor will there ever be in the future. God is the origin of all things, and has no beginning. God possesses all things but is possessed by none.

His Son Jesus Christ has been with the Father before the beginning, and through him everything was created, all beings and realms, spiritual and material. Christ became human, conquered death, and returned to the Father in Heaven.

The Father has given his Son power over everything in heaven, on earth and beneath the earth, so that every tongue might rejoicingly say that Jesus Christ is Lord.

He has poured down his Spirit upon us, and we overflow with the Spirit. It is his Spirit which brings us the promise of eternal life. Through the Spirit we learn to trust and obey the Father and with and through Christ, become sons and daughters of God.[6]

This is a somewhat different understanding of humanity's relationship with Christ than the Roman Christian model of the Trinity, which was strongly influenced by the traditions of Roman rigor, Greek philosophy, and Persian dualism. In Patrick's world view, we are members of a loving family, bound by ties of affection and compassion. In the Roman Christian model, there is a focus instead on hierarchy and power. We can see this in the hard, legalistic, precise language of the Nicene Creed, concerned more with defining the nature of Christ exactly than with expressing the love which holds the Trinity together:

> We believe in one God,
> the Father, the Almighty,
> maker of heaven and earth,
> of all that is, seen and unseen.
> We believe in one Lord, Jesus Christ,
> the only Son of God,
> eternally begotten of the Father,
> God from God, light from light,
> true God from true God,
> begotten, not made,
> of one Being with the Father;
> through him all things were made.
> For us and for our salvation
> he came down from heaven,
> was incarnate of the Holy Spirit and the Virgin Mary
> and became truly human.
> For our sake he was crucified under Pontius Pilate;
> he suffered death and was buried.
> On the third day he rose again
> in accordance with the Scriptures;
> he ascended into heaven
> and is seated at the right hand of the Father.
> He will come again in glory to judge the living and the dead,

and his kingdom will have no end.
We believe in the Holy Spirit, the Lord, the giver of life,
who proceeds from the Father [and the Son],
who with the Father and the Son is worshipped and glorified,
who has spoken through the prophets.
We believe in one holy catholic and apostolic Church.
We acknowledge one baptism for the forgiveness of sins.
We look for the resurrection of the dead,
and the life of the world to come. Amen.

All forms of Christianity are fusions of the story of Christ with other traditions, but I believe it is sad that the British tradition did not grow further, for it had great wisdom and gentleness. This was not some form of romantic Christianity; it arose from a scholarly priesthood and austere monastic tradition rivalling anything Rome could offer.

To appreciate something of this British Church, we should look at perhaps its greatest centre, Llantwit Major in South Glamorganshire.[7] Today it is a small but busy town. The nearby Atlantic College brings an international air to what is otherwise a country place. The heart of the town is the beautiful, stone Norman church, which is almost as large as a cathedral, and an indication that this was clearly a place of some importance. In Llantwit, the size and beauty of the Norman building indicates that they felt a power here that they wished to encase in stone and make their own. The Normans tended to clad in stone places of sacred power in Wales, St David's being perhaps the best example, as will be seen in Chapter 9. Inside the church is one of the most important collections of British Christian carvings, inscriptions and crosses anywhere, dating from the mid-fifth century. Visitors stare in wonder at the intricate carvings and the fusion of British/Celtic artwork with Christian themes.

The area around Llantwit Major had been settled and developed from early times. A large Roman villa has been excavated nearby and shows evidence of having been converted to Christian use. It is even possible that St Illud lived in the villa during the late fifth century. Llantwit Major was certainly a large Christian establishment, and may well have been the first university in Britain. Here the Romano-British Christians came, first to be strengthened in the faith, but then to settle as they lost their lands in England. Here were trained some of the most outstanding of the early British saints, who then in turn created the Church that withstood the physical and psychological shocks of the disasters that hit Britain during the sixth century. St Samson, a pupil of St Illud, who died in north France c. AD 565, was a classic example of the influence of this holy place. An outstanding student at Llantwit, he then became a monk, possibly even the abbot, of a monastery on nearby Caldy Island. From there he went to be a hermit somewhere by the River Severn and then set off on a series of missions to the British in Cornwall, Brittany and the Channel Isles. Churches dedicated to him are to be found in all these places, almost certainly marking places where he preached or lived.

Llantwit's crosses and inscriptions bear witness to a vibrant, local Christianity. The inscriptions are still in Latin, but it is poor Latin.[8] Mixed in with the Latin is Ogham, the Celtic alphabet invented by monks and based upon the runic tradition. The crosses fuse figurative art derived from Roman prototypes with Celtic knot patterns. In particular, the beautiful remains of the Cross of Iltyd, Samson, Samuel and Ebisair embodies this fusion, dominated as it is by some of the most intricate and varied of the knot patterns. The vigour lies not so much in the inscriptions, but in the artwork. It is this fusion of earlier traditions and the energy of the Christ story that, from Scotland to Brittany, is the hallmark of British Christianity.

Crosses such as these, which were erected not just in Wales but also in other parts of Britain, still stand. They bear witness to the way that the British Church resanctified the land by either taking over places which were already sacred to the older religions, or creating new sacred places in accord with the changing needs of the time. Andrew Patterson, historian and explorer of ancient pilgrimage routes, sums this up well when talking about one of the standing stone crosses now in the museum at Whithorn in Dumfries and Galloway, southern Scotland.

> The tallest, most imposing of the carved stone crosses which now rests in the little museum in Whithorn once stood beside the White Loch. It marked a preaching place where bread was broken and the wine poured in divine communion. Outdoor worship among the fellow creatures of nature was a feature of the Celtic Church which saw the whole created order as suffused with the divine, the eternal breaking into the mortal with every

indrawn breath. It was only after many centuries that Norman inspired stone vaults were raised to hem worship behind walls, so that the call of the winter geese was no longer intertwined with the liturgy.[9]

In fact, stone churches were being built much earlier, but he has a point.

ST COLUMBA

Hundreds of miles north of Llantwit is one of the most important sites of this period, Iona. This strange, mystical island requires a long journey to reach it, one that many make today, and have done for centuries. It lies off the much larger island of Mull, off the coast of western Scotland.

Iona is a lovely place: it is hard in winter, but in the summer, when most people come here, it basks like a quiet whale in the sunlight, floating just above the surface of the sea. For thousands of years people have come to bury their dead here, as shown by Bronze Age burial mounds near the abbey. This far western isle would have been a popular place for British burials, because the land of the dead was thought to lie to the west, in the direction of the setting sun; perhaps this was a mortuary island where the great were brought to be laid to rest.[10]

One might think that it was this symbolism that in AD 563 brought St Columba and a small band of followers to Iona, but this is not the case. Arriving from Ireland, Columba came from the west, and therefore went east to the island, and chose it because it was the first place from which he could not see Ireland, his homeland, and because there were Irish Celts who had moved into this area and he was continuing the British tradition of bringing the Gospel only to his kin. On Iona he founded a monastery which, over the next few hundred years, was to be the powerhouse of the Christian faith not just in Scotland but through much of England and Ireland as well.

Columba is a complex figure, who embodies the contradictions that are such a feature of the British Churches. Born c. AD 521, he was a scion of a noble Irish family, an aristocrat brought up in a culture focused around judgement, raiding, diplomacy and war. He was also a foretold sage. His biographer, Adomnan of Iona, the ninth abbot of the monastery after Columba himself, told this story in the seventh century:

> Earlier still, many years before the time of his birth, by revelation of the Holy Spirit to a soldier of Christ, he was marked as a son of promise in a marvellous prophecy. A certain pilgrim from Britain, named Mochta, a disciple of the bishop Patrick, made this prophecy about our patron which has been passed down by those who learnt it of old and held it to be genuine:
>
> In the last days of the world, a son will be born whose name Columba will become famous through all the provinces of the ocean's islands, and he will be a bright light in the last days of the world.[11]

Adomnan goes on to give a thumbnail sketch of Columba:

> Since boyhood he had devoted himself to training in the Christian life, and to the study of wisdom: with God's help, he had kept his body chaste and his mind pure and shown himself, though placed on earth, fit for the life of heaven. He was an angel in demeanour, blameless in what he said, godly in what he did, brilliant in intellect and great in counsel. He spent 34 years as an island soldier, and he could not let even an hour pass without giving himself to praying or reading or writing or some other task. Fasts and vigils he performed day and night with tireless labour and no rest, to such a degree that the burden of even one seemed beyond human endurance. At the same time he was loving to all people and his face showed a holy gladness, because his heart was full of the joy of the Holy Spirit.[12]

Although it may contain a certain amount of devout exaggeration, this account offers us a glimpse into the austere, rigorous life of Celtic Christianity. It may have been closer to nature, but it still stressed the dislike of sexuality and the punishment of the body through fasts and vigils, which is a feature of much of early Christianity, from Persia to Ireland, though not of the Christianity of Central Asia, China and India, interestingly.

Though a gentle man, and much loved, Columba could also be very stubborn, and this brought about his initial downfall. Quite what happened is unclear, but it seems that somewhere around AD 560–1 a battle took place between Columba's kinsfolk and the High King of Ireland. Columba's kin won, but at a terrible cost to all. It is even suggested in later documents that Columba was the cause of the conflict.[13] Whatever the truth, either Columba felt he could no longer stay in Ireland or he was exiled, and he left the monastery that he had founded there.

Today, you can walk from the site of Columba's monastery on Iona to St Columba's Bay at the southern end of the island. This is where Columba landed on Pentecost, AD 563. To the west of the bay is the small hill known as the Hill of the Back to Ireland, so called because Columba and his followers climbed it to see if they could see the coastline or mountains of Ireland. They could not, and thus felt that they were truly in exile. Columba's white martyrdom – the Celtic martyrdom of sacrifice and cutting oneself off from loved ones and home – had begun.

Columba was famed for his gift of prophecy – one entire Book of Adomnan's *Life* is concerned only with recounting prophecy after prophecy. He was also a remarkable organiser, and his monastery was soon active not just with the Irish settlers in Scotland, but also with the native peoples of Scotland itself. Columba himself rather delightfully referred to his mission as 'I began to live in pilgrimage in Britain'.[14] In AD 574 he converted and baptised the King of the Picts, and his missionaries spread out across Scotland. Iona swiftly became the leading educational establishment of Britain outside the great monasteries such as Bangor and Llantwit. To Iona were sent the tribal chieftains' sons, the future leaders of the British and, as we will see later, the sons of Anglo-Saxon rulers. People accepted the Christian faith because it brought with it both greater spiritual security and material advancement through literacy, good buildings, and links to the emerging Christian world of the Mediterranean. Iona soon became the burial place of the kings, for it was believed that the land was a gateway to heaven.

It was from here that Christianity began its long journey back to mainland Britain, for Columba's mission eventually continued from Scotland into England. Unlike many of the Christian saints, and even though he had gone to Iona to reach out to his own, Columba included non-British peoples in his mission. It was to be one wing of a pincer movement by two very different forms of Christianity, the other being the return of Rome-centred Christianity in AD 597 with the mission of St Augustine. Together they were eventually to bring the whole of the land back into the Christian faith, but not before the faith was almost extinguished as the result of disasters which were to arise at the end of the eighth century.

Iona today is a treasure house, not just the restored abbey, or as a focus of a thriving and international network of active Christians, and not just because of the crosses, stones, shrines, pilgrimage routes and churches that make this a holy island, but because you can feel the sacred in the land. If you have never been then, like a Muslim who must go on Hajj to Makkah once in his or her life, go to Iona.

I went to Iona once when I had very little time as I was due to fly to China, and I had a lot on my mind. On the last night I went into the abbey church for a few moments of quiet. A single candle burned in the side chapel reserved for prayer, and the moon cast a pale light through the ancient building – a Norman church, but imbued by the spirit of the older churches that once stood here. I have a special passion for China's Taoist temples and sacred sites. Indeed, it was while working on them that I realised we had our own lost tradition of such places that link the natural and the sacred, which then led to the founding of the Sacred Land project. But that night, as I spontaneously knelt in the quiet gloom, I knew that I was in a place I could call home and that this was why I was still a Christian. There was an earthiness, a centring, and a power there that moved through me and owned me. I could understand the Britishness of this place, and yet in a strange way it also prepared me for the journey to China and another faith world.

Perhaps the true achievement of Iona was to take a wet, windswept little island, far from the civilised world of the Mediterranean, and reveal it to be where Christ could walk as surely as he had in Palestine and where the ordinary Briton could touch the face of God. I really do not know quite how else to describe the power of this place.

CHAPTER SEVEN

THE WARRIOR AND
THE CHRIST

TO GILDAS, GRUMPY SACRED HISTORIAN of the British, the Anglo-Saxons were little short of being the very devil, the forces of the Anti-Christ. Yet he could, in true Old Testament style, see them as the unwitting instrument of God in chastising the slothful and sinful British Christians. In the mid-fifth century, as the hordes of invaders rampaged across the land, this was an understandable view. Yet it was to be these invaders who were to produce one of the most astonishing Christian cultures of Europe, a culture which itself was to face a life or death struggle in the ninth century to preserve the faith they themselves had once despised and almost destroyed.

By the early seventh century the Anglo-Saxons had taken most of England either by force or by occupying abandoned land. They had brought their families over or married British women, had settled and were busy creating the network of villages that are now a feature of the countryside. They had brought with them their own deities, traces of which can be found today in place names.[1] For example, Wednesbury in the West Midlands, Wednesfield in Staffordshire, and Woodnes-borough and Wormshill in Kent were named after the god Woden. We have already encountered the god Wayland Smith at Wayland Smithy, while Thundersley in Essex and Thursley and Thunderfield in Surrey are all named after the god Thor. Though few such names have survived, there are enough to indicate the spread and extent of the worship of the Anglo-Saxon deities.

These deities were not nature spirits; they offer no immediate sense of the sacred in the environment. They were war gods, brutal and demanding; Woden did not care who won a battle as long as there was blood. They came to be associated with places primarily because temples or shrines were established. The deities were closely akin to those of the Vikings who later raided and then invaded Britain. Excavations of Viking sites have shown that the temples were probably established for purposes of animal, and occasionally human, sacrifice. Anglo-Saxon deities as such lack the all-embracing and naturalistic elements of Celtic religion, or the cosmic vision of Christianity.

Anglo-Saxon religion was not only warrior-dominated but also dynastic. The deities were gods for the nobility; the great royal families all prided themselves on being descendants from Woden, and drew some of their authority from this claim. This tradition was to carry over into the culture of the Christian Saxons, who remained obsessed with their own bloodlines and claimed descent from all kinds of biblical figures. Take the family tree of the royal family of Wessex, as recorded in *The Anglo-Saxon Chronicle* of AD 855. The lineage of the then king, Aethelwulf, is traced back to Christ himself, who is described as 'our father who is Christ'. From Christ the lineage goes via Adam and Methuselah and other great biblical figures, such as Noah, and yet also includes the god Woden.

The Anglo-Saxon's world was heavily peopled by evil spirits, elves, ghosts and so on, all of whom were determined to cause trouble, and had to be constantly guarded against and warded off. In many ways the Anglo-Saxon's religion, with its war motifs, its elaborate funerals, and its curses and charms, was best suited to a people on the move, battling against a tough environment. Their settled life in England both unsettled them in their faith and opened up new worlds to them. The progress of the Christian mission was as much a result of a loss of confidence by the Anglo-Saxons in their traditional religion as it was about conversion to Christianity.

The Anglo-Saxons were missionised from both north and south. In the late sixth century Rome sent the very reluctant St Augustine to Canterbury, at the invitation of the Christian queen of the pagan king of Kent; and in the early seventh century, St Aidan of Columba's mission in Iona was invited by King Oswald to come to Northumberland and bring the Gospel to his people.

ST AIDAN AND ST CUTHBERT

Oswald had taken refuge on Iona *c.* 610 when a child and grown there into a young man while a civil war raged in his kingdom. He became a Christian and returned to Northumberland to try to civilise his people and introduce Christianity to his kingdom. He begged the monastery at Iona to send him a monk to help him do this. A very unhappy monk called Aidan was chosen and, despite his protests that he did not speak the language, was sent to Northumberland. Aidan was an Irishman who had come to Iona to lead a life of prayer and contemplation. The very last thing he wanted was to be made a bishop and then sent off to the barbaric Anglo-Saxons in order to try to convert them.

Aidan need not have worried, for the king translated for him. Soon a deep friendship grew between the two men, and side by side king and priest travelled the kingdom, preaching and teaching together. The impact was enormous. Within a few years the Church had been re-established in Northumberland; there had been churches there in Roman times but they had perished along with the Christians in the Anglo-Saxon invasions. There had even been a Roman mission a few years earlier but this had failed to take hold. This shared ministry of king and priest, so touching in its personalities and humility, sets a pattern which runs through the whole Anglo-Saxon period, and which stands in stark contrast to the post-Norman invasion relationship between Church and state.

Central to Aidan's work was the creation of the monastery on the island of Lindisfarne, just off the Northumbrian coast. Here, in what was clearly a centre modelled directly on Iona, Aidan established himself and trained his monks and lay people. Here a pattern of rigorous Christian ascetical life and celebration of artistic creativity emerged which drew people to the faith. Aidan, the reluctant missionary, became one of the most successful because of his ability to inspire friendship, his love of beauty and his focus upon prayer as the heart of the faith.

Today Lindisfarne is the place to go to touch this sacred history. Here, on one of the tiny islands off Lindisfarne, a retreat was created where the monks could escape the demands of the secular world and enter into long periods of meditation, surrounded by the wonders of creation itself. In particular, there came one man, Cuthbert, to this holy island of Lindisfarne and especially to the retreat island of the Farnes. If Aidan was a man of shining grace, Cuthbert was the model of what the Anglo-Saxons thought a true Christian really should be. Indeed, until the Norman Conquest, he was the patron saint of England. Cuthbert was born in the early part of the seventh century somewhere in Northumbria. He became a monk in AD 651 and was at Ripon in Yorkshire in the late AD 650s where, as Bede recounts in his *Life of St Cuthbert*, he entertained an angel, unbeknown to himself.[2] He was a man who in his own self embodied the great tension of his time. Born probably into an Anglo-Saxon family he was trained by the Celtic Church and it is its spirit of nature, humility and grace which he most embodies. Yet when the Council of Whitby, AD 664, agreed that the Churches in Britain should come under Rome, Cuthbert did what he could, within his conscience, to assist that transition, though he opposed the heavy-handed approach of some who sought to snuff out the Celtic Church tradition.

In AD 676 Cuthbert, uncomfortable with the demands of running a major monastery, withdrew to the tiny neighbouring island of Farne. Here he spent eight years praying, fasting and seeking God in the solitude of nature and the ascetic life. Something of the sensitive theology of this remarkable man can be heard in the prayer of St Columba, who also sought a life of prayer. It is perhaps the most telling prayer of the British Christians:

Delightful I think it to be in the bosom of an isle,
on the peak of a rock,
that I might often see there the calm of the sea.
That I might see its heavy waves over the glittering ocean, as they chant
a melody to their Father on their eternal course.
That I might see its smooth strand of clear headlands, no gloomy thing;
that I might hear the voice of the wondrous birds, a joyful tune.
That I might hear the sound of the shallow waves against the rocks; that
I might hear the cry by the graveyard, the noise of the sea.
That I might see its splendid flocks of birds over the full watered ocean;
that I might see its mighty whales, greatest of wonders.

That I might see its ebb and its flood tide in their flow; that this might
be my name, a secret I tell 'He who turned his back on Ireland'.
That contrition of heart should come upon me as I watch it; that I might
bewail my many sins, difficult to declare.
That I might bless the Lord who has power over all, Heaven with its
pure host of angels, earth, ebb, flood tide.
That I might pore on one of my books, good for my soul; a while
kneeling for beloved Heaven, a while at psalms.
A while gathering pulse from the rocks, a while fishing, a while giving
food to the poor, a while in my cell.
A while meditating upon the Kingdom of Heaven, holy is the
redemption; a while at labour not too heavy; it would be delightful![3]

Cuthbert's life, teachings, miracles, foretelling of events and humility all endeared him to the English. When he died in AD 687, his body was laid to rest at his beloved monastery. Lindisfarne became the greatest pilgrimage centre in Britain and the literary, educational and spiritual heartland of Anglo-Saxon culture was found there. Cuthbert, both in his life and perhaps even more so after his death and the rise of the cult of pilgrimage to his holy places, helped elements of the old British/Celtic Church tradition find a *modus vivendi* with the new Order of Rome. Through his own life, lived according to the values of the British Church and yet also later according to the rules of the Roman Church, he embodied the best of both worlds. Through pilgrimage to his holy places, especially Lindisfarne, the traditions of the older, British Church were explored anew by each generation of pilgrims.

Cuthbert achieved a special place in the heart of the Anglo-Saxons and indeed of the Celts and British that few other saints achieved. Stories of his humility and generosity help one to understand why. For example, when he introduced the codes of conduct of the Roman Church to Lindisfarne, some there made his life very difficult. As Bede puts it in his *Life of St Cuthbert*:

At chapter meetings he was often worn down by bitter insults, but would put an end to the arguments simply by rising and walking out, calm and unruffled. Next day he would give the same people exactly the same admonitions, as though there had been no unpleasantness the previous day. In this way he gradually won their obedience.[4]

But in some strange way, it was his 'home' of Lindisfarne and the quintessential link between spirituality and nature there that seem to have made Cuthbert so important. Today it is certainly this link that has caused a huge revival of his veneration. Lindisfarne is dominated by the ruins of the medieval abbey and, to some extent, by the castle, but there are places here where you can feel the old link between land and faith.

For me, Aidan and Cuthbert are the very heart of sacred Britain. Humble men, quiet yet strong, friends of kings but fighters for the rights of the poor, travellers, teachers and soul friends, they embody what I love most in my faith. They walked in wonder through the natural world, which the God they adored created. All this and more is what draws me, as it draws and has drawn so many others, to stand in the gentle light which shines from these men of God, companions of Christ, and friends of the poor.

THE ROMAN MISSION

While Aidan was busy in Northumbria in England, the Romans had returned. In AD 597, a group of damp and worried Roman clergy arrived in Canterbury, including St Augustine. Formerly the abbot of St Andrew's monastery in Rome, St Augustine had been chosen as leader of this mission by Pope Gregory the Great. Gregory was one of the dynamic figures who redrew the outlines of faith and society in the old Roman Empire after the collapse of the Roman Empire in the West, and he it was who gave new life to the Roman Church.

Through sheer force of personality and brilliance of mind, Pope Gregory the Great was forging for the first time a sense that the Roman Church was the absolute standard, the one normative Church to which all others had to conform. Earlier popes had acted as if this was the case, but until Gregory, none had the power to try to make it so. Augustine shared his mentor's vision.

It has long been claimed that Augustine converted Britain, or brought Christianity to Britain. This was not the case, for as we have seen Christianity was probably the majority faith by the time the Roman Empire fell in Britain and it continued in many areas: in terms of renewal of the faith, Aidan and Cuthbert brought it to the north, but

St Augustine did bring Roman Christianity back to Britain. Augustine's mission was explicitly to the Anglo-Saxons (or English), not to the British, who were considered to be Christian but deviant in their traditions. Augustine's new order took a very different view of the land and of the sacred from that of the British Church. In the late seventh century, one of Augustine's successors, Theodore the Greek, divided England into the dioceses and parishes that have persisted to this day. The British Church had no such structures; the churches grew where people wanted them, and bishops wandered as monks and members of a monastery, rather than ruling from a central point. The diocesan model, however, saw the whole of the land as being under the jurisdiction of the Church, and gave everyone the right to belong to a church, which exists to this day. If you want a church wedding, you have the right to be married in your parish church, and there is not an inch of Britain that is not in a parish.

Another difference between the two models of Christianity was observed by the Venerable Bede, the first truly sacred historian of Britain. Through his history, written in AD 731, he describes a vision of the English Church (by which he means Augustine's Roman model) and people that is rooted in a sense that their history was as sacred as that of the kings and kingdoms of the Old Testament, and as destined to find its fulfilment in the Gospel of Jesus as was that of the people of Israel in the Old Testament. From him comes the sense that to be of this land is to be specially blessed, and yet also part of something much bigger.

Bede did not see this sense in the old British Church. He complained of the state of the British c. AD 440 when there were no foreign invaders but the people were torn by civil war: 'Among other unspeakable crimes, recorded with sorrow by their own historian Gildas, they added this – that they never preached the Faith to the Saxons or Angles who dwelt with them in Britain.'[5]

In contrast, Bede shows that, while the English Church developed a unique culture, it also played its part in a wider world and a wider history. This is the first time in the sacred history of Britain that a faith developed in Britain whose believers perceived it to be of importance beyond just its own people. Not even the Druids, praised as they were by some Romans and Greeks, had had a wider sense of their role. From now onwards, the story of the sacred history of Britain is always in dialogue with the wider sacred history of at first Europe, and later the world.

It was inevitable that Augustine should make contact with the existing British Church. In AD 604, St Augustine of Canterbury and the British bishops met. Legend has it that this meeting took place on what is now College Green in Bristol, just beside the later cathedral of St Augustine. However, it is more likely that it was at Aust on the somewhat bleak coastline of the Severn Estuary, for the River Severn had effectively become the boundary between the British and the Anglo-Saxons.

The meeting was designed to forge an alliance between the newly re-established Roman authority Church and the existing Church of the British. In a gripping account of the occasion, Bede writes that Augustine declared:

> There are many points on which your customs conflict with ours, or rather with those of the universal Church. Nevertheless, if you will agree with me on three points, I am ready to countenance all your other customs, although they are contrary to our own. These three points are: to keep Easter at the correct time; to complete the Sacrament of Baptism, by which we are reborn to God, according to the rites of the holy, Roman and apostolic Church; and to join with us in preaching the word of God to the English.[6]

The British bishops, offended by the fact that Augustine, who had been seated when they arrived, and had not stood up to greet them as equals, refused. They did not seem to feel that the English were worthy of the Gospel. Augustine then made it very clear that it was this above all else that brought the wrath of God upon them through the invasions of their enemies, 'and if they refused to preach to the English the way of life, they would eventually suffer at their hands the penalty of death'. And, Bede continues, 'by divine judgement, all these things happened as Augustine foretold'.[7] It is in the light of this incident that Bede saw the destruction of the ancient monastery at Bangor and the murder of its 2,100 monks as fulfilment of this dire prediction.

The next showdown came in AD 664 at Whitby. By then, British churches had been established from Scotland to the Midlands and Essex. Meanwhile, the Roman Church had expanded from Kent up into the Midlands, and even as far north as Northumbria. Britain was now effectively a Christian land, but there were differences between the two camps. At Whitby Abbey, ruled by the formidable Hilda, abbess of both a monastery and nunnery, a meeting took place. The British Church was essentially on trial for not conforming to Roman orthodoxy. The core issue was the date of Easter. Different methods of calculating the date of Easter had arisen in the various churches and, indeed, to this day, the Catholic Church and the Protestant churches follow one method of calculating this, while all the Orthodox churches follow another method. The pretext for calling this council was that the King of Northumbria had married a princess from the south. She followed the Roman date for Easter, he the date of the British Church, and it was to resolve this conflict that the Council met. Describing the debate between the defender of the British tradition, Colman, and the defender of the Roman position, Wilfred, Bede gives us a loving portrayal of the British Church and its leaders, despite being strongly in the Roman camp. In particular, he says:

> During Aidan's lifetime these differences of Easter observance were patiently tolerated by everyone; for it was realised that, although in loyalty bound to retain the customs of those who sent him, he nevertheless laboured diligently to cultivate the faith, piety, and love that marks out God's saints. He was therefore rightly loved by all, even by those who differed from his opinion on Easter.[8]

In the end the King went against the British Church, opting for the Roman Easter and thus the authority of Rome on spiritual matters. The key issue in his decision seems to have been Wilfred the bishop of Ripon's claim that the Roman Church, and only the Roman Church, held the keys of St Peter that would admit the King into heaven. Wilfred's intemperate words illustrate how uncompromisingly the Roman Church viewed its supremacy:

> But you and your colleagues are most certainly guilty of sin if you reject the decrees of the Apostolic See, indeed of the universal Church, which are confirmed by Holy Writ. For, although your Fathers are holy men, do you imagine that they, a few men in a corner of a remote island, are to be preferred before the universal Church of Christ throughout the world?[9]

After the Council of Whitby, the days of the independence of the British Church in England were numbered. Over the next few decades, monasteries were taken away from the British Church and given to the Roman Church. Bede relates how Colman and his followers left Lindisfarne and handed it over to the Roman party. Wilfred also took over monasteries, such as Ripon, where he removed all those monks who would not conform to the Roman practices, which led, as Bede puts it, to 'the result that the Catholic Rite daily gained support and all the Scots then living [Bede uses Scots to describe the Church of Aidan, who came from Iona, Scotland] among the English to either conform to it or return to their own land'.

It was a long time, however, before the victory of the centralist Church of Rome was complete. In England, the British Church was soon swallowed up, but in Wales, the British Church continued in some form or another right through to the fifteenth century, even though most of it had been subjected to Rome by the Normans. In Scotland it was to be many centuries before the British Church there was tamed. St Margaret, who married King Malcolm III of Scotland in 1070, reformed the British Church and brought it under the loose control of Rome.[10] However, it continued underground, rising up when the Scots launched their bid for independence from the English under Wallace and Robert the Bruce in the fourteenth century. The British Church priests performed the coronation service of Robert the Bruce, furtively and illegally.

Even so, with Whitby in AD 664, the British Church had begun the long slide out of sight and in England only the Anglo-Saxon Church, an almost faithful child of Rome, remained.

CHAPTER EIGHT

A CHRISTIAN COUNTRY

ROM THE COUNCIL OF WHITBY IN AD 664 to the dreadful year of 793 when the Viking raids began, much of Britain was drawn into the orbit of Rome, finding its place within the growing and consolidating Christianity of Europe. Elements of the older pagan and warrior Anglo-Saxon traditions survived, and these were woven into the emerging religion that was to become Anglo-Saxon Christianity. Britain still saw itself as a special place, even as part of the bigger story of faith, and Bede, writing in the early eighth century, when the Church and kingdoms were at their most harmonious, still viewed his Church and people as, in some indefinable way, uniquely special and sacred.

To some degree he was right. The Anglo-Saxon Church was different and special because it maintained a balance between the narrative of the Gospels, if you like the core insights of the traditional Christian beliefs, and the old pagan Anglo-Saxon beliefs and values, modified to be sure, but nevertheless absorbed rather than rejected out of hand. As before, the dying of the older traditions took place gradually and included an element of transformation, of incorporation into the Anglo-Saxon version of Christianity. The way the Anglo-Saxons took on the Gospel within their own cultural context is wonderfully highlighted in the story told by Bede about the discussion King Edwin of Northumbria held in the year AD 627. Recent archaeology has probably revealed to us exactly where this discussion took place.

The attractive village of Kirknewton in Northumberland is dominated by the nearby hill, Yeavering Bell, the summit of which is topped by an Iron Age fort. Bede thought it was here that King Edwin had his palace and pagan temple. In fact, a remarkable archaeological excavation in the valley, now marked by a stone monument, has revealed where the palace and temple once stood. The excavations at Yeavering have uncovered a 27 metre (90 foot) long Great Hall and the burnt remains of a temple. This is very similar to Iron Age temples, and the remains of sacrificed animals have been found there. It seems the site was a compound of banqueting hall, workshops, ancillary buildings and temple. It was almost certainly here that one of the most famous sacred and theological expressions of Anglo-Saxon culture was made. The Roman missionary Paulinus was trying to convince the King to convert. Bede describes how, during the discussion, one of the King's chief men said:

> Your Majesty, when we compare the present life of man on earth with that time of which we have no knowledge, it seems to me like the swift flight of a single sparrow through the banqueting-hall where you are sitting at dinner on a winter's day with your thanes and counsellors. In the midst there is a comforting fire to warm the hall; outside, the storms of winter rain or snow are raging. This sparrow flies swiftly in through one door of the hall, and out through another. While he is inside, he is safe from the winter storms; but after a few moments of comfort, he vanishes from sight into the wintry world from which he came. Even so, man appears on earth for a little while; but of what went before this life or of what follows, we know nothing. Therefore if this new teaching has brought any more certain knowledge, it seems only right that we should follow it.[2]

This thoughtful statement is typical of the English attitude (indeed I would even argue, quintessentially Anglican attitude) to the usefulness of faith, with the combination of fatalism and hope that characterises the gradual and undramatic way in which Christianity won over the Anglo-Saxons. Incidentally, Paulinus converted the King, but when he died in AD 633 his people turned again to their old ways and it then fell to his son Oswald, who came to the throne after many tribulations in AD 635, to invite Aidan, whose very different form and style of Christianity finally won the day for the Church, creating an extraordinary fusion of cultures.

An example of just such fusion is at Ruthwell village, which lies beside the Solway Firth just over the border from England in Dumfries and Galloway, Scotland, battered by the gales off the Firth. It is a very ordinary-looking village, but its church, set back from the salt winds and almost hidden in surrounding trees, holds one of the greatest treasures of Anglo-Saxon Britain. The church has a most unusual shape, for it has been designed to focus upon the Ruthwell Cross, which is positioned where an altar would usually be. Standing 6 metres (20 feet) high, the cross was erected some time in the eighth century – the golden age of the first flourishing of Anglo-Saxon Christianity. While the sheer height and beauty of the cross more than justifies a visit here – for it is one of the best such crosses anywhere in Britain – it is the text inscribed upon it in Anglo-Saxon runes that is of greatest importance.

Carved here is the earliest known selection from the greatest spiritual poem of Anglo-Saxon Britain. The text is from the 'Dream of the Rood', an account of the crucifixion from the point of view of the tree (rood) to which Christ was nailed. It is an astonishing poem, not least for the boldness of its theology and the welding together of the Christian image of the Son of God being crucified with the Germanic or Anglo-Saxon image of Woden, the one-eyed god who voluntarily hung from a tree to gain knowledge. The key section of the poem carved on the cross (according to my own version of the translation) is as follows:

Men bore me
on their shoulders and set me on a hill.
Many enemies held me fast there.
I saw the Lord of All coming swiftly
and with such courage to climb upon me.
I did not dare to bend or break then
when I saw the surface
of the earth tremble,
for it was against my Lord's desire.
Tumbling I could have felled

all my enemies.
but I stood firm and true.
Then the young warrior,
God Almighty Himself,
stripped, and stood firm
and without flinching.
Bravely before the multitude
He climbed upon the cross
to save the world.
I shivered when the hero clung to me,
but I dared not bend to the ground,
nor fall to the earth.
I had to stand firm.
I was a rod raised up,
I bore on high the mighty King,
the Lord of Heaven.
I dare not stoop.
They drove nails into me –
see these terrible injuries,
the open wounds of malice.
I dared not injure the enemies.
They insulted us both and I was soaked in the blood
that ran from the Man's side after He set his spirit free.
On that hill I saw and endured much.
I saw the God of Hosts stretched on the rack.
I saw darkness covering the lifeless body of the Ruler with clouds.
Against His shining radiance
shadows swept across the land,
strange powers moved under the clouds.
All creation wept,
weeping and moaning for the death of the King.
For Christ was on the cross.[3]

Christ becoming a warrior and mounting the tree by choice and the weeping of the whole of creation are elements from the Odin story, here fused with elegant skill in the narrative of the Passion to produce what for me is one of the most moving pieces of religious poetry.[4]

This poem illustrates how the Anglo-Saxon Church incorporated elements of earlier cultural traditions into the Christ story, just as the earlier British Church had done. The Anglo-Saxon Church did the same with the sacred landscape. Many of the holy wells of today have names associated with Anglo-Saxon saints, such as East Dereham in Norfolk, where the holy well is associated with St Withburga. Another delightful Anglo-Saxon well, lovingly restored, is at Binsey, just beside Oxford. Here the ancient church lies at the end of a single track, just a few hundred yards from the rush and noise of the A34, but a million miles away in terms of peace and quiet. Approached through an avenue of great trees, a cathedral of nature, the little church lies almost sunken in the ground it is so old. Behind it still flow the waters of the holy well of St Frideswide, who settled here at some time in the eighth century. Here you can feel what Anglo-Saxon Britain must have been like.

By the late eighth century, the Anglo-Saxon peoples had largely abandoned their original faiths. The shrines to their gods were deserted or had been removed following the conversion of the kings and the people through the extraordinary efforts of the British Roman missionaries. The Anglo-Saxon world of deities was a localised, militaristic world view. It did not have the vision to respond to a universal religion, such as Christianity. The process of tribes converting to Christianity was occurring right across Europe, as the tribes sought a role in the wide social world of emerging Christendom. The benefits of education, travel and trade, and the social benefits which accrued by becoming part of this new world block of Christianity, far outweighed any advantages of clinging to the old ways. That which could be accommodated – charms, beliefs, imagery – was, and that which could not was quietly dropped.

The skill of the Anglo-Saxon Church lay in its ability to incorporate the old culture into a wider and ultimately more sacred network of saints, holy hills, sacred wells, and sanctified buildings, even towns and cities. These were all linked by the magical web of pilgrimage, ritual and ceremony. England had settled into being a Christian country. It had its own sacred geography of the landscape, from holy hills and sacred rivers to wells, shrines and the great education and artistic centre at Lindisfarne. It also had its own sacred history which saw the kings and queens of England as modern-day versions of the kings and queens of the Old Testament. Gildas, our first sacred historian in the fifth century had bemoaned the dying of his world and cast Britain as the scene of tragedy. Bede saw things radically differently. For him Britain, but especially England, was a land especially blessed and held in the love and even purpose of God. Its Christian artwork and poetry, weaving the old with the new, and the older traditions of magic and spells, were incorporated into the rituals and services of the Church. Bede says at the very end of his *History*:

> As such peace and prosperity prevail in these days [*c.* AD 730], many of the Northumbrians, both noble and simple, together with their children, have laid aside their weapons, preferring to receive the tonsure and take monastic vows rather than study the arts of war. What the results of this will be the future will show.[5]

Centuries later the Normans noted when they had conquered England that every village seemed to have its own saint or specially revered holy man. They were astonished at the extent to which the most mundane places were revered as sacred. Pilgrimage played a great part in opening up what could have been rather provincial, even parochial, sacred places. Great pilgrimage centres grew, such as Crowland, Lincolnshire, where the cult of St Guthlac emerged from the mid-eighth century onwards, or Threckingham in Lincolnshire, burial place of St Weburga until she was moved to Chester in the tenth century to escape the Vikings, both of which drew pilgrims from across England. Anglo-Saxon England was a veritable maze of pilgrimage routes, and the landscape, whether it was springs and wells such as the one at Burnsall, North Yorkshire, which was orignally called Thorskeld – dedicated to Thor – but was rechristened St Helen's Well, hills and rivers such as the Tor at Glastonbury or entire new towns such as Bristol, itself laid out as a cosmological city protected by saint deities, was accepted as a manifestation of the essential sacredness of the land.

It seems that the fundamental nature of the sacred geography of Britain, so many traces of which still shape the land today, was a result of the brilliant vision of the creators of sacred Anglo-Saxon Christian Britain. Bede contributed to it with his *History*, Archbishop Theodore, of the seventh century, created the system of parishes and dioceses which covered all of England with a spiritual network rooted in the parish church and priest, and the poets contributed through their writings. Alongside, and as a result of these magnificent over-arching visions, came the confidence to see a spring as a manifestation of the sacred and thus to dedicate it to a saint, or even to the Virgin, the sense of being which inspired the creation of high shrines to St Michael to protect the towns and settlements below, as happened, for example, at St Michael's Mount, Cornwall, or Bristol's St Michael On the Mount Without church, protecting the city from the north; and the feel for the Divine which meant that all life was seen as a sacrament, as worthy of praise.

The old cults of warfare, of the trickster religion of Woden, who has been described as 'a combination of hard-faced impudence and low cunning in getting out of awkward places',[6] and the somewhat confusing family relationships between the old pagan deities of the Anglo-Saxons, which seems at times to resemble nothing more than a supernatural and rather more vicious version of *The Archers*, fell easily to the more sophisticated, frankly more civilised and gentle saints who lived amongst the people and brought the sacred into everyday life.

Christian Britain had survived the collapse of the Roman world and the subsequent disasters. It had converted the invaders and had created again a profound Christian culture. It was in this sense of confidence that Bede ended his book with 'What the results of this will be the future will show.' Never in his wildest dreams could he have imagined what happened next.

THE COMING OF THE NORTHMEN

On 8 January AD 793 this world fell apart. *The Anglo-Saxon Chronicle* tells us why:

> 793: Here terrible portents came about over the land of Northumbria, and miserably frightened the people: there were immense flashes of lightning, and fiery dragons were seen flying in the air. A great famine immediately followed these signs; and a little after that in the same year on 8 January the raiding of heathen men miserably devastated God's church in Lindisfarne island by looting and slaughter.[7]

The Vikings had appeared from nowhere. Suddenly Christian Britain was under attack in a way that it had never experienced before. These 'heathen men' deliberately targeted the churches, where they knew there would be people to seize as slaves, treasures to sell and books to burn. The attack on learning was one of the things that most shocked the Anglo-Saxons, Welsh, Scots and Irish generally. The celebration of learning that came with Christianity was central to the sense of civilisation, as can be seen in the art of the time, such as the Lindisfarne Gospels, the *Book of Kells*, or the *Lichfield Gospels*. A wonderful example is the delightful picture at the top of the cross slab at Nigg, Easter Ross in the Scottish Highlands, where two saints are leaning forward, totally engrossed in reading books.

For nearly 100 years the Vikings wrought terrible destruction on the settlements on the coastlines and rivers of Britain, sacking cathedrals, monasteries and homesteads with ease. Christian Britain reeled and very nearly lost its faith.[8] Gradually, some Vikings began to settle. Then came the fateful year of AD 869, when the Vikings came in such numbers that they overran most of England, and they did not leave.

The timeworn remains of the Saxon cathedral and abbey at Soham, Cambridgeshire are a visible reminder of those terrible years. Here, in the AD 630s, St Felix had founded a vast abbey, which grew to be one of the mightiest monasteries in England and a place of great learning. Then in AD 869, the Vikings struck deep into East Anglia and reached both Ely and Soham, destroying both towns, amongst many others. The economic strength of East Anglia was destroyed by the Viking invasion and, in some places, has never returned to the level it was at in the mid-ninth century. As was the case with many of the great churches destroyed by the Vikings, it was 100 years before the area was sufficiently calm and English rule re-established for the abbey at Ely to be rebuilt. But no one rebuilt Soham. The times were too hard and too precarious for a full-scale rebuilding of that which Viking violence had so swiftly destroyed. The ruins at Soham are silent witness to the sheer scale of the devastation that the Vikings brought.

The Vikings proceeded to sweep through England, defeating kings, overrunning kingdoms, destroying every army sent against them, ravaging churches and monasteries in their wake, until by the mid-870s eventually only Alfred, the young King of Wessex, stood in their way.

KING ALFRED

Let me declare a passion. I am intrigued by Alfred. In my personal world of heroes, there are two Greats: Alexander the Great and Alfred the Great. I am hugely fascinated by Alexander, but also repulsed by him. In Alfred, though, I see a man I can really sympathise with, a man of determination and a great heart, but one who was also flawed. He is an English version of St Peter, big and powerful but also aware of his own weaknesses.

Born in AD 849, Alfred's childhood was a tough one, caught in the cut and thrust of Anglo-Saxon power struggles, but lit by the sheer wonder of his visit to Rome as a child, aged four or five. Here he was treated as a representative of a country that the Pope valued and admired for its steadfastness to the faith in the heat of the Viking attacks. Yet Alfred was never intended for the kingship. He had four elder brothers, all of whose names contain that quintessential Anglo-Saxon name, now somewhat hard for us to take seriously, of 'Ethel' (noble). With four older brothers, Alfred was never expected to rule. It was perhaps with an eye to Alfred entering the Church that his father sent him to Rome as a kind of ambassador. Certainly, the glories of Rome and of Christian civilisation had a lasting effect on the very young Alfred. His entire life as a child and young man was overshadowed by the increasing violence and incursions of the dreaded Vikings, so much so that the first 20 years of his life, as related by his biographer Asser, consists largely of descriptions of these attacks with only odd snippets about Alfred. During this period, his father and his brothers all died, leaving Alfred in AD 871 unexpectedly as the King of Wessex.

The Alfred one meets is a gentle giant. Illiterate until his teens, there is a story that he won a coveted copy of a book of poems not by actually learning to read as his elder brothers were trying to do, but by memorising the whole book, thus appearing to his mother to have excelled his brothers. Here is a man whose first loves were learning and compassion, but whom circumstances forced to become perhaps the greatest war leader we have ever produced. A warrior capable of rousing his people to fight for his freedom, but who also sought peace at every turn and used victory to heal divisions and reconcile different peoples. A man who planned systematically, building the first navy since Roman

RIGHT The market square Saxon crosses and stones of Sandbach, Cheshire, are the direct descendants of the ancient stone circles. Most stone circles were probably trade and market places rather than purely ritual or sacred. (*English Heritage Photo Library*)

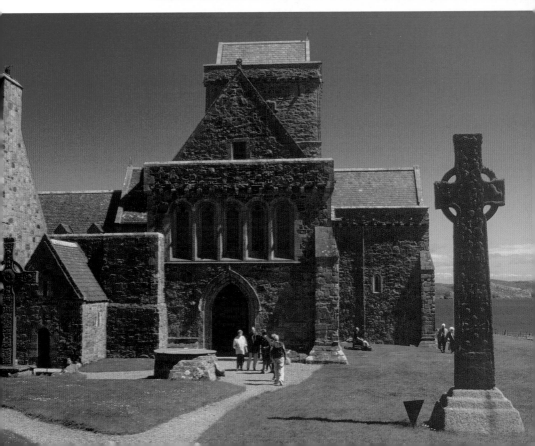

BELOW The rebuilt medieval abbey of Iona, Scotland sits on the original site of St. Columba's monastery, founded in 563 AD. From here the Christian faith first entered Scotland and from there down into Northern England. (*Circa Photo Library*)

incipit
eccl'iaca
...

liber primus
dicens historiae
anglorum

OPPOSITE PAGE This glorious title page from Bede's *History of the English Church and People* is a marvellous example of early Anglo-Saxon design, love of literature and art. It is our earliest extant Sacred History of Britain. (*The British Library/Heritage-Images*)

RIGHT The news of the death of St. Cuthbert in Lindisfarne is dramatically portrayed in this illuminated 12th century manuscript. The monks in the foreground stand in Lindisfarne island and signal with beacons to lay people on the mainland. (*The British Library/ Heritage-Images*)

BELOW In the 9th century AD, the body of St. Cuthbert, driven from its original resting place of Lindisfarne by the Vikings, rested here. Today St. Cuthbert's Church, Corsenside, Northumberland bears witness to this but this medieval church also tells another story. The village it served has gone bar one farm – a victim of the destruction of entire communities by the 14th century Black Death. (*Alan Brooke*)

LEFT Lindisfarne, the great scholarly, monastic and missionary centre of British and Anglo-Saxon Christianity was reduced to ruins twice. First in 793 AD by the Vikings, sending the body of its beloved St. Cuthbert on its long journey to refuge in Durham: and then by Henry VIII in 1538 when all the monasteries were dissolved. (*John Smith/Circa Photo Library*)

BELOW The ruins of the medieval abbey at Whitby, on the side of the Anglo-Saxon nunnery and monastery founded 654 AD. Here the Council of Whitby met in 664 AD to decide on the fate of the British Church. (*Victoria Finlay/Circa Photo Library*)

times to patrol English waters in order to beat the Vikings at their own game and fortifying his new towns so they could withstand Viking sieges. He was rooted in the warrior culture of the Anglo-Saxons but was also beginning to work out that sheer bravery is not enough: proper planning can prevent needless death and destruction. In this he was inspired by his love of Christianity and its vision of a world without war. Nothing illustrates this more clearly than the events that followed the dramatic sweep of the Vikings through England in the AD 870s. As we have seen, they landed, firstly, in Anglia in AD 869 and crushed the Christian kingdoms there, yet that was only the beginning. Over the next nine years they raged across England. The 'raiding army', as *The Anglo-Saxon Chronicle* calls them, seemed beyond the power of any to control let alone stop. Indeed, for a few months in 878, it seemed that even Alfred had become a victim of their sweep across the land.

By AD 878 the invaders had pushed Alfred out of most of Wessex and as *Asser's Life of Alfred* recounts, most of the countryside had accepted Viking rule while many had fled overseas. Christian England seemed doomed as the ruins of the monasteries and the churches stood silent witnesses to the destruction of Anglo-Saxon Christianity and in particular its great treasure houses of learning. Alfred now seemed to be a lost leader, harried almost to extinction, and with a small band of men he hid in the swamps and marshes of Somerset. It is here, in hiding and disguise that the famous story of his having burnt the cakes takes place. Whether true or not, it indicates that his people recalled him with affection and humour – the true sign I would argue, of a great and loved leader. In a medieval version of Alfred's life it is said that when he was at his lowest point, he had a vision: St Cuthbert, the great saint of the British Church – indeed, at this time the patron saint of Britain – came to him in a dream and urged him to fight back.[9] British saint and Anglo-Saxon king made common cause to defend the faith, their people and their lands.

Just after Easter Alfred, emerging from his swampy refuge on the isle of Athelney in Somerset, rose up to fight back, calling to him the men of Wessex. Raising his standard at Egbert's Stone in the forest of Selwood he declared war on the Vikings. Three days later his army overwhelmed the Vikings at Edington, Wiltshire. But physical victory was not ultimately what Alfred sought. Not only did he defeat the invading leader Guthrum, but he also baptised him and many of his men, for he saw that if he was to regain his lands he needed to win the invaders over to the faith and restore learning and education.

The little church of Aller, Somerset nestles alongside the manor house, about 1.5 kilometres (1 mile) from the village of Aller itself. Standing in the churchyard and looking east, you can see that, once upon a time, this was a small island in the marshy watery wastes of the Somerset levels. The Poldan hills run down towards it, but stop about 1.25 kilometres (¾ mile) away. The land then dips down and only starts to rise about 90 metres (295 feet) from the church on its little island. This is still a damp and watery site, as shown by the dragonflies that dart about on a warm summer evening. The church stands as it has stood since the time of Alfred, though his church was probably a wooden one. Today only the occasional visitor comes here.

Yet this ought to be one of the greatest pilgrimage sites in England, a place to celebrate the survival and the recovery of Christianity in England after the Viking invasion. For it was here in 878 that King Alfred, having defeated the Vikings, stood as godfather to the Viking leader Guthrum and twenty-nine of his main warriors. Here, in this now forgotten corner of Somerset, the first Viking Christians were baptised, perhaps in the very font which lies within the church, but more likely in waters drawn from the lakes and streams which made this an island. The church, according to popular belief, stands over the site of the baptism, with the altar on the exact spot where it took place.

Entering this delightful church, you feel its age. The doorway is fine Norman and the arches within the church thirteenth century. The tower is a grand affair, built as stage one of a major expansion planned at the start of the fifteenth century by the lord of the manor. However, his untimely death in a tournament in 1405 put paid to that. Though restored by the Victorians, the church remains a model of a village church. Yet without Alfred both defeating the enemy and converting them, we might well have never had such parish churches that adorn villages across the land. Aller, in its beautiful simplicity and its layers of history visible and invisible, is truly the origin, the starting place for the recovery of Christianity in England.

Alfred is called the Great not only because he was a great fighter, but also because he rebuilt the foundations of civilised life in England. He founded new monasteries and nunneries, as well as schools, new towns, the navy and the English law system, writing personally to famous church scholars in order to persuade them to come to England and aid him in this task. He learnt Latin in his thirties, and went on to translate a number of works into Anglo-Saxon, such as Boethius' *The Consolations of Philosophy*, and Gregory's *Pastoral Care*, the first reflecting Alfred's concern for his soul, the second his concern for his people. Alfred also translated parts of the Bible and key Church documents to encourage the re-establishment of British culture. His legal codification, based upon Anglo-Saxon law models rather than the continental Roman law, laid the basis for the modern English legal system.

Slowly, slowly he and his descendants pushed the Vikings back. He built a strategic alliance with the neighbouring state of Mercia, an old enemy of Wessex, never exploiting his reconquest of its traditional lands or cities such as London, but anxious to create a sense of being English rather than belonging to either Wessex or Mercia. By the time of his death in AD 899, Alfred could look on a land that, while shared with the Viking settlers, was largely at peace, with learning and faith restored and growing. He may not have expected to rule, but without him it is unlikely that England *per se* would ever have come into being. He truly deserves the epithet 'Great'.

The Viking settlers were converted fairly quickly to the Christian faith, often long before the Anglo-Saxons had taken back political control of a region. The reasons for this are the same as the reasons for the conversion of the Anglo-Saxons. The crude, violent and warlike deities of the Vikings, which they largely shared with the old Anglo-Saxons, were no match for the universal and all encompassing nature of Christianity. Furthermore, the Vikings had now come to settle. They wanted to be civilised, to live quiet lives of farming and trading and, ultimately, to be accepted into the wider society of Britain and of Europe. To do this they had to be more like the English and this included becoming Christians.

CHRISTIAN VIKINGS

It took on average just three generations for the Vikings to pass from 'heathen men', who destroyed, to become Christian priests and lay folk. A strange development at this time was the cult of St Edmund. As King of the East Anglians, he bore the brunt of the invasion of AD 869.

His army was defeated and he was murdered, or martyred, by being tied to a tree and shot to death with arrows, then his head was cut off. When the invading Vikings had moved on, his body was collected and eventually found its way to the town of Bedricsworth, where it was buried. The town changed its name to Bury St Edmund's. The remains of the enormous abbey there, within which, in just one little corner, the present cathedral nestles, bear witness to the power this saint had, and soon his cult had became a major one. He was particularly popular with Viking Christians: and often we know exactly where Vikings settled because the parish church in a place would be called St Edmund's. Pilgrimages to shrines associated with St Edmund were very popular not just with the Viking settlers, but also with Scandinavians, right up to the Reformation. The Vikings soon became missionaries to their own people back home and the Christian faith spread into what is today Finland, Sweden, Norway and Denmark. The speed with which the Vikings went from killing the poor man to being amongst his most enthusiastic devotees shows how swiftly the faith came among the Vikings and how readily they accepted it.

But the Vikings also brought their own ideas with them. Viking Christian crosses in Cumbria, for example, combine pre-Christian and Christian imagery. Of these the most dramatic is perhaps that at Gosforth in Cumbria. Standing 5.5 metres (12 feet) high, this superbly carved cross has on its western side a depiction of the god Loki. He is bound to a rock where he was tied for his sins against the rest of the Norse gods, and a serpent is suspended above him dripping poison into his mouth. His wife Sigyn catches the drops in a cup, but has to turn away to empty it, and so a few drops fall each time into Loki's mouth. Also on this side is depicted a warrior slaying a monster, a scene from the Norse legend of Ragnarok – the final battle when the gods all die. The eastern side shows a crucified Christ, and a Celtic cross tops the whole thing. Here British, Anglo-Saxon and Viking fuse into one, yet each brings something of their own.

While Christianity in Britain at this time thus blended with other ideas to develop into a form that suited its local needs, it still participated in the international world of Christianity, sending pilgrims to Jerusalem, and having a whole Quarter in Rome known as the English Quarter, so many Anglo-Saxons lived there.

In rebuilding the Christian culture of England, Alfred saw himself as a faithful son of the Pope. Having visited Rome himself, he had a great respect for the wider traditions of the Church. However, the realities on the ground required him to synthesise the various cultural strands in Britain. For example, the Anglo-Saxon Church was a largely hereditary church, reflecting the family and dynastic nature of Anglo-Saxon culture. Abbeys were passed down through the ruling family, while kings and their families provided not only the finances for the rebuilding and founding of churches and monasteries, but the personnel as well. King's sons, daughters, aunts and sundry other relatives had dynastic roles in the Church as much as in the royal family. Alfred founded the immensely powerful nunnery at Shaftesbury for his daughter, and he endowed it as he might have endowed a dowry for a dynastic marriage.

When Asser came to write his account of the great king's life and struggles in AD 893 he had this to say about the state of the monasteries at the start of Alfred's reign: '... for the monastic life had been totally lacking in that entire race (and in a good many other peoples as well), even though quite a number of monasteries which had been built in that area still remain but do not maintain the rule of monastic life in any consistent way'.[10]

The struggle to reinvigorate the monastic model of Christian life was obviously hampered, as Asser goes on to note, by invasion and destruction. Alfred did his best to rectify this by creating or restoring monasteries with schools as part of them, thus encouraging learning. Anglo-Saxon monasticism, however, had deteriorated, and the laxity Asser noted seems to have increased in the first half of the tenth century. In the mid- to late tenth century, however, this was reformed by another of those king/priest combinations of which Anglo-Saxon Britain was so rightly proud.

ST DUNSTAN

Born in AD 909, ten years after the death of Alfred, St Dunstan embodied as a priest exactly what Alfred looked for in his clergy. Dunstan came from a royal family closely associated with the Church – his Uncle Athelm was the first Bishop of Wells, and then became Archbishop of Canterbury. After finishing his education at Glastonbury

Abbey, Dunstan was appointed as a young man to the court of King Athelstan of Wessex. His asceticism made him unpopular there and, after some unpleasant bullying had brought on a serious breakdown, he withdrew to Glastonbury and became a monk. It is clear that his illness had brought him to reflect upon life and from this he derived the strength of vision that was to guide him for the rest of his life.

At Glastonbury St Dunstan began a life that combined scholarly studies, energetic reform, and arts and crafts. He made bells and cast vessels for the church. He was also very musical and composed hymns and chants. One of these, the 'Kyrie Rex Splendens', is still used to this day. Dunstan was recalled to court by Athelstan's successor, King Edmund. In AD 943, the King, as a thanksgiving for escape from death while hunting, appointed Dunstan as abbot of Glastonbury. From this date onwards Dunstan began his life's work of reforming the monastic communities, and then the Church itself. Dunstan continued to pursue his goal of reform during the next three reigns – of Edmund, murdered after six years on the throne, Edred, who died after just a couple of years and then the strange boy king, Edwy, whose poor behaviour Dunstan criticised. As a result he was humiliated and exiled abroad.

In AD 959 following the overthrow of Edwy, Edgar became king. He immediately recalled Dunstan, and one of the most remarkable friendships between king and priest since the time of Aidan and Oswald emerged. Side by side they travelled the land, reforming both Church and state. It was the second golden age of the Anglo-Saxon Church. Edgar appointed Dunstan Archbishop of Canterbury, and Dunstan became his firm advisor, even when Edgar committed an act of physical sacrilege in violently ejecting priests from Winchester in order to reform the Cathedral. Dunstan imposed penances on Edgar, who accepted them. Together with Edgar, he ensured that some of the laxity and corruption that had crept in to the Church was banished. Together, King and archbishop worked to reform, educate, and enlighten the people through reforming the monasteries and encouraging libraries and scholarship, and to bring them into a much closer alliance with the forces of Christendom that were shaping Europe at that time.

Their contemporaries revealed more eloquently than I why these two are such fascinating figures of the renaissance of Anglo-Saxon Christianity in the tenth century. In *The Anglo-Saxon Chronicle* for the year AD 959, the writer in Peterborough says of Edgar:

Far and wide he exalted God's praise and loved God's law, and improved the people's security much more than those kings who were before him within the memory of men ... He became greatly honoured wide throughout the land of the nation, for he readily honoured God's name, and deliberated God's law over and again, and promoted God's praise far and wide, and counselled all his nation wisely, very often, always continuously, for God and for the world.[11]

As for Dunstan, 'When he sang at the altar', wrote a contemporary, 'he seemed to be talking with the Lord face to face'.[12]

These descriptions paint a somewhat rosy picture, for conflict and raids and the settlements of the Northmen continued to tear Edgar's England. Nevertheless England was moving towards a greater sense of unity.

Although Dunstan and Edgar pushed England and its sense of the sacred back towards the model of the Roman Church and discourse with Europe, the Anglo-Saxon Church was still to some degree set apart, different from other Churches. It did not quite walk at the same pace as the rest of Europe, and was proud of its distinctiveness. It saw its own history as divinely inspired – after all Christianity in Britain had survived and triumphed over two separate invasions of non-Christians. As we have seen, it had developed its own sense of significance, of sacred history, of its own sacred topography and its own style, traditions, and art, which freely combined Christian and Norse mythologies and beliefs. For example, just before the Norman invasion of 1066 St Cuthbert's biographer described a vision that came to Bishop Eardwulf, which led to the choice of a new king, Guthfrith: St Cuthbert instructed the bishop to place upon the arm of the chosen Guthfrith a gold armlet – a sign of the pagan Viking source of power – to indicate his right to rule. The bishop did this, and then led the king to the tomb of St Cuthbert where the new king and his nobles swore loyalty. This vision, with its mixing of cultures and religions, did not strike Cuthbert's biographer as at all odd.[13]

To much of the rest of Europe, Britain was an enigma. The English Church (and of course the continuing British Church, still active and in control in most of Scotland and Wales) was viewed askance by Rome and its allies. So it was that when the end came for this strange Christianity, and for the sense of a unique sacredness to the land, the invaders came bearing the holy, blessed banner and best wishes of the Pope. They came as Crusaders, to crush heresy.

CHAPTER NINE

THE CONQUERORS

A BROKEN UNITY

IT WAS A COLD, CLEAR CHRISTMAS EVE, when the noise, bustle and slight mania of the day before Christmas had faded into the darkness of the evening. Now as the clocks struck eleven o'clock, the streets of the ancient city of Rochester in Kent were filled with people making their way to and from parties or the pub, and with others on their way to the cathedral for Midnight Mass. As I walked that evening to the great Norman cathedral, towering up in front of the houses clustered around it, I suddenly understood the difference between the temporal and the spiritual.

Rochester is dominated by two huge Norman buildings, both essentially built by one man who combined the roles of priest and warrior – a man both spiritual and secular. Bishop Gundolf, a faithful supporter of William the Conqueror, built not only the Norman cathedral at Rochester but also the great keep. (He was also responsible for building the original Tower of London.)

On that Christmas Eve in the mid-eighties, as I wandered down the hill from my parents' house, I looked with new eyes on what Gundolf had done and, in a sense, what the Normans as a whole did. That night, the cathedral was ablaze with light, people were pouring in and out, music could be heard drifting from it and the great bells in its spire tower were ringing out. This was the living heart of a worshipping community that had been here long before the Normans – St Augustine of Canterbury created his second diocese here in AD 604 – and it has long outlived them. The cathedral seemed like some great living beacon of light and joy. Opposite and just as tall and massive, the castle lay shrouded in darkness. No lights shone from its broken windows. It sat heavy and dark, lifeless against the night sky. No joyous crowds surged through its portals. No music was to be heard. Light and dark. Living and broken. Spiritual and secular. Prayer and war. The contrast was staggering.

I began to realise how the balance of power between the spiritual and the temporal had shifted. At one time the castle must have seemed far more threatening, permanent and awesome than the cathedral. Yet it was now a thing of the past, while the cathedral was a thing of the present. The difference between the two was that the spiritual was the more enduring.

Rochester endorses my belief that with the Norman Conquest of 1066, secularisation began in Britain. The sacred, which for so many millennia had been indistinguishable from the mundane, began to be forced apart from the 'ordinary' aspects of life.

For example, as we saw earlier, the lineage of the royal families of the Anglo-Saxons was both sacred and temporal, many of them claiming descent from both tribal gods and Christian figures. Saints and temporal power groups were also closely related. Take the royal family of East Anglia. In the seventh century King Anna had a sister-in-law who was a saint, St Ebba, three daughters who became saints, Sts Etheldreda, Sexburga and Withburga, and a great-granddaughter, Werburga, who became a saint. Think also of two of the most charming images of the spiritual and temporal powers of the Anglo-Saxon era: St Aidan and King Oswald converting Northumbria together in the seventh century, and St Dunstan and King Edgar reforming the church in the tenth century.

The sacred and the temporal were part and parcel of the same world view. This is not to say that the relationship was always honoured! The Anglo-Saxon kings and queens were quite capable of behaving like other human beings, driven by jealousy, anger, greed and pride, as indeed were many of the priests. But the conceptual world within which they lived was one overseen by God in Heaven and the Church on Earth. It was a sacred world, which transformed Britain into a sacred island. It was a place where, as William of Malmesbury, writing c. 1120–30 states of the then fast disappearing Anglo-Saxon England, 'Does not the whole island blaze with such numerous relics of its natives, that you can scarcely pass a village of any consequence but you hear the name of some new saint, besides the numbers of whom all notice have perished through the want of records?'[1] It was a sacred vision that saw Britain as being just as holy as Jerusalem or Rome, but which also delighted in being in touch with and a part of a wider European faith. Indeed there is evidence that the Anglo-Saxon Church and the Irish Church were in touch with Churches beyond Europe. For instance Coptic monks from Egypt visited Ireland and the graves of six of them have been found. At the wonderfully preserved Anglo-Saxon churches and monastic buildings at Deerhurst in Gloucestershire, one window is unique in design, at least in Europe. But its exact equal can be found in the rock cut church of Gondar in Ethiopia.

I think the opening of King Alfred's will sums up the sense that God was intimately involved with the land: 'I, King Alfred, by the grace of God and on consultation with Archbishop Aethelred and with the witness of all the councillors of the West Saxons, have been inquiring about the needs of my soul and about my inheritance which God and my elders gave me . . .'[2]

With the coming of the Normans, the bond between the spiritual and the temporal was broken. The two buildings at Rochester I believe testify to this. The bishop/knight Gundolf is as much a temporal ruler as a spiritual teacher. Indeed, more so, for he even built a military tower into the very fabric of his new cathedral building! Instead of the Church being the dominating influence over the castle, we now find the castle dominates the Church. This was so much so at Old Sarum in Wiltshire that the two parted company. In 1092 Old Sarum, a fortified Anglo-Saxon town, was chosen as the site for a new cathedral. At the same time, the Normans also built a major castle. For a variety of reasons, the relationships between the castle and the cathedral were often tense and this led to abuse of the cathedral and its staff by the soldiers. So serious did this become that in the reign of Richard I (1189–99) the bishop decided to move his cathedral away from the vicinity of the castle. Thus it was that the magnificent cathedral of Salisbury arose from the water meadows some five miles away from the troubles and secularity of the castle of Old Sarum.

With the powerful baron bishops of the Conquest, such as Gundolf and Bishop Odo, half brother of William the Conqueror and Earl of Kent after the invasion, the mould is broken of the king and priest travelling together. Instead, we find increasingly that the bishops were part of the secular, political structures and that when priest and king met they were often in conflict.

NEW MASTERS

The Normans saw themselves as overrunning a rather old-fashioned country with a church that was not properly integrated into the wider power structures of the Roman Church – a view endorsed by the Pope, which was why he declared William's invasion a Crusade and sent a Papal banner to lead the invading forces. This was equivalent to the Pope's support of the Crusades in Spain – which were directed against Islam.

Within a very short period of time after the invasion, no Anglo-Saxon occupied any position of real authority within the Church, even at a local level. This lack of power is also reflected in land ownership. By the time the Domesday Book was compiled in 1086, only two of the king's leading tenants were of Anglo-Saxon descent. One of the first actions of the Norman Archbishop of Canterbury, after he ousted the Anglo-Saxon archbishop, was to declare as non-saints a list of Anglo-Saxon saints, even including a former Anglo-Saxon Archbishop of Canterbury until he was persuaded otherwise.

The ties between the land, the sacred, and political authority were already being cut. The most dramatic evidence of this severance is to be found in the horrific actions of William in the north-east. Here resistance to the invasion was very strong. In 1069 the brutal new lord of Northumbria, Robert, was murdered in Durham along with hundreds of his men. William's response was to march north and devastate Durham, sparing not even the cathedral, the great resting place of the patron saint of England, Cuthbert. William and his men then laid waste to the north, so much so that some historians have referred to this as 'the devastation of the north'. Whole swathes of countryside were cleared of farms, hamlets and villages. People were driven from their lands and the land was put to torch. Then William created a vast parkland for himself and his followers, where he could hunt. Where churches, monasteries, homes and farms had once stood, a king now hunted for sport.

These actions can only be compared to the devastation caused by the Vikings in the terrible raids on Lindisfarne in AD 793 or their sweep through East Anglia and across southern Britain from AD 869 onwards. The fusion of gospel, land and people, which the English Church had created and had struggled hard to preserve and develop through the invasions of the previous 500 years, was once again under dire threat. This time it was not pagan invaders who threatened to destroy the balance of people and Church, but fellow Christians albeit still invaders, who saw the Church as an arm of their control. As such they had no time or stomach for the older traditions or even saints of the Anglo-Saxon Church. Nor did they have much time even for the physical fabric of the Anglo-Saxon churches. While there are hundreds if not thousands of churches with Norman arches, doorways, pillars, etc., there is but a handful of Anglo-Saxon churches. The Normans replaced the older churches with their own churches as a further sign of conformity to Rome. Gone is the more idiosyncratic layout and style of the Anglo-Saxons. From now onwards, British churches would be modelled on European trends.

In Durham, the Normans rebuilt the cathedral, producing one of the greatest treasures of sacred Britain, and at the same time they built a huge fortress, imposing their rule on a rebellious area. Here the temporal, political and spiritual roles of church prelates were fused, for the new Norman bishops of Durham were also made rulers of the north on the King's behalf and created prince bishops, combining the role of lord and priest, and even having their own army.

It is quite clear that the Normans did not see England as their sacred land. Indeed, so alien did they find it and so much did they hanker after their own homelands that they imported their own saints. St Denis is the patron saint of Paris, and was very popular with the Normans. To this day you can trace the presence of the nostalgic Normans in England by the villages and parish churches that were renamed in honour of St Denis, such as Coln St Dennis in Gloucestershire, St Dennis, Cornwall and the cathedral church in Manchester, St Denys.

ONE CHURCH, ONE AUTHORITY

If Anglo-Saxon sacred Britain was a mass of local saints, holy wells, shrines and ancient pilgrimage routes, Norman sacred Britain was about control, centralisation and domination. This reflected increasing efforts by the Church in Rome to establish its authority. All across Europe, the older, local churches, with their plethora of local saints and holy wells, were being streamlined, usually as part of a process of gradual tightening of controls from Rome. The process reached its apex in the Fourth Lateran Council of AD 1215, which imposed stringent new regulations on such issues as the creation of saints. In Britain, such changes were brought about earlier and more quickly by the Norman invasion.

To some extent, the papacy used the disruption of all traditions and precidents of local churches that took place in England and Wales as a result of the invasion as a testing ground for controlling local churches. The concept of 'One Church' still had to fight for acceptance. The Orthodox Churches had gradually distanced and then cut themselves off from the papacy, the last such schism taking place formally in 1054, when the Patriarch of Constantinople excommunicated the Pope and the Pope excommunicated the Patriarch. As the Roman Church claimed total jurisdiction, increasingly it came into conflict with the power and traditions of local churches from Spain to Ireland. This led to the development of the doctrine that outside the one Roman Catholic Church there was no possibility of salvation, which had been strongly hinted at by Wilfred in his debate with Colman in AD 664 at Whitby. The Popes made this point increasingly explicit, and it reached its fullest development under Pope Boniface VIII when, in 1302, he issued his famous Bull, *Unam Sanctum*, in which he made clear the papal position of authority over all life everywhere:

> We are compelled, our faith urging us, to believe and to hold – and we do firmly believe and simply confess – that there is one holy catholic and apostolic Church, outside of which there is neither salvation nor remission of sins; ... Therefore of this one and only Church there is one body and one head – not two heads as if it were a monster: Christ namely, and the vicar of Christ, St Peter, and the successor of Peter.[3]

The Normans also saw themselves as bringing civilisation and proper, mainstream, orthodox and well-behaved Christianity to a land of superstitious and credulous people. William of Malmesbury is perhaps the best mouthpiece of this view, even though he was also quite sympathetic to the fast-disappearing Anglo-Saxon Church:

> Nevertheless, in process of time, the desire after literature and religion had decayed, for several years before the arrival of the Normans. The clergy, contented with a very slight degree of learning, could scarcely stammer out the words of the sacraments . . . The monks mocked the rule of their order by fine vestments, and the use of every kind of food. The nobility, given up to luxury and wantonness, went not to church in the morning after the manner of Christians, but merely, in a careless manner, heard matins and masses from a hurrying priest in their chambers, amid the blandishments of their wives.[4]

The coming of the Normans was seen by William as a blessing from God for the benighted Anglo-Saxons, whom he depicts as sunk in drunkenness, unable to build proper towns and dressed in a barbarous fashion: 'their arms laden with golden bracelets: their skin adorned with punctured designs'. Having commented upon the fact that every little village seemed to have its own sacred place and its own local saint, he paints a picture of the Norman building programme that was transforming the face of much of Britain:

> They [The Normans] revived, by their arrival, the observances of religion, which were everywhere grown lifeless in England. You might see churches rise in every village and monasteries in the towns and cities built after a style unknown before; you might behold the country flourishing with renovated rites; so that each wealthy man accounted that day lost to him, which he had neglected to signalise by some magnificent action.[5]

The Anglo-Saxon version of this story is somewhat different. The Peterborough manuscript of *The Anglo-Saxon Chronicle* has this to say under the year 1086, the year of William the Conqueror's death:

> *He had castles built*
> *and wretched men oppressed.*

The king was so very stark
and seized from his subject men many a mark
of gold, and more hundreds of pounds of silver
that he took by weight, and with great injustice
from his land's nation with little need.
He was fallen into avarice,
and he loved greediness above all . . .
Alas, woe, that any man should be so proud,
raise up and reckon himself over all men.
May the Almighty God shew mercy to his soul
and grant him forgiveness of his sins.[6]

The truth is that reality probably lies somewhere between the propaganda accounts of William and the nostalgic view of the Anglo-Saxon scribes writing *The Chronicle*. What is clear is that both sides saw the coming of the Normans as a breaking point, a seismic shift in the social and sacred life of England. The Normans had a determination to hold the land for themselves, for their people and for the 'universal Church', of which they were blessed sons. It was for these purposes that they used the magnificence of Norman architecture to encase and build upon the sacred in Britain.

Nowhere is this more clearly to be seen than in South Wales. The Norman incursions into and then invasions of Wales began the year after the Battle of Hastings. Although the Welsh princes were initially able to regain much of the land seized in the twenty years after Hastings, by the early part of the twelfth century much of South Wales was either already 'legally' owned by Norman lords or under *de facto* Norman domination.[7] Even the Welsh/British Church, which had defied Augustine 500 years before and defended its independence from Rome and Canterbury, buckled under the pressures of the Normans and the rising centralism of the Catholic Church. Two places in particular tell this story and highlight the way the Normans both promoted and weighed down the religion of Britain, and sought to capture and control the sacred powers of the saints and sacred sites.

In or around 1107, an ambitious Norman bishop was appointed to the see of Glamorgan. He was the first bishop in Wales to acknowledge the Archbishop of Canterbury as his archbishop. Ironically, he probably did this to harness the authority of the archbishop in his struggle to protect Church lands from the Norman barons. This bishop's name was Urban and, true to his name, he was dissatisfied with the ramshackle, rural and localised nature of the churches in his area. Taking the model of the great metropolitan dioceses of Europe, he set about creating an urban and urbane Church. This meant that he needed not the humble little church that he found but a proper cathedral.

Where once there was a major yet physically quite humble monastery at Llandaff, now on the outskirts of Cardiff, Urban began to build the first great cathedral in the history of Wales. From *c.* AD 1115 onwards a vast edifice began to rise, the main arch of which you can still see to this day. But Urban needed to harness more than just modern technology and architecture. He needed to capture and draw authority from the great saints of Wales, who were probably turning in their simple graves at the grandiose and un-Christian pomp and expense of the new bishop. If they were turning in their graves, it appears Urban wanted to find out. For Urban proceeded to dig up, steal and buy some of the most important saints' bodies in Wales. He claimed that he was the spiritual descendant of Sts Dyfrig and Teilo, and that any of the churches named after them were his. He 'found' the body of St Teilo and 'discovered' a holy well. He borrowed – some said stole – the body of St Dyfrig from its simple, hermit-like resting place on windswept Bardsey Island in North Wales. He also claimed to have the body of St Euddogwy, also known as Oudoceus, the supposed nephew of Teilo and his appointed successor. Unfortunately no one else had ever heard of this saint and despite some skilful editing of older traditions and the creation of a 'Life' of this supposed saint, he is still to this day classified as 'supposed'.[8]

Having thus exploited the spiritual powers of some of the greatest figures in Welsh sacred history, Urban began to claim other areas around his diocese. He fabricated manuscripts which claimed to show that Llandaff controlled most of South Wales from the sixth to seventh centuries onwards. The mischievous, fascinating and occasionally illuminating *Book of Llandaff*, also known as the *Llandaff Charters*, has caused confusion and chaos and fuelled endless speculation about early Christianity and early Wales by those who have taken the documents to be authentic.

Urban was thwarted principally by Bishop Bernard of St David's. It is to St David's that we must now go to see how the Normans sought to dominate physically the old sacred sites and capture their power. When Bernard arrived in St David's in 1115 he found a world that had changed little from the sixth-century world of David – Dewi – himself. The little church at St David's was still surrounded by the simple buildings of a classic Celtic Church monastery, where the lifestyle was based on the examples of the great saints, blending simplicity with scholarship.

Bernard hated all this, and dissolved some 600 years of tradition at a stroke. In the place of the monastery he created a formal Chapter of Canons. The simple church was immediately demolished, and a grand Norman cathedral began to arise. Beside it rose a splendid bishop's palace – indeed a palace worthy of even an archbishop. For despite the fact that Bernard was the first bishop of St David's to take an oath of allegiance to Canterbury, he also sought permission from the Pope for St David's to be made into an archbishopric.

Then the site took its poetic revenge! It had been originally chosen by David because of the fast-flowing stream in which it is thought that he baptised people and because of the many springs and holy wells in the area. It is essentially a watery and marshy site, suitable for small wooden or even stone and wooden churches and huts but not for building heavy stone cathedrals and palaces. Bernard weighed the site down with heavy dressed-stone walls rising high into the air and, ever since, the cathedral authorities have had to prop up the building, watch it sink, level it out, dry it out, rebuild it and eventually in the nineteenth century, fill in, divert or cover all the holy wells on the site. The sacred ground of Dewi has undermined the mass of the Norman aspirations, and has been a constant reminder that the holiness of the site lay in its simplicity and its sacred waters.

However, the solidity of the Norman centralising of sacred and the temporal power survived, embodied in the cathedrals of Llandaff and St David's and the castle/cathedral pairings of Rochester and Durham. As a result, today the memory of many of the Anglo-Saxon saints has been lost or is only slowly being recovered. Sacred Britain had been reconfigured. Gone was the sense that saints walked everywhere and that every area had its holy ground, its sacred place.

Until the twelfth century, the task of deciding who was and who was not a saint lay in the gift of the local church. This is still the case in the Orthodox Churches of Greece, Russia and central Europe. If a congregation decides that its priest or local monk or nun is a saint and can show how in his or her life, the person embodied Orthodoxy and shone with saintliness, the wider Church will usually accept its verdict. But from the twelfth century onwards, and especially after the great reforming meeting held in 1215 in Rome, the permission and authorisation of the Pope was required before any saint could be officially recognised. Consequently, whereas saints galore arose in Anglo-Saxon Britain, after the Norman Conquest the number of British saints can almost be counted on one hand. And it was no easy matter creating a saint. Take, for example, the canonisation of poor old St Osmund.

Osmund was the Norman bishop who was the second bishop of the see of Old Sarum/Salisbury, and is remembered as being generous towards the Anglo-Saxon clergy and people of his diocese. Soon after he died in 1099, miracles were associated with his tomb and it became a place of pilgrimage. In 1228, somewhat in need of their own saint to draw crowds and thus cash for the building of their new cathedral, away from the soldiers of Old Sarum, Salisbury began the process of lobbying Rome for the canonisation of Osmund. By 1387, despite numerous visits to Rome and some considerable 'gifts' to key bishops and clergy in the Eternal City, nothing had happened. In 1387, King Richard II brought pressure to bear upon the Pope, but to no avail. In 1406 a further push was given to the cause. Again, there was silence from Rome. In 1412 the then Bishop of Salisbury, Robert Hallam, established what is possibly the first known advertising budget in English history. He set aside one-tenth of all the income of the canons to fund the promotion of the canonisation of Osmund. Kings Henry V and Henry VI were drawn in as advocates and at last a commission came from Rome to examine the case. Finally, in 1456, over 350 years after his death, Osmund was canonised. It had cost the diocese £731 13s – the equivalent today of perhaps several hundred thousand pounds. Had Osmund been bishop fifty years earlier, under the aegis of the Anglo-Saxon Church, and had the people wished it, he would have been declared a saint within perhaps ten to twenty years of his death – and for free.

The Norman Conquest solidified the Catholic Church's control over Britain, as manifested in the great cathedrals, and the Normans used this and their castles built alongside each other to encapsulate their control of their newly conquered lands. The Normans made it quite clear that the Church was a useful arm of the state, not as, for example, Alfred the Great had seen the Church – as the leading light which showed the pathway the state should walk. Gradually, but on a smaller scale, this pattern was repeated across Britain, as the feudal system of lord, serfs and peasants took over the old villages, and where previously a small wooden church had sufficed, there rose the jewels of British Christianity: stone churches. Beside these arose the castles or manor houses of the lords and nobles who ruled the land and hundreds of new monasteries. It was a colossal building programme, involving a huge commitment of skilled workers, resources and money.

To appreciate the significance of these churches and cathedrals we need to recall the roles of the megalithic tombs – the long barrows – and the stone circles. Just as they played a central role in a community's life, so to did the parish church and the great cathedral, often the largest stone buildings other than the castle in an area. Unlike the castle, they were open to all. Within their premises meetings were held, trading took place, festivals were celebrated, rites of passage undertaken, school lessons taught, books kept for consultation and priests available for advice or confession. The church was the physical and spiritual hub of life because it was dry, large, open, sometimes even heated and most of all useful. It was also often beautiful, inspiring and peaceful. People poured their money or their skills into creating these wonderful buildings because they were important to them.

It was also the main training ground of craftsmen and women. The great cathedrals in particular created schools of architects, carvers, weavers, embroiderers, designers, gardeners, builders and painters whose work still delights the visitor today. Here local children could learn a craft that would ensure a decent standard of living for them and their families. While the great lords and ladies were the major benefactors, it is important to remember that local communities took great pride in the creation of their cathedrals and churches. These were local centres as well as embodiments of the international faith of Christianity. They functioned as community centres for they were often the only stone-built and thus dry and relatively warm building in the community. And they had been carved and decorated to express local pride as well as local humour, as can be seen in the capitals and misericords in cathedrals – the builders of churches saw humour as part and parcel of the Divine.

The new churches, wonders of art, construction, piety and authority, were no longer dedicated just to local saints. They tended instead to be linked to great international saints such as Mary, John the Baptist, Peter and James – saints whose cults spread around the European Christian world, with shrines, pilgrimage centres and relics to support them. Saints had by now become big business, and the pilgrimage trade was a major economic force. This can be clearly seen as evidenced by the differences between those churches and cathedrals that had marketable saints and those that did not. Canterbury, for example, is obviously the most successful saint centre. It was able to rebuild itself completely from the proceeds of the cult of Thomas Becket (of whom more later). Rochester, on the other hand, just up the road in Kent and the younger sister of Canterbury, founded just a decade later, had no such major saint and its attempts to create one were somewhat pathetically unsuccessful. When a pilgrim to Canterbury, William of Perth, who may even have been on his way to Jerusalem, was murdered just outside Rochester, the monks at Rochester seized upon this 'pilgrim martyr' and began to vigorously promote his cause. However 'St William of Rochester' was never recognised by the Pope and his cult remained very low key. There were even stories (possiby spread by Canterbury in an early example of industrial espionage) that William was a drunk who died in a fight. Whatever the truth, this failure to find a marketable saint is why Rochester Cathedral is still essentially a Norman and Romanesque building, while Canterbury was able to redesign itself in classical Gothic.

I love the fruits of the great Norman rebuilding of the sacred in Britain. It has provided us with some of the most sublime buildings in our history. But as I have travelled and explored into the older sacred landscape of the Roman, British, Anglo-Saxon and Viking Churches, I have had to come to terms with how much was literally and metaphorically squashed under these great stone buildings. Essentially, Norman Christianity was driven by secular power concerns and control. Yet the older tradition of the Church as defining force for the betterment of society and of the people was still there, running like the troubling stream undermining the massive structures of the Norman cathedral at St David's. This stream of opposition was to erupt at odd times and places and for very varied reasons throughout the medieval period. Its influence can be felt in the upheavals of the Reformation, the battles – physical and spiritual – of the Civil War and through into the modern period in the social conscience of so many Christians who have shaped Britian, from Trades Unions to the Aid movements.

CHAPTER TEN

KING AND CHURCH –
THE STRUGGLE FOR
THE SACRED

HENRY II AND THOMAS BECKET

THE MOST FAMOUS CONFRONTATION between church and State of the entire sacred history of Britain is that between Henry II and his Archbishop Thomas Becket. Let us stand where the shrine of St Thomas Becket once stood, for this small, empty space tells a fascinating story of the continued separation between the sacred and the temporal.

Becket was born in London of a Norman family in around 1118. Legend has it that his mother was a Muslim who had met his father in the Holy Land, then converted and came to England with him. Until the destruction of the old St Paul's Cathedral in London during the fire of London of 1666, the tomb of Becket's parents, itself a place of pilgrimage, had the Muslim crescent-moon symbol hanging above it as a reminder of her origins.

Becket grew up to become a well-educated young man who was part of the court circle and was friends with Henry II. In 1162, at Henry's behest, the Pope made Becket Archbishop of Canterbury. This appointment seems to have had a startling effect on Becket. From being, as he described himself, 'a patron of play-actors and a follower of hounds' he became, again in his own words, 'a shepherd of souls'. He became a transformed man, living simply and seeking to fulfil the pastoral and educational role of the Church.

However, he soon came into conflict with Henry. In 1164, after a furious row, Becket fled to France and went into hiding. Thomas's arguments with the King were concerned with the authority and powers of the Church in relation to the authority and powers of the King. For example, a major bone of contention was the exemption of the clergy from criminal law. As the *Images of History*, written by Ralph of Diceto, a canon of St Paul's London, puts it:

> 1164. The king of England [Henry II] wished, so he said, to inflict severe punishment on individual members of the clergy who were guilty of crimes, considering that for such men to receive less punishment than they deserved derogated from the dignity of the order as a whole.[1]

Gerald of Wales, a historian of the late twelfth century, puts a slightly different interpretation on this issue:

> He ventured upon many detestable usurpations in things belonging to God, and through a zeal for justice (but not according to knowledge), he joined the rights of the Church to those of the crown, and therein confused them in order to centre all in himself.[2]

Becket's quarrel was primarily with issues of the rights of the clergy against the rights of the ruler rather than issues about which ordinary people might be concerned. Yet after his death, in the public perception he became the champion of the Church against the state and of the ordinary people against the rulers. The reasons for this are difficult to comprehend, but they offer a glimpse of the concept of the sacred, in defensive mode, confronting the growth of secular power.

After six years in exile, Becket returned to England in 1170. Within weeks the quarrel between him and the King had erupted again. It was possibly during a drunken fit while at his court in Normandy that Henry uttered the fateful words 'Who will rid me of this turbulent priest?' Four knights, thinking this to be a command and hoping to curry favour with the King, took to horse and then ship, arriving in Canterbury in the late afternoon of 29 December 1170. Becket was at prayer in a side chapel of the cathedral when the knights burst in. He was cut down in front of the altar and killed along with one of his priests.

The shock this murder produced throughout Europe was extra-ordinary. Not only had a king apparently ordered the murder of his own archbishop, but this had taken place within the sanctity of a cathedral. Under Church Law, no weapons were supposed to be brought into a church and those taking shelter within were under the direct protection of the Church. Even those accused of crimes were allowed to take sanctuary in a church and could then ask the Church to investigate their case before the secular powers of the state could claim them back. Thus the horror of the murder *per se* was compounded by the venue and sacredness of the place of murder. That Thomas was also at prayer added even more to the offence.

By 1173 the Pope had declared Becket a saint, and pilgrimages to the site of his death were well under way. The cult of St Thomas Becket began and Canterbury became the most important pilgrimage destination in England and one of the top three or four in Europe. Henry II was forced to pay compensation to the Church and to walk barefoot to the cathedral while being beaten by clergy. It was the single most humiliating moment in the relationship between the Church and the monarchy in the history of Britain. It was also a defining moment in British sacred history. From this debacle St Thomas Becket became the symbol of the defiant and autonomous Church, which had considerable rights and authority and to which the monarchs were to be servants.

The shrine of Thomas became a key place of opposition to the powers of the monarch and the most fabulously wealthy in England. In a sense it confirmed the split between secular and religious, and from then on the kings of England sought to have as much control as possible over the bishops, turning them effectively into civil servants, albeit of the highest order.

The cult of St Thomas increased the wealth and power of the Church, speeding up the growth of corruption and indifference to the poor that was to bring the Church to its knees in the sixteenth century. What in fact happened was that the Church lost out in the long run. Posts within the Church became so profitable that the secular state and its principle families sought and obtained monopoly of the key appointments, turning the Church into effectively a family business for the aristocracy. It also made it clear that one or other, court or Church, had to be in charge: gone was the partnership. Instead the higher echelons were locked economically into the higher echelons of the state, while the poor were left with impoverished priests, many of whom were illiterate but at least were there for the ordinary people. In Henry's humiliation were sown the seeds of the Reformation.

Why should a stroppy, aristocratic churchman, defending the rights and property of the Church, be transformed into the saint of the age – the very model of the Church as counterpoint to the state? Perhaps there is a hint of the answer in the letter Thomas sent to Henry in 1166:

> In that you are my lord I owe and offer my counsel and service, such as a bishop owes to his lord according to the honour of God and the holy Church. And in that you are my king I am bound to you in reverence and regard. In that you are my son [spiritual son] I am bound by reason of my office to chasten and correct you.[3]

In the previous centuries of the Church in Britain, attacks upon the rights and powers of the Church only came from invaders. Essentially the Church had become the authority from which the converted royal families of the Angles, Saxons and Vikings received their right to rule – as for example in St Cuthbert's visionary command to chose Guthfrith (see Chapter 8). Under the Normans, the use of secular power by the Roman Church to bring the British Churches into conformity with Rome left an ambiguous legacy. It is not without significance that Pope Boniface VIII, who asserted the Church's absolute power over all secular forces, was eventually a victim of power politics that focused upon his opposition to the forceful king, Philip the Fair of France, from 1296 onwards. The Pope was pushed from pillar to post, perhaps best symbolised by his celebration of the Jubilee Year of 1300, which he conducted with enormous expense and pomp, but to which not a single major ruler of the Christian kingdoms of Europe came. The Church had gone a long way towards bedding down with the secular authorities. It now found it difficult to remind them of their due place in the Christian order – the order outlined by Thomas in his letter above.

In challenging Henry, Thomas was not so much defending the

rights of the clergy as reminding him of his rightful place in the Christian order.

This perhaps explains something of what the shrine and cult of Thomas came to symbolise. There is, however, another dimension: magic. The Thomas cult illustrates perhaps more clearly than any other the power of the magical associations of Christianity in the minds of ordinary people. What do I mean by magical? We tend today to see Christianity as the foe of magic, of astrology and of other forms of what are often rather unhelpfully lumped together as superstitions. Yet in the Middle Ages most Christian kings had their court astrologers who saw no problem in weaving together astrology and the Christian faith. Most people wore talismen against disease, evil and misfortune. Given the medical facilities of the Middle Ages, this was probably wiser than visiting a doctor. Spells, charms and curses were part and parcel of the religious life and although much of this would never have received the formal approval of the Church *per se*, it nevertheless was accepted as one of the means by which the Church offered help and succour to the distressed or the worried. It was of course completely forbidden for Christians to practise abuse of such forces by, for example, seeking to harm people for no good reason, but that apart, magic was part of the world view which Christianity both embraced and created. One only has to think of the stories surrounding the consecrated bread and wine which were so popular in the later Middle Ages. Eamon Duffy in his study, *The Stripping of the Altars*, has a whole chapter on 'charms, pardons and promises' and has this to say:

> ... it would be a mistake to see even these 'magical' prayers as standing outside the framework of the official worship and teaching of the Church. The world-view they enshrined, in which humanity was beleaguered by hostile troops of devils seeking the destruction of body and soul, and to which the appropriate and guaranteed antidote was the incantatory or manual invocation of the cross or names of Christ, is not a construct of the folk imagination. Such ideas were built into the very structure of the liturgy, and formed the focus for some of its most solemn and popularly accessible moments.[4]

In *Religion and the Decline of Magic*, Keith Thomas lists in his chapter 'The magic of the medieval Church' the miraculous effects of just looking at paintings or statues of certain saints. For example, to look at a picture of St Christopher gave a day's protection from illness or even death.

St Thomas was thought to be so powerful that it was unnecessary to touch his bones or even visit Canterbury for a cure, as phials of water from his shrine were sufficient. A Cheshire nobleman brought back to his family church of Whitchurch in Shropshire a collection of what we would see today as pilgrim mementoes from the shops at the shrine of Thomas, which in a short period of time were credited with producing twenty-two cures.[5] A French noble who was cured at the shrine in Canterbury went home and built an oratory as a thanksgiving and on the night it was opened, a local paralysed woman was cured. The cult of Thomas allowed all sorts of unfocused popular magical beliefs to find a respectable focus, in much the same way as, for a brief period in the twentieth century, the death of Diana, Princess of Wales did. For example, the tradition of tying fragments of cloth or paper to a tree near the site of a 'holy' or 'blessed' one is one which is associated with holy wells and shrines but was last recorded in the first decade of the twentieth century. Yet it emerged full formed again in response to Diana's death. The remarkable thing about Thomas is that this focus lasted for nearly 400 years, and was only ended by the arrival of the Reformation, when the shrine was demolished.

Significantly, when Henry VIII eventually brought the Church under his authority, the first shrine to be demolished was that of St Thomas. The secular had struck back with a vengeance.

After the debacle of Thomas and Henry II, the Court tried to make sure that the Church was to be largely at the beck and call of the State, but there were exceptions and the most striking of these embodies all the virtues of the older Christian traditions, which seem to have found a voice again in this remarkable man. With Hugh of Lincoln, saint, defender of the poor, protector of the Jews and friend but also critic of the Royal Family, we see what the best of Norman Christianity could look like.

STANDING BETWEEN KING AND PEOPLE

I want you to come with me to the village of Witham in Somerset, where, beside the main street, there are a most unusual church and a dovecote. The church looks as if it has been moved lock, stock and barrel from France. It is one of the purest examples of the dramatic and simple building style of the early Carthusian monks. The church leaps straight up from the roadside, soaring upwards without anything of the graduated style of the usual village church. The church and dovecote were probably lay buildings, designed to serve the lay community that serviced the larger monastery, Witham Abbey, about a mile up the road. Of that monastery nothing now remains. When I went there with friends looking for some sign of this once great monastery, we found virtually nothing. A few depressions in the ground may mark the fishponds, but even these are fading over time. Yet here the sacred stood up to the secular and for a brief moment won. The man who did this was one of the greatest saints England has produced, yet he was not even English.

In 1178 Henry II founded Witham, the first Carthusian monastery in Britain. The Carthusians were part of the eleventh-century reformation of the religious orders, and were renowned for the austerity and simplicity of their lifestyles and their focus on individual contemplation. Their austerity is probably why Henry chose to found their first house in England, as the building of Witham was an act of contrition by Henry II for the murder of Archbishop Thomas Becket.

Henry invited Hugh of Lincoln to become the first prior of the completed monastery in 1175. Hugh was born a son of the manor in Avalon, Burgundy and was about thirty-five when he became prior of Witham. But Henry had not really taken stock of the man he had asked. Hugh discovered that while Henry was keen to proclaim his contrition in building the monastery, he was not so keen on either paying the workers on the building or in compensating the peasants and farmers whose lands he had taken. Publicly, and at considerable personal risk, Hugh refused to take up his role until the King honoured his debts and treated the dispossessed locals fairly. When Hugh was reminded in later life of how blunt he had been to one of the more ferocious kings of his time, he always blushed with embarrassment. But his stance did the trick and Henry honoured his commitments. The incident was to be the first of many stand-offs between Hugh and Henry.

In 1186 Hugh was made Bishop of Lincoln, then one of the major trading towns of England and a large and powerful diocese. It stretched far up into the north, where the impact of the Norman destruction 100 years earlier was still visible. The Normans had created a series of unjust laws, which they enforced with brutal efficiency, concerning the right of the king and nobles to hunt and the creation of royal forests, which cut across established farmland, villages and even towns. The imposition of these laws was highly disruptive and created poverty, abuses and violence. Hugh discovered this and became the champion of the ordinary English farmer and villager against the nobles and their sheriffs. His stance eventually came to the attention of Henry and a row of dramatic proportions broke out. Luckily Hugh had a strong sense of humour, and by using this but standing firm on principle, he was able to argue the King into a corner. He teasingly refered to the reputed humble origins of Henry's great-great grandmother, reducing a furious Henry to tears of merriment and ensuring that Hugh's case would be heard properly and with due respect for ordinary people. Thus through Hugh the Church was able to assert its values, its laws and its sacred understanding of the land and people over the secular, militaristic and aristocratic values of the King and his court.

It had been a tricky moment for Hugh but was as nothing in comparison to what he then had to face in defence of the Jews. The Jewish community in England dates from at least the time of the Norman Conquest, possibly earlier. By the time of Hugh, a contemporary noted:

> Under our first three sovereigns they had been to a certain extent left alone; they had been loyal and industrious subjects and had ministered much to the prosperity of the country of their adoption; they worshipped in their synagogues in peace, bought land and amassed riches; their lives had fallen in pleasant places and they concluded that the future would be as the past had been.[6]

Indeed, relationships were so good that in Bristol, which boasted one of the larger and more influential Jewish communities, the crypt of the parish church of St Giles was given to the Jews as their synagogue.

However, this pleasant state of affairs was to be shattered by events in the Holy Land when in 1187 Jerusalem together with most of the Holy Land was recaptured by the Muslim leader, Saladin, from the Crusaders. The fall of Jerusalem and the surrounding Crusader states, which had been captured in 1099 during the first Crusade, caused a huge shock in Europe. It raised the spectre that the Anti-Christ would be coming and produced much heart-searching, manifesting in major new outbreaks of unorthodox Christianity and in reform and self-abasement movements within the Church. The Crusading Orders, such as the Knights Templar and the Knights of St John, along with much of the more hysterical preaching of the ordinary but frightened clergy, whipped up a frenzy of apocalyptic expectation.[7]

The Jews had been given a degree of protection by Henry II, but he died in 1189 and the same protection was not afforded by his son, Richard I, also known as The Lionheart. Despite his later mythology, Richard was a thorough going thug and bully. He terrorised the nobles and kings around him and used brutality where others might have just used cunning. He had also sworn to go on Crusade following the Fall of Jerusalem. It is doubtful that Richard himself believed as many did that the Fall of Jerusalem pressaged the coming of the End of Time or the heralding of a New Age. But he was happy to exploit these beliefs. They had been fuelled not only by the classic expectations of the coming of an Anti-Christ based upon the Book of Revelation, but also by a new twist to these traditions by a contemporary writer, Joachim of Fiore, who had devised a Trinitarian reading of history – a sacred history in fact of sorts. He saw Time as divided into three great periods. The First Age was that of the Father, when humanity lived according to the Law. The Second Age was that of the Son, when humanity lived under the new dispensation of the New Testament. Joachim estimated that this Age would last forty-two generations of thirty years each; thus he calculated that the Age of the Son was due to end in or around 1260. The Third Age, that of the Spirit would then be inaugurated and would combine the best of the two previous Ages and humanity would live freely, unconstrained except by love. The transition period, however, would be a time of upheavals and struggles by evil before this perfect Age came into being. Joachim's writings and teachings became bestsellers and the stuff of populist preaching and performance. As a result, when Jerusalem fell, this was for some a sign of the coming of troubles before the Third Age, for others a sign of the coming of the Anti-Christ. Emotional and psychological confusion were the order of the day. Mobs in England looked for signs of the Anti-Christ in their midst and found the Jews. By 1190, all the major Jewish communities in England were under attack of one sort or another and hundreds died. The most terrible of these outrages was in York.

Today, Clifford's Tower in York stands as a bleak reminder of Norman fortifications, now isolated and alone on its mound. It is a stark place, all the more so for Jews. I have visited it with Jewish friends and colleagues and they have visibly paled. For here in 1190, well over 100 Jews took refuge when a mob rampaged through York. They hoped for protection from both the Archbishop and the King's representatives. But the crowd's demands for blood grew over a number of days. To their eternal shame, these potentates withdrew and hid, and it was clear that the mob was on the edge of breaking into the tower. The Jews decided to commit suicide rather than fall into the hands of the mob and this they did, every single person dying at the hand of another, until only the rabbi was left, who then took his own life.

Clifford is a place of shame, and yet it is also a sacred place. For here England as a sacred land failed itself and failed the Jews. This shame was to be repeated in pogroms and killings, extortion and cruelty towards England's Jews until in 1290 they were all forcibly expelled from England – the first time in history that a country in Europe so abused and mistreated the Jews. It is a sacred place because here we need to recognise that the sacred is not just about the nice parts of life but also touches massacres and horrors when innocent ones died for their faith.

It is in this context of an almost apocalyptic lawlessness that Hugh's actions have to be seen for the remarkably brave actions that they were. There was a large Jewish community in Lincoln, living primarily in an area halfway up the hill towards the cathedral and bishop's palace itself. When news of the attacks on other Jewish communities reached Lincoln, this led to attacks on the Jews there. Soon an ugly mob was gathering and it was clear that it meant to harm, even kill, if it could. Hugh appealed to the King's representatives to protect these innocent citizens. When he realised that they were not going to do so, he sent his own representatives to invite the Jews to come to his palace and there to find sanctuary and safety. The mob, robbed of its intended victims, stormed up the hill and surged towards the bishop's palace. Hugh, furious at the mob's actions, strode out and confronted it: a lone priest standing before the fury of the mob. His actions could easily have cost him his life, but he faced the mob and shamed it into going home and leaving the Jews in peace. Not only did he do this, but later he went on to remonstrate with the local leaders and even with the King. Hearing that similar trouble was brewing in Northampton, he rushed there, confronted the mob and ensured that the Jews were protected by the local church.

Sadly, Hugh stands as a remarkable exception. Elsewhere in the country the sanctuary of the Church was rarely extended to protect the Jews and ultimately the Church stayed silent or was compliant with the increasing persecution of the Jews.

In 1290, when the Jews were finally expelled from all of England, the synagogue in Bristol, one of the biggest communities, was destroyed. Many Jews were also murdered. In the 1990s the site of this desecrated synagogue was discovered and in the blackened ruins was found a poignant reminder of the sacred in Judaism. A broken lamp used to commemorate the dead was found. It was smashed even as the Jews of Bristol were being murdered and thus was never lit to commemorate those who died in this most shameful episode. Perhaps it is time to light that lamp again, to recall, honour and heal the scars, the lives lost and blighted, and this most terrible failure of Sacred Britain.

By standing between the oppressed and the oppressor, maintaining the integrity of all sides in the tripartite structure of Church, nobles and peasantry, Hugh epitomises in my view all that is best about the sacred and the Church in Britain. His role as defender against the powers of the King, the mob and the forces of oppression is a last great stand against the subservience of the sacred in Britain to the secular powers. Thereafter, while solace was sought at the tombs of the great defenders, Thomas of Canterbury and Hugh at Lincoln, the reality was that to all intents and purposes the Church leadership became a branch of civil administration. At a local level it continued its old role of maintaining the old traditions of holy places, holy people, healing and the alleviation of poverty. But essentially the leadership of the Church never again challenged the secular leadership. By the end of the twelfth century sacred Britain was at the start of a long road of destruction and neglect which the majesty of the great cathedrals and glorious parish churches of the medieval period covers up, but cannot completely hide.

Hugh returned to the monastery in Witham each year for a silent retreat. It was destroyed during the Reformation and the remains were turned into a grand country house, which eventually fell down and was finally destroyed in the nineteenth century. Today, as I found when I went searching, virtually nothing remains except the parish church built to meet the needs of the local people. Perhaps this is the best monument to the basic simplicity of holiness which Hugh embodied.

This era, the 150 years of Norman rule, is often portrayed as a golden age for the Church. The figures are certainly impressive. It has been estimated that there were roughly 60 monasteries and nunneries in England in 1066 with around 1,000 nuns and monks. By 1216 there were around 700 monasteries and nunneries and roughly 13,000 monks and nuns.[8] The scale of the Church was enormous and its influence vast. Yet it was already fighting a battle for supremacy, which it was to lose stage by stage. Today we stand and wonder at the scale of the cathedrals and parish churches of the Middle Ages, and so we should, for they are a glorious part of our heritage. But we should also look at the empty sites, such as the barely visible hints of the great monastery at Witham and the bare patch of ground in Canterbury Cathedral where Becket's shrine stood, and wonder about the forces that took the might of the Church away. They remind us that at the same time that the Church was consolidating the sacred in stone, in the growing separation between Church and state that also characterised the age, lay the seeds of the forces that would eventually shatter that world for ever.

CHAPTER ELEVEN

THE BLACK DEATH

DEAD VILLAGES

I CANNOT TAKE YOU TO THE NEXT SITE on our pilgrimage through the Sacred History of Britain – because it no longer exists. Its loss is part of the greatest disaster to ever visit Britain. In the Bishop of Durham's rent rolls for 1352 there is a one-line entry which is, in effect, the obituary notice for a community. It simply says, 'No tenant came from West Thickley because they are all dead.'[1]

It may be that a local could point out bumps in the ground where West Thickley once stood, but you will look for it in vain on a contemporary map of Britain. For this village was wiped out by the greatest pestilence that ever struck Western Europe, greater even than the sixth-century plagues that nearly destroyed Constantinople and helped spell the end of Romano-British life in England. This was the Black Death.

Unlike West Thickley, you can visit the pleasant seaside resort of Weymouth, Dorset. Here, you can wander along the seashore, shop in the arcades, play on the sand and climb up on to Portland Bill to admire the views. Above Weymouth the Romans built a temple and in its harbour kept ships to ward off pirates and invasions. But nothing could have prevented the invasion force which arrived in 1348. Here, in June 1348, some rats came ashore from a ship that had come from an area where the Black Death, which had already cut a swathe through Europe, was taking hold. With the landing of those rats and their deadly passengers, plague-carrying fleas, the Black Death came to Britain. By the time it died down in the 1350s one third, at least, of all those alive in 1348 had died of the plague – probably a minimum of two million people.

The old centre of Bristol, in the mid-fourteenth century fast rising to become the second city of England, is where Corn Street, Wine Street, Broad Street and High Street meet and churches rise around you like the masts of ships. This is a good place to read this description of Bristol in 1349, from *The Little Red Book of Bristol*, a contemporary record of affairs in the city: 'The plague raged to such a degree that the living were scarce able to bury the dead ... At this time the grass grew several inches high in the High Street and in Broad Street; it raged at first chiefly in the centre of the city.'[2]

The English writer Henry Knighton, writing in about 1350, traces the plague back to India, from whence it swept through the Muslim lands until it came to Europe. It appears that Bristol was the first major English city to be afflicted. Knighton gives a dramatic account of its spread:

> Then the most grievous pestilence penetrated the coastal regions ... and came to Bristol, and people died as if the whole strength of the city were seized by sudden death. For there were few who lay in their beds more than three days or two and a half days; then the savage death snatched them about the second day. In Leicester, in the little parish of St Leonard, more than 380 died; in the parish of the Holy Cross, more that 400, and in the parish of St Margaret in Leicester, more than 700.[3]

Tens of thousands of domestic animals, sheep, pigs and cows also died; Knighton graphically portrays the collapse of the rural economy. Interestingly, he links the Black Death to the Yellow Plague of the sixth century as his quote from Bede illustrates, even if he places it, wrongly, at the time of Vortigern:

> And the sheep and the cattle wandered about through the fields and among the crops, and there was no one to go after them or to collect them. They perished in countless numbers everywhere, in secluded ditches and hedges,

for lack of watching, since there was such a lack of serfs and servants that no one knew what he should do. For there is no memory of a mortality so severe and so savage [as that] from the time of Vortigern, king of the Britons, in whose time, Bede says, the living did not suffice to bury the dead.[4]

Much has been made by some historians of the ultimately beneficial effects of the Black Death. Not, obviously, for the poor souls who died such terrible deaths, but for the death of feudalism which the Black Death also caused. Feudalism had bound the serfs – peasants – to the land and had made of them virtual slaves. The Black Death changed all this by making labour so rare that it could afford to demand new rights and freedoms. Feudalism never recovered from the Black Death. Nor did the Church.

In terms of sacred history, the Black Death can be seen as the first moment when the old pact between medieval religion and the people began to break down. This plague might have led to the death of the faith altogether, as the Yellow Plague did to the last remnants of the pre-Christian faiths in Britain in the sixth century AD. It might have left the churches as empty and meaningless as the environmental collapse of *c.* 1000 BC left the stone circles. That it did not is because religion was now not an indigenous local faith but a universal one, capable of being revived by the sheer scale and universality of the Church. But the old version of the Christian faith took a severe knock, which laid the foundations if not for a new faith, then for a radically new version of the old faith.

Psychologically the world view of the later medieval period is very different from that of the earlier part. Until the coming of the Black Death, the arrangement that had evolved between state and Church since the Conquest had been pragmatic: broadly speaking, it was that the state, or more precisely the king and his court, working with the Church, would take care of this world, and the Church alone would take care of the next. That the Church was also the almost sole provider of hospitals, dispensaries, schools, social welfare for the impoverished, lodgings for the homeless and refuge for the wanderer was seen as part and parcel of its role in this life which would find its greatest fulfilment in the next. Yet in a strange way the next world hardly impinged upon the Church of the earlier part of the medieval period. The bishops were busy being statesmen and Chancellors of the Exchequer or ambassadors, the local clergy were busy taking care of the everyday pastoral needs of their communities, the monasteries were big businesses and the main expressions of the social concern of the Church for the people. Heaven and hell, and even death itself, were not that major a concern, as is evidenced by the fact that there is very little artwork or writing about them in contemporary culture.

Where Heaven, Hell and the Last Judgement did appear was often over the western entrance to a great cathedral. It was traditional to make the West Front a series of scenes of the Last Judgement. This might sound like a fascination with death and hell. In fact, it was the reverse, for the West Front led you into the church and thus to salvation. The geometric layout of the great cathedrals takes you from the fear of Judgement to the safety and security of the incarnation, Crucifixion and resurrection for it leads you to the High Altar where the blood and body of Christ are celebrated, and usually ends ultimately, at the extreme East End in the Lady Chapel. Here, through prayers to our Lady, Mary, the Mother of Christ, all could be saved. Indeed, so unfearful is the usual medieval vision of the Last Day that at Wells Cathedral, all the dead being raised look cheerful and are heading to Heaven. No sign of the damned here. That wonderful West Front was carved in the mid-thirteenth century – at the height of early medieval confidence in the covenant that existed between God, the saints, Christ, the Church and humanity. It seemed to be a covenant set in stone. Today the battered fragments of this vision can be seen at Wells and at other such churches throughout Britain. The truth is that the vision itself was soon to collapse and fade, breaking apart even faster than these fragile statues.

This situation changed radically with the Black Death – as can best be seen in the monuments to the dead. Look at a stone effigy of a knight and his lady, or a priest carved on a brass, or a merchant and his wife made of alabaster, from the period prior to the Black Death, for example the magnificent brass monument at Westley Waterless, Cambridgeshire. Here lie Sir John de Creke and Alyne his wife. The monument was created *c.* 1325 and is one of the finest brasses in England. A delight to rub and set in a quintessentially English country church. The two, husband and wife, knight and lady lie side by side hands together in prayer and confidently looking out at the viewer, sure that they were secure in their future beyond death.

Look at the magnificent stone tomb of William, Lord Graunson in Hereford Cathedral, created *c*. 1335. Here lies a noble knight above whom the saints cavort. Or study the calm repose of the lady whose tomb is to be found at Ledbury church, Herefordshire *c*. 1340. There is a serene quiet and certainty about them. They appear as they were in life, clad in their finest armour, priestly robes or rich clothes, confidently awaiting the Resurrection in a quiet, rather comfortable sort of way.

Then look at the monuments in the decades after the Black Death and you will see less of this confidence. Indeed, in certain cases there is a horrible realism. Take, for instance, the tombs of the bishops of Bath and Wells in Wells Cathedral, Somerset. The rather flat and incised images of the early medieval bishops show men resting, lying in their vestments and clasping their badges of office, confident of the afterlife and of their place there, while later bishops such as Bishop Drokensford – 1329 – ran to large tombs with fine canopies, again with an air of quiet confidence.

Then go and look at the tomb of Bishop Bekynton in the south chancel aisle, in a chantry chapel and dedicated in 1452. At first glance, this is just as grand and elaborate a tomb as any of his predeccesors. It is ornate, large and beautifully carved, and at the top shows the bishop in all his robes, hands together in prayer – just as his predecessors are shown. Then look again, for below the elaborately carved effigy of the bishop in his robes, apparently confident of the Resurrection, lies a cadaver, a rotting body crawling with insects, worms and rats. It is the very embodiment of decay, showing the triumph of death and the mortality of the body. This tomb, like many others of this time, and especially those of wealthy and successful priests or bishops, cries out uncertainty. No longer does being a priest mean the certainty of eternal life after death; instead death is a moment of a ghastly reckoning.

This view of death was even more starkly realised in Hexham in Northumbria. Here, on the rood screen where for centuries the images of Christ crucified, watched by his mother and St John, had been considered sufficient, in the mid-fifteenth century the church erected a painting of the *Dance of Death*, known as the *Danse Macabre* (after the Maccabees of Old Testament fame who were believed to have been the first to pray for the dead). This image first originated in Paris and drew its inspiration from the shock of the Black Death. In it the figure of

Death either dances with or scythes down kings, popes, bishops, merchants, knights, beautiful women and peasants, illustrating that all die, no matter how powerful they are.

As often happens in times of great distress, the poor saw the rich and powerful as surviving in greater numbers and resented their indifference to death and their apparent disregard for what the poor saw as a punishment from God. Thus William Langland in his poem *Piers Plowman,* written just after the Black Death, says:

> Since the time of the plague, friars and frauds like them have been dreaming up difficulties as a diversion for the sneering upper classes. Out of sheer clerical bloodymindedness they deliver sermons at the cross outside St Paul's, the effect of which is to undermine people's faith, so that they cease to give generous alms or feel sorry any longer for their sins. In the religious orders, and indeed in all sections of society, rich and poor alike, pride has reached such proportions that prayers have lost all efficacy as a means of stopping the plague. These days, God seems to be deaf – he can't even be bothered to open his ears. Because of *their* sins he snuffs out little children. And yet, these incorrigible materialists can't even take the hint from what's happening to their own number. Not even fear of the Black Death itself can make them abandon their pride. Oh no, they won't be kind to the poor as simple charity demands; instead they greedily go through their wealth, buying fancy clothes and extravagant meals.[5]

It was to be more than 100 years before this grumbling and loss of faith overturned the old order, the old alliance between Church and State, the reliance upon faith in the religious orders and their prayers. But in Langland's powerful complaint we hear the death knell of the old way of faith.

To my mind, the relationship between a crisis such as the Black Death and the collapse of a system of belief takes two apparently contradictory forms. Firstly, it breaks down trust in the existing order, as is witnessed by Langland. Secondly, it drives people to try and reinforce traditional patterns, such as a return to healing shrines. For example, the number of pilgrims to the shrines of healing saints, such as St Thomas at Canterbury, rose considerably during the time of the Black Death and for some time after. Furthermore, the growth of reliance on religious orders, hierarchy and the priesthood, and the transcendent, manifested itself in a surge of mysticism following the Black Death, such as the increased interest in the Body of Christ as expressed in the Communion bread, which was carried in a procession through the streets. Known as the Corpus Christi, this predates the Black Death by about thirty to forty years but only really became popular after the Black Death. Although we have seen how tombs exemplify the breakdown of trust in the existing order, approaches to death also illustrate an adherence to traditional patterns. The historian Philippe Aries writes:

> However, the reaction to the shock of the epidemic does not always take the realistic form of the cadaver or the description of death. Millard Meiss has shown that in Florence in the late fourteenth century, the mendicants were instructed to idealise the traditional religious representations rather than load them with realistic details, and they were also to exalt the role of the Church and of the Franciscan and Dominican orders by emphasising the hieratic aspects of the sacred and the transcendence in an archaic, abstract style.[6]

This phenomenon can be seen in England with such things as the creation of the Guild of Corpus Christi in Kings Lynn, which arose as a direct result of the numbers of deaths during the plague, and concern that the rituals and ceremonies of the Church were not sufficiently funded and organised to properly honour the dead.[7] Now, too, came the golden age of the building of chantry chapels, such as the magnificent one in the parish church of Tiverton, Devon. Chantry chapels increasingly became a feature of churches, for example the first recorded one at Ledbury Church in Herefordshire was that of St Anne, founded in 1384. But by 1412 two more, of the Virgin Mary and the Trinity, had also been built.

At the same time, however, chantry chapels represent the demise of the old certainty of automatic reward in heaven. The idea of a chantry chapel was that you built a special chapel and altar where, for a fixed fee settled in your will, priests would chant for you every day in order that you might escape hell, spend a short while in purgatory and then find yourself in heaven. Uncertainty had become the name of the game and the Church exploited it ruthlessly. It promoted the idea of purgatory – the condition of a person's soul who had died in a state of grace but who had not been purged from sin before entering heaven – and developed the concept of indulgences by which you could pay money to escape, or assist your relatives to escape, the horrors of hell or purgatory and go straight to heaven. This market for pardons, as indulgences were popularly known, gave rise to a much disliked group of professional salesmen of pardons, who often acted without the full blessing of the Church or as freelance's for an abbot or bishop who needed more money. The pardoners do not get a good press in English literature of the late fourteenth and fifteenth centuries – witness the Pardoner in Chaucer's *Canterbury Tales* who mocks his own goods and relishes the tricks he plays on ordinary folk. In his disdaining voice, we can hear the preachers whom Langland condemned:

> *'My lord,' he said, 'in churches where I preach*
> *I cultivate a haughty kind of speech*
> *And ring it out as roundly as a bell . . .*
> *I speak some Latin – just a few –*
> *To put a saffron tinge upon my preaching*
> *And stir devotion with a spice of teaching.*
> *Then I bring all my long glass bottles out*
> *Cram-full of bones and ragged bits of clout,*
> *Relics they are, at least for such are known . . .*
> *Why copy the Apostles? Why pretend?*
> *I must have wool, cheese, wheat and cash to spend,*
> *Though it were given me by the poorest lad*
> *Or poorest village widow, though she had*
> *A string of starving children, all agape.'*[8]

In the literature of the end of the fourteenth century and early fifteenth century there was a profound sense that the Church had become almost so corrupt as to be a problem rather than a solution. The papacy itself had periods of schism: two popes ruling from Rome and Avignon in France supported for purely political and economic reasons by different kings and emperors. The abuses within the Church were primarily financial. The wealth of the Church attracted people to its 'service' who were quite simply in it for the money. Many priests had more than one parish – some even as many as seven or eight. From these parishes they extracted the tithes – 10 per cent of all produce –

which could generate quite an income. With this practice of simony – holding more than one ecclesiastical appointment – came corruption. (Simony was so called after the story of Simon Magnus in the Acts of the Apostles in the New Testament who tried to offer money to the Apostles in order to learn what he believed to be the magical secrets of the Church.) The really wealthy parishes, even bishoprics – for some clergy held more than one – were openly bought and sold on the ecclesiastical market. Wealthy families would put younger sons into as many rich positions as possible to gain status and money.

The sexual laxity of the clergy is an issue of great debate. It is clear from the enquiries of archbishops and bishops in the fifteenth century that many priests were living with women and had children. This was often done quite openly; although clergy celibacy had been made compulsory in 1215, in many parts of the Church it was ignored and not considered to be particularly important.

The famed sexual laxity of the monasteries and nunneries has to be taken with reservations, however. The Protestant reformers loved to mock the nuns and monks, as those who are different from the bulk of the population in their habits are often mocked and derided. However, the monasteries and nunneries had become either immensely wealthy – it was said that if the Abbot of Glastonbury were to marry the Abbess of Shaftesbury, they would own half of England between them – or had become very poor, as inflation ate into their original funder's bequests. Certainly, monasticism in the fifteenth century was in a poor state.

Such abuses tend to emerge most strongly when a hierarchy is in decline. The history of the Church after the Black Death and up to the Reformation is one of its bleakest and worst times. This is not to say that there were no good priests, nunneries or monasteries, which kept the fabric of society together; many were still inspired by the Church. But increasingly the Church became tainted by abuses and the link between the official Church and the sacred began to unravel.

Equally serious was the pastoral care of the Church congregation. When clergy were more interested in the amount of money a parish could produce, they tended not to bother too much with the spiritual or physical needs of the parishioners. Every major ceremony of the Church had to be paid for by those seeking baptism, confirmation, marriage or burial. There were of course many good priests. But at the highest level, with a few exceptions, the spiritual oversight of Britain was in the hands of financiers and power politicians, not men who cared too much for the physical and spiritual state of the ordinary person in the church.

From the ferment of corruption and confusion that, in the wake of the Black Death, was changing the physical and spiritual landscape of Britain in the late fourteenth and early fifteenth centuries the Lollards emerged, the first significant new expression of the sacred that Britain had seen for perhaps 600 years.

The origins of the Lollards date back to John Wycliffe, a priest and scholar who was active in the last half of the fourteenth century. By the time he died in 1384, he had been condemned by the Church for his teachings and activities and, although not physically persecuted in his lifetime, his bones were dug up and burnt in 1415. He began the work of translating the Bible into English, believing that it should be available for people to read and interpret for themselves. He was called a 'lollard' by one of his opponents – a name derived from *lollaer*, a mumbler of prayers but became a name used about anyone who questioned the authority of the Church. The power of the clergy, and of the Church as an institution, was challenged by the idea of anyone being able to read the Bible, for it took away the authority of interpretation and opened access to all, regardless of ecclesiastical status.

From the 1390s onwards the Lollard movement, about which even to this day it is hard to find details, had created a secret society which spread throughout England and Scotland. The Lollards rejected many of the mainstays of medieval Christianity, targeting especially the celibacy of the clergy, which they saw flagrantly abused everywhere; transubstantiation – the belief that the bread and wine of the mass literally became the blood and body of Christ; indulgences and the right of priests to conduct the sacraments. They also rejected pilgrimage.

Some 16–19 kilometres (10–12 miles) south west of Buxton in Derbyshire there is a site called Lud's Chapel. To find it you need to know it is there, as it lies almost completely hidden on the top of a wooded hill. The hillside is covered with mature trees, stunted by the strong winds that sweep over the hill. It is behind one of these trees that you will find Lud's Chapel. Turning aside from the trackway you find a small opening which begins to lead you inexorably downwards. Within a few feet you look straight down into what is in effect a hidden gorge. Descending the slippery stone steps, you enter an incredibly narrow gorge, which runs for maybe 0.5 kilometres (¼ mile) in total. The walls are covered with ferns and mosses, a botanist's delight. The light that filters through trees above and the fronds of the ferns gives the whole place a greenish tinge. This is somewhat appropriate for it is believed that the confrontation between Sir Gawain and the Green Knight, so vividly told in the medieval book of that name, took place here.

But that is not why we have come. In the mud at the bottom of the gorge you can still see the bottom half of a late-medieval carved cross cut into a slab of rock. Here in the open air, hidden from prying eyes, Lollards met to read the Bible in English, to pray and to dispense with the services of priests, rituals and church. For the Lollards the failure of the rites of the Church, hinted at in Langland, seemingly confirmed by the devastation wrought by the Black Death, became the basis for a radical new understanding of the sacred, which rejected the intercessory and mediatory role of the Church. The Lollard text *The Twelve Conclusions* of 1395 says: 'That exorcisms and hallowings, made in the Church, of wine, bread, and wax, water, salt and oil and incense, the stone of the altar, upon vestments, mitre, cross, and pilgrims' staves, be the very practice of necromancy, rather than of the holy theology.'[9]

It is hard to know how serious a movement the Lollards were. Either they were one of our most widespread, successful secret movements and remained largely undetected, or they were not that numerous and were discovered, exposed and persecuted by the Church. I suspect the truth lies somewhere in between. The Lollards were active in Kent, the north-west and the Midlands. Bristol, associated with Wycliffe, who was a priest at the nearby college of Westbury-on-Trym, was a major centre, as was London. Persecution, leading to execution, drove them underground, but it is very difficult to estimate their numbers. Ultimately, it was not their numbers but the boldness of their ideas that was important – ideas that predate and in all likelihood partially created those of the Reformation more than 100 years later.

The Lollards were the forerunners of the English Reformation. They were also the first clearly identifiable group to step outside the sacred bounds of the Church as established under the Anglo-Saxon kingdoms and subsequently developed under the Norman and later kings. As such they were essentially expressing a belief that the sacred was other than that which they had been taught. In former millennia they might have been the harbingers of a whole new religion. Perhaps in some ways they were, for their wholesale rejection of the core elements of medieval Christianity put them outside the conventional Church and led to them being officially declared heretics.

As a result of the Black Death, English life was changing. In particular, the old feudal patterns were collapsing, and this freed many to make decisions of their own. Feudalism had been, to all intents and purposes, a form of slavery: serfs were not allowed to leave their lands without permission from the lord of the manor. When the Black Death made labour scarce, the serfs flexed their financial muscle and, to some degree, renegotiated their terms of employment. This was combined with a breakdown of order, which meant that people were suddenly free to go almost wherever they wanted.

Along with physical freedom came intellectual freedom, and the exploration of freedom is fundamentally linked to the sacred. The Lollards are the first evidence of this. Their movement was part of a new version of the relationship between people and faith that began to emerge in response to the crisis and opportunity that the Black Death and its assault on the old bonds had created.

As the overlay of feudalism began to break up, there was a remarkable rediscovery of interest in the older Christian sacred geography of Britain at this time, as Eamon Duffy has shown. He records a rise in visits to sacred springs, holy wells and saints' shrines; however, the popularity of certain saints and their sites also rose and fell according to fashion. Rituals such as the Corpus Christi, that elevated the bread as the actual body of Christ, provided a powerful vision of the sacred as a physical manifestation, leading to a greater awareness of the sacred in the physical landscape. Many of the most beautifully decorated churches date from this time, especially the Wool churches of central and south-west England, built upon the riches of the wool merchants. But it was to be a brief last blaze before the old world of saints, wells, pilgrimages, ritual and magic was assaulted by new forces, and all that they embodied was overthrown.

It is no coincidence that the physical landscape was changing radically as well as the social, spiritual and economic landscape. At the end of the fourteenth century the power of the nobles was still considerable and they made most of the important decisions. And key amongst these was that sheep were more important than human beings. Vast areas of English countryside were turned over to sheep, which required little in the way of workers to care for them, and also needed to be able to graze widely. Old field systems, farms and villages were removed or abandoned as the sheep took over. Consequently poverty and unemployment among the people became a major problem, land rights enshrined in tradition diminished and land was taken from many of its traditional uses by the powerful and wealthy for rearing sheep. Once again, environment, lifestyle changes and religion were walking together uncomfortably in sacred Britain.

In the vicinity of Buxton it is said that the Bible was first read publicly in English in Lud's Chapel. In the natural beauty and atmosphere of the defile in the Derbyshire hills, the sacred of the land and the sacred of the word, which was to shape the next centuries, were meeting for the first time. The words of Isaiah as read by Jesus and quoted in Luke 4: 18–20 must have sounded to the Lollards both fascinating, heard at last in their own language, and possibly even challenging:

> The spirit of the lord on me for whiche thing he anoyntid me: he sente me to preche to pore men, to heele contrite men in herte, and to preche remyssioun to presoneres: and sizt to blynde men, and to delyuer broken men in to remyssioun, to preche the zeer of the lord plesaunt, and the dai of zeldynge azen, and whanne he hadde closid the book: he zaf azen to the mynystre, and satte, and the izen of alle men in the synagoge weren biholdynge in to hym and he bigan to seie to hem for in this daie this scripture is fulfullid in youre eeris.[10]

The Lollards' work precipitated the production of that masterpiece of the sixteenth and seventeenth centuries, the Bible in English, which was to play a significant part in the Reformation.

Against a backdrop of social and religious change caused by the Black Death, Britain stood on the edge of its own cultural revolution. And what was about to be unleashed was far more devastating, far more destructive than anything that had gone before.

Ironically, it was to be a cultural revolution which drew much of its inspiration from, and was supported by, a royal family, which depended upon a vision of the sacredness of Britain which had been slowly evolving over the last 200–300 years. A vision of the sacred of Britain which rooted itself aetiologically in the mystic past of King Arthur but which also found its fulfilment in the triumph of a British king, a king of Celtic–British stock. Before we can move into the beginnings of the modern age, which is the Reformation, we need to explore a strange story of gods and prophets, visions and storytelling, which is as much part of the origin of modern Britain as is the coming of printing.

CHAPTER TWELVE

MYTHS, LEGENDS AND HISTORY

T
O UNDERSTAND A PEOPLE and a time, it is not enough to know only the dates and names. It is also important to attempt to understand what the world looked like to them, and what beliefs and myths they used to explain and manage the world around them. On the eve of the modern world, at the end of the fifteenth century, we can, for the first time, do this. We have the stories and books, and we have the visible outcomes, which together allow us to attempt to see through the eyes and beliefs of those who took Britain dramatically into a new era. The consequences of those actions – Reformation, empire, colonialism, education, royalty and even the New Age – are with us today.

I grew up in Bristol, where my family has lived for centuries, and I felt great pride as I walked its ancient streets. Sadly I never saw the city in its full splendour: Bristol probably lost more historic buildings in the Second World War than any other city apart from London. As a child I wandered through bomb sites, and ran down into great pits that were overgrown with buddleia and brambles where 50 years before people had lived, worked and worshipped. In the late-medieval period, Bristol was the second city of Britain, but its medieval treasures had gone up in flames a decade before my birth. It is still a wonderful place to wander, though. I particularly adore the old churches and the city walls, although virtually nothing survives of the walls now. However, if you know where to walk you can trace their shape and size, catching glimpses of fragments embedded in church walls, overgrown court-yards and basements.

The only remaining church over a city gate, St John on the Wall, at the end of Broad Street, has a special attraction for me. This beautiful little church sits gracefully on the wall, its thin spire rising as a delicate counterpoint to the curving arch beneath it. Sadly it is almost always locked, but just looking at it is enough for me.

Two brightly coloured and fiercely posed statues fill the niches that would normally be occupied by saints on the tower over the gate. But these statues are not of saints. They are clearly kings and, as a child, I thought they were two of the three kings of the Nativity, but this proved not to be the case. The two statues are of Brennus and Belinus, sons of the legendary founder of Bristol, and were erected during the mid- to late fifteenth century. As a child I was fascinated but completely flummoxed by these two figures. Nowhere in my motley but good collection of history books could I find a single reference to them. Who on earth were they and why were they there when they did not seem to exist?

It was years before I found an answer, and when I did it only made things more confusing, for they are not part of ordinary history. They are the manifestations of a sacred history, a mythology which helped to define the ruling family who would most affect the sacred in Britain: the legends of Merlin and Arthur and the Red Dragon of Wales.

THE ONCE AND FUTURE KING

In one form or another, the legend of King Arthur is familiar to most of us. A great and chivalrous king, he was hidden as a child and only revealed by the wizard Merlin. He headed the Round Table of heroic knights, and was eventually destroyed by the tragic love of his wife Guinevere for his best friend Lancelot, and the insurrection by his bastard, incestuous son Mordred.

Curiously enough, this version of the most British of tales was forged in France. Between the eleventh and fourteenth centuries, the French troubadours became obsessed with the tale of King Arthur, which they called 'the matter of Britain'. They added many of the elements familiar to us, in particular the character of the French knight Lancelot and his affair with Guinevere, and the quest for the Holy Grail. The tales came to exemplify the highest ideals of knighthood, a shining example that stood in somewhat brutal contrast to the realities of the feudal system. Everything within them was perfect, at least until the end of the tale: Arthur was the perfect king, Gawain the perfect knight, Lancelot and Guinevere the perfect lovers.

In the fifteenth century Thomas Malory, a knight imprisoned for political reasons or possibly for rape, translated and revised these versions back into English as *Le Morte d'Arthur*. Malory's version of the story has many fascinating elements that are too complex to explore fully here. But one of the most interesting is how the events seem to parallel the Plantagenet dynasty that, in Malory's time, was tearing itself apart in the Wars of the Roses. Malory seems deliberately to have drawn parallels between the Arthurian story and Plantagenet history, emphasising the civil wars that marked both, and ending his book with a revolt that uses cannon. His version of the Arthurian myths has undoubtedly been deeply influential on the British. Whenever the Victorians needed to invoke a true British hero, they would turn to Arthur. For example, Disraeli used to flatter Queen Victoria by claiming that she was descended from Arthur. Yet the earlier versions of the Arthur story have, perhaps, had an even more powerful influence on the sacred history of Britain.

The historical Arthur, if he existed at all, was probably a fifth-century Romano-British leader (or possibly two leaders merged into one mythological figure) who maintained a small kingdom against the invading Saxons. However, in the Welsh *Mabinogion* Arthur is a great fighter and chieftain, leading a band of warriors whose powers seem almost superheroic, such as leaping nine hills in a single bound and standing as high as oak trees. These stories echo many of the Irish tales of heroes, such as Cuchulain, and possibly reflect stories of earlier, pre-Christian chieftains. The name Arthur may come either from *arthos*, meaning bear, or from the Gaelic *ard rhi*, meaning the high king.

Ironically, Arthur's greatest knight in these stories is Sir Kay, who is depicted in many later versions as something of a poltroon, bully and coward. This is because whenever writers wanted to introduce a new character of their own devising, such as Sir Gawain or Sir Lancelot, and show that he was 'the best of all knights', they would have him beat Kay in a fight. Even later authors then read these stories, in which Kay gets repeatedly done over by other knights, and not unnaturally, concluded that Kay was evidently something of a wimp; a classic example of how a story can shift over the centuries. Another, sadder example of this is the story of Black Annis, a child-eating hag of Shropshire, who seems to have been a perverted memory, created by Protestant anti-Catholic monasticism propaganda, of a saintly anchorite, Agnes, of the fifteenth century. Myths, like everything else, change with time.

But the single most influential version of the Arthurian mythos, portrayed as 'history', was that of Geoffrey of Monmouth, a twelfth-century canon, eventually Bishop of St Asaph who, in 1136, wrote an extraordinary book entitled *Historia Regum Britanniae*; the *History of the Kings of Britain*. From reading Geoffrey I sense an enthusiastic, patriotic and slightly gullible man who was a great storyteller, never unwilling to suspend disbelief or invent in order to further his story. He was probably of mixed Norman–Breton–Welsh blood but he was most certainly a Briton in spirit. Geoffrey's work when read as strict history needs to be taken with a large dose of salt.

As an attempt to forge a sacred history of Britain, however, it is fascinating. The culmination of earlier attempts by writers such as Gildas and Nennius who, in Geoffrey's opinion, were clearly too bound by such paltry considerations as a vague sense of historical accuracy, Geoffrey goes to great lengths to draw parallels between Britain and Rome in order to demonstrate that Britain was the new sacred kingdom, a Holy Empire.

The great poem of Roman mythology and history, Virgil's *Aeneid*, claims that Rome was founded by Aeneas, a refugee Trojan prince who, guided by the gods, fled Troy after it was sacked by the Greeks. Gildas, the sixth-century writer we encountered in Chapter 6, claimed that Britain was also founded by a refugee from Troy, Brutus, who founded a new Troy in Britain and whose descendants made up the kings of Gildas's own age. Brennus and Belinus, the two figures over the gate in Bristol, were Brutus's sons. Geoffrey picks up this theme with enthusiasm, determined to show that Britain has been a place guided by God from the first. His Britons are tough, slaughtering thousands of Romans with cunning tricks when they try to invade, establishing ancient codes of law, and generally proving themselves a fine and worthy people. Geoffrey claimed, with absolutely no evidence, that it was Britons and not Gauls who sacked Rome in 390 BC, that they had a great and civilised kingdom and code of justice, and that they had amphitheatres, baths and central heating.

Out of the line of these British princes, according to Geoffrey, sprang King Arthur, the son of Uther Pendragon, and the final pages of the book are dedicated to telling his story. Geoffrey emphasises the role Arthur played in uniting Britain under, effectively, one rule, and his important role in beating back the Saxon invaders in a long series of wars. Geoffrey even claims that Arthur, after being insulted by Roman envoys, invaded Europe and conquered the remnants of the Empire, eventually being crowned Emperor by the Pope in Rome.

Geoffrey's own contemporaries were somewhat suspicious of his stories, questioning why, if Arthur was so great a conqueror, his name was not known throughout Europe. William of Newburgh, a careful and accurate historian, bluntly called Geoffrey 'the father of lies' and said that he 'cloaked fables about Arthur under the honest name of history'. Gerald of Wales, a historian of the late twelfth century, can never resist making a dig at Geoffrey. At one point Gerald tells a story about a great soothsayer called Meilyr who could see people's true natures, and because of this was the subject of attacks by demons. To defend himself, he would place a copy of St John's Gospel on his lap, forcing the demons to flee. Gerald then goes on to have a crack at Geoffrey:

> If the Gospel were afterwards removed and the 'History of the Kings of Britain' by Geoffrey of Monmouth put there in its place, just to see what would happen, the demons would alight all over his body and on the book too, staying there longer than usual and being even more demanding.[1]

The book, however, was a huge success, eventually becoming known simply as the 'Brut', and was accepted as the standard history of Britain right up to the sixteenth century. It was also the major spur for the invention of the Arthurian myths and, as we shall see, quite possibly put the first Tudor king on the throne.

WHITE DRAGON, RED DRAGON

One of the most ambiguous and powerful figures in Geoffrey's mythic history is the wizard Merlin, whose magic aids Arthur's rise to power.

Merlin, according to Geoffrey, was a mighty soothsayer, and his prophecies, as recounted by Geoffrey, were to prove a powerful influence on British history. To see the impact of these prophecies, we must travel into the Lleyn Peninsula of North Wales, one of the most dramatic and sacred of landscapes. Along here runs an old pilgrims' route, 'the way of the Saints', which leads to Bardsey Island where legend says no less than 20,000 saints are buried. At the church of Llanaelhaearn you can see Romano-British tombstones of the sixth to eighth centuries, including one inside the church linking this ancient Christian site with the strange kingdom of Elmet in Yorkshire.

In this wonderful landscape we find the hill of Tre'r Ceiri, soaring up to 485 metres (1,591 feet) and topped by one of the best-preserved Iron Age towns in Britain, containing the remains of at least fifty clearly visible houses. From here you can look down on a valley today known as Nant Gwrtheyrn. This strange place, lying at the base of the mountain known as The Forks (Yr Eifl in Welsh) is the setting for one of Geoffrey's most powerful inventions, for its alternative name is Vortigern's Valley.

We have met Vortigern before. He was the last Roman ruler of London and the south-east, who invited the Saxons to settle in Kent, a disastrous decision that allowed the Saxons a fatal foothold in England. From Gildas onwards, British historians have tended to see Vortigern as the British Anti-Christ, or as the unwitting instrument of God's punishment on the British. Vortigern has been, both mythologically and historically, central to the story of Britain.

It is no surprise, then, that Geoffrey, drawing on earlier legends and histories, such as that of the ninth-century monk Nennius, uses the stories of Vortigern to create a dramatic prophecy for the future of Britain. According to him, Vortigern built a palace in this tiny valley, where he was hiding from the invading Angles and Saxons he had accidentally unleashed on his land. He tried to build a strong tower for protection but, for unknown reasons, the ground would simply swallow it up each night. Desperate to know why, he consulted his magicians, who told him that if the blood of a fatherless boy was sprinkled upon the earth, the curse would be lifted.

This boy was the young Merlin (who was supposed to have been begotten by the Devil upon a novice nun but, generally speaking, took after his mother's side of the family), who was brought to the valley and led before Vortigern. The figure of Merlin is a powerful one, largely invented by Geoffrey to act as a voice for his vision of Britain. He is a combination of the fatherless boy, Ambrosius, who plays the role of the potential victim in Nennius's stories, and the prophet Myrrdin, who appears in *The Black Book of Carmathen*, a collection of Welsh fables.

Anticipating Vortigern's desire to murder him, Merlin told the king that the true cause of the collapse of the tower was a magical pool beneath the earth. Vortigern dug down and, upon finding it, two great dragons emerged from the water, one white and the other red. The moment they saw each other they launched into a terrible battle. At first the White Dragon drove the Red Dragon back against the mountains, but then the Red Dragon turned and fought back, eventually forcing the White Dragon to flee.

Vortigern called Merlin to explain this and, as Geoffrey graphically puts it:

> Merlin immediately burst into tears. He went into a prophetic trance and then spoke as follows:
>
> Alas for the Red Dragon, for its end is near. Its cavernous dens shall be occupied by the White Dragon, which stands for the Saxons whom you have invited over. The Red Dragon represents the people of Britain, who will be overrun by the White One: for Britain's mountains and valleys shall be levelled, and the streams in its valleys shall run with blood.
>
> The cult of religion shall be destroyed completely and the ruin of the churches shall be clear for all to see. The race that is oppressed shall prevail in the end for it will resist the savagery of the invaders.[2]

There are many other prophecies that Geoffrey claims to have translated from 'the British tongue' into Latin at the request of the Bishop of Lincoln; I suspect he harvested some from local folklore, and made up the rest. However, the prophecy of the dragons, which predicted that the British – or the Welsh, if you like – would rise again and throw off the Anglo-Saxon yoke, has been a powerful one for many centuries. Its influence can still be seen in the present-day flag of Wales. Closer to Geoffrey's time, however, the prophecies were combined with local folklore to predict a 'son of prophecy', a liberator who would rise up and restore the glory of Britain.[3]

The first person to claim he was this son of prophecy was the Welsh prince Owain Glyn Dwr, who rose up in revolt in 1400 and declared he was the one spoken of in the prophecies, the liberator who would restore the glory of the Red Dragon. He used the dragon on his banners, and at the height of the rebellion in 1401, when it seemed quite possible that Glyn Dwr might destroy Norman rule in Wales, he wrote to Robert III, King of Scotland, proposing that they ally, as they were both descendants of Brutus and the royal line of Britain.

There is no doubt that this was a powerful story. Owain Glyn Dwr fought on until around 1415, although the revolt had failed by 1406, but this did little to dampen the enthusiasm. Legend has it that Owain never died, but continues to live in a cave on Plynlimmon Mountain, from which the River Severn flows. I have met Welsh shepherds who will quite casually talk of crossing the mountain and meeting Owain riding or striding across the moors.

In 1485 another contender for the title son of prophecy arose: Henry Tudor, the eventual victor of the War of the Roses. As he was of partial Welsh descent the Welsh gentry, who had been spurred on two generations before by the near-success of Glyn Dwr, placed their hopes in him as being the true fulfiller of Merlin's prophecies. That he was seen as the true son of prophecy and Owain's rightful successor is contained in a Tudor story told by Ellis Griffith of Calais. It tells how Owain was out walking one day in the Berwyn Mountains and here met the abbot of Valle Crucis Abbey: '"You are up betimes, Master Abbot," said Owain. "Nay sire," was the answer, "it is you who have risen too soon – by a century." '[4]

In Henry the Welsh gentry and the powerful bardic network believed that they had found 'the British king who would once again rule in London', as the songs and prophecies put it. Henry was consequently able to ignite the Welsh upon his landing at St Ann's Head in 1485, drawing massive support to him in Wales. Preachers and bards alike linked Henry to the old stories, giving hope to those who flocked to his Red Dragon banner. The rest, as they say, is history. There were, of course, other forces at work – military, economic and social – but the initial success of Henry in his march through Wales lies more in the realm and influence of a sacred history than has been previously imagined. Within a few months, at the Battle of Bosworth Field, Henry VII defeated Richard III and the reign of the Tudors began.

DANGEROUS MYTHS

Perhaps the true descendants of Geoffrey of Monmouth are the numerous, and rather silly, books of 'conspiratorial history', which generally have about as much historical validity as Geoffrey's claims of Arthur sacking Rome. One of the most powerful themes of these books tends to be a longing for a chosen people, a sense of specialness, which can also be seen in Geoffrey's patriotic elevation of the British. It is no coincidence that many of them focus around Arthur, or that by far the most popular and successful has been the bestselling *Holy Blood, Holy Grail*, which claims, through a splendid mixture of misreadings, half-truths, and complete invention, that the Merovingian rulers of France were, in fact, descendants of Jesus Christ. Frankly, the thought of the French as descended from the Son of God seems to me a rather implausible one! Two other favourites of mine are *Holy Grail Across the Atlantic*, which makes any number of splendidly daft claims about the Templars, a perennial favourite of conspiracy historians, founding castles in Nova Scotia in Canada, and *The Holy Kingdom*, which accepts not only Geoffrey, but also the faked Llandaff Charters, at face value, creating a pseudo-historical myth around Arthur and the 'holiness' of Britain.[5]

These books may seem rather silly, but they have a more sinister side. The story of Henry Tudor shows the powerful forces that a sacred history can unleash, and perhaps the most powerful and dangerous sacred history forged in our time was that which motivated the bombers that devastated Bristol's medieval buildings: the terrible mythology of Nazi Germany. The Nazis created a powerful sacred history for themselves, that of the Aryan people, destined by evolution and the gods to rule the world over the lesser races. It was this sense that Germany was a chosen land, and the Germans a chosen people, that helped justify their brutal aggressive wars and the slaughter of millions of 'inferiors'. Himmler, a keen mythological and occult enthu-siast, even tried to invoke a sense of the SS as the new Knights of the Round Table, building a bizarre castle that was full of the imagery of 'Camelot'.

Indeed, the Second World War involved massive use of sacred histories by almost all sides. The Japanese invented strange stories of their descent from ancient Chinese rulers, and that their true destiny was to 'liberate' Asia from European oppression. The Nazi invasion of Russia was named 'Barbarossa', after the Holy Roman Emperor who was supposed to lie buried beneath Germany and, like King Arthur, would rise again to fight Germany's foes. In turn, Stalin invoked the stories of the Russian King Alexander Nevsky and his battles against the Teutonic Knights, and handed out new medals named after him. The war as a whole, of course, has become a powerful new mythology itself; indeed, the whole British sense of being 'special', of patriotic identity, is now considerably formed around our defeat of Nazi Germany, and the time when we 'stood alone'.

Sacred histories are powerful, and you play with them at your peril. The Thousand Year Reich, mercifully, lasted only fourteen years, but those were quite bad enough. The nationalistic, even racist, overtones of many of these histories is highly disturbing, and they can have disastrous effects.

Henry Tudor's invasion of Britain was to have its own devastating consequences. Within two generations, this family was to undo and destroy virtually everything religious and sacred that had been born and treasured since the White Dragon – the Saxons – became Christians. It was almost as if the Red Dragon of the Tudors is returning to an earlier, simpler and purer vision, but what the Tudors actually unleashed was the most traumatic change to English, Welsh and Scottish culture that there has ever been, as we shall now see. The mythology went dramatically wrong!

CHAPTER THIRTEEN

'Bare Ruined Choirs'

AN UNCHANGED CHURCH

THE EXQUISITE VILLAGE CHURCH OF St Mary the Virgin in Childrey, Berkshire, is one of those remarkable places where time seems to have stood still. Tucked away at the end of a lane beside the ancient manor house, it is one of the most perfect churches I know. Its setting – manor house, farm and fields – has probably not been significantly altered for 500 years or more. The church itself was complete by 1500 and the changes to it since have been minor. The doorway is late twelfth century while the nave is twelfth century, modernised in the fifteenth century. The chancel is thirteenth century and the two old chantry chapels to the north and south were both built around 1325. The glorious tower, sturdy as faith itself, dates from 1450.

The Victorians had only a minor impact on this church and as you enter it, it is as if you had stepped back 500 years. To your left is the ancient font, with a lead frieze of abbots running around it, symbols of the monastic control of this church by the hugely powerful Abingdon monastery. Still crossing the church, dividing the nave from the chancel, is the rood screen, dating from the late fifteenth century. Looking into the north transept, one of the old chantry chapels built *c.* 1325 by the local lords of the manor for prayers to be said for their ancestors, you can see faded medieval stained glass which still exudes the lightness and grace of the storyteller's art.

In the chancel, the choir pews are medieval, and to the left of the altar is one of the most attractive Easter sepulchres in Britain, with charming carvings of dogs and a delightful hedgehog in the spandrels above it. On Good Fridays before the Reformation, the consecrated Communion bread and the altar crucifix were placed here and often covered by a black cloth. From then through to Easter Sunday a vigil was kept. It was as if the church had its own Holy Sepulchre as in Jerusalem, from which Christ could arise on Easter morn.

The collection of monumental brasses in this church is among the largest and most important in Britain and it was rubbing these that first drew me, as a teenager on my faithful bicycle, to this wonderful church. There are twelve, ranging from knights in armour, through to civilians, priests dressed in Eucharistic vestments, and corpses rising from their graves. Uniquely, there are also three brasses of the Holy Trinity, being devoutly worshipped by other brass figures.

Five hundred years ago, most churches would have been like this, adorned with Easter sepulchres, rood screens, symbols of the Holy Trinity, chantry chapels and stained glass. Today Childrey is one of the very few remaining churches where all these features survive. Most Easter sepulchres were destroyed in the sixteenth century, when they were believed to be superstitious objects, and replaced by monumental tombs – ironically known as sepulchre monuments – dedicated to late-sixteenth or early-seventeenth-century local gentry. The place of the Host and the risen Christ were taken by the Patron of the Church and the rising bourgeoisie. The rood screens were torn down and often burnt or, as in the case of Childrey, used for other purposes in the church. Symbols of the Trinity were ripped out and the elegant saints in the glass windows were smashed to pieces

Most of this destruction was unleashed by the events of the Reformation, and the breaking away of England from the Catholic Church. Before we investigate further the extent and fury of this destruction, and the profound issues it raises for any understanding of sacred history in Britain, let's look at what the Reformation was in Europe, and why it had such a dramatic and sudden impact upon Britain.

In Chapter 11 we saw the changing social conditions, changing attitudes to faith and corruption of the clergy that sowed the seeds for the Reformation in Britain. These events were also influenced by what was happening in the wider context of Europe. Before the Reformation, there was only one Church throughout the majority of Europe, the Catholic Church centered upon Rome and the Pope. For Western Europe, religion was the Catholic Church, whose complete unity was thought to be a sign of its divine origin. Sadly such power had tended to produce popes from powerful families whose main interest was money, power and personal indulgence. Of course, contrary to later Protestant fantasies, by no means was the whole of the Church corrupt.

The Church ran hospitals, homes for the elderly and leper colonies; it protected the weak against the powerful, and sought to mediate in wars to bring peace. Monasteries still provided the only serious education available to ordinary people. In parishes across Europe, local priests offered spiritual and practical help to the depressed, distressed and unemployed.[1] But as well as widespread abuses among the clergy of the kind seen in Britain, there was such corruption at the centre that it put the rest of the work of the Church at risk. For example, the popes had their own kingdom and their own army, which was often the cause of warfare in Italy and beyond – hardly the practices of those following the humble carpenter from Nazareth, the Prince of Peace. Added to this was the fact that the popes often acted as if the Church was their private property. They bestowed lucrative posts such as archbishoprics on their somewhat earthly relatives, they aggrandised themselves and their families through the wealth which flowed from the Church, and at times they openly kept mistresses.

There were consequently many who wanted to reform the Church. Apart from the Lollards, whom we have already met, there were the Waldensians in Italy itself or Hussites in Bohemia, both of which groups reformed the Church in areas they dominated. However it was the broadside launched by Martin Luther that finally cracked open the unity of the Catholic Church and precipitated the movement known as 'the Reformation'.

Martin Luther was a monk whose explorations of the Bible and exposure to the greed throughout the ecclesiastical structures led him to despair altogether of the Church. In 1517, he nailed ninety-five theses to the door of the main church in the German town of Witten-berg. These particularly addressed the issue of the sale of indulgences. He questioned the authority of the Church to determine access to the grace and love of God, arguing his belief that there was nothing humanity could do of itself, which could bring salvation. The gift of forgiveness was a gift from God through Christ, which was gained not by what a person did, but by what they believed. He saw salvation as coming through the justification of faith in God, not through any action or institution of man.

In challenging the Church in this way, Luther opened a door that would not shut. He became the centre of a vast shift in attitude towards the Catholic Church. He had hoped to reform the Church from within but it soon became clear that the ecclesiastical powers wanted nothing to do with this. As a result, and encouraged by the support of ambitious princes in Germany who wanted greater power in their own lands, he turned to these rulers and then to the Scandinavian kingdoms, to help reform the Church. The result was the creation, from the early 1520s onwards, of state churches, which divorced themselves from the control of Rome and the authority of the Pope, and whose loyalty was not to the Pope, but to the prince or king.

While much of this change was inspired by genuinely pious motives, it was also done for reasons of power and money. Funds that had traditionally gone to Rome, such as the fee charged for authorising the Church in each country, known as Peter's Pence, now flowed into the coffers of the princes and kings. The lands that had belonged to the great monasteries was now 'reclaimed' by the state, and sold off to the rising new merchant class. The result was the breakdown of the unity of the Church as well as the opening of debate about the meaning of the Gospels, and the condemnation of many beliefs and traditions of the medieval Church, such as pilgrimage, shrines and the high role of the priest. These events also unleashed terrible and violent warfare, as Catholic princes sought to destroy Lutheran princes, and vice versa. Soon Lutheranism was also splitting, with other ideas emerging: notable amongst these was Calvinism with its creation of what was in effect a theocracy, based upon the belief in predestination.

THE CREATION OF THE ANGLICAN CHURCH

At first Britain remained aloof from all this; indeed, Henry VIII sided with the Pope. On every British coin, beside the head of the Queen, appear the letters 'D.F.', which stand for 'Defensor Fidei' – Defender of the Faith. Many assume that this refers to the monarch's role as head of the Church of England, which the Queen swore to uphold at her coronation. In fact the words refer to a title bestowed by the Pope on Henry VIII in gratitude for Henry's book attacking Luther, which he published in 1521, and which became quite a bestseller not just in England, but also on the Continent.[2] Luther was anathema to Henry as a good son of the Church – until the Church tried to stop Henry having a son of his own.

In 1527 Henry VIII began efforts to divorce his wife, Catherine of Aragon. Although they had a daughter, Mary, later to be Queen Mary, they had failed to have a son. Henry was desperate to have a male heir, and he had also fallen in love with another woman, Anne Boleyn. He therefore appealed to the Pope for an annulment of his marriage. An annulment was given, in theory, on the grounds that a marriage had broken some law of the Church concerning consanguinity or the proper seriousness of the partners, but in fact it was normally given purely on grounds of the power and influence of the parties involved. As Catherine had been briefly married to Henry's older brother Arthur, now dead, Henry claimed that he had inadvertently committed a sin by marrying his brother's wife. However the Pope, influenced by Catherine's nephew Charles V, the Holy Roman Emperor, did not agree, and refused Henry an annulment.

In frustration Henry, in a series of Acts of Parliament between 1530 and 1534, transferred the Supremacy of the Church in England and Wales from the Pope to himself and his successors, thereby creating the Church of England.[3] It is doubtful whether Henry had any idea what forces he was unleashing. As has been seen so vividly in recent decades, once a powerful system collapses – Communism in the former USSR, dictatorship in Indonesia, the regimes of megalomaniac rulers such as Mobutu Sese Seko in Zaire – all sorts of long-repressed forces are suddenly unleashed, and chaos often follows.

Henry seems to have tried to be a good Catholic even as he took over the role of the Pope and resisted Protestant reforms. For instance, as late as 1535 he was persecuting those who wanted the Bible to be translated and published in English. However, the desire to reform a manifestly corrupt Church was overwhelming, and was also linked to the rise of a new class, the middle classes, who wanted land and authority. Under the old covenant between the court and the Church, this was not possible and so, for the middle classes to rise, the status quo had to go.

Once the idea of one binding Church authority was challenged, the question became: what is the true source of authority? This issue, combined with profound questions of theology, ripped across Britain as a result of the Reformation. Much that was bad about the old Church structures and practices went, and most people did not lament it.

By the time of Henry's death in 1547, the Church of England looked like a push-me-pull-you. At one end it was still a Catholic Church, cut off from the Pope, reformed of some of the worst abuses, but essentially an English-speaking version of the Catholic Church. At the other end, there were extremist reformers for whom anything that smacked of 'Catholicism' was anathema. They were chaffing at the bit, wanting to institute a purge of all Catholic elements in order to produce either a full-blown Lutheran Church or even going towards the kind of Puritanical theocracy Calvin was to establish in the 1550s in Geneva. In the middle was the bulk of the clergy and people – confused, alarmed and just hoping life would calm down and return to normal.

Tragically, however, this Reformation of the Church included the destruction of Catholic artefacts, symbols and artwork, as well as the closing of all monasteries and nunneries. Childrey, while still having much that has been lost in other churches, nevertheless lost a great deal itself. Most of its medieval stained glass was destroyed, and what remains is but a fraction of that which existed until *c.* 1538. The year 1547 saw the forced closure of the two chantry chapels and the seizing of the lands that had paid for the chantry priest. The role of these chapels – as places where daily prayers and Masses were said for the dead – ceased and the chantry priest at Childrey lost his job. At the time he was one of four priests in the church, along with the rector, his curate and the family chaplain of the lord of the manor. In 1548 the huge figure of Christ on the cross with Mary his mother and St John to either side was taken down and destroyed. In the same year all the statues of saints and images painted on the walls were taken away or whitewashed. It was shorn of much that would have made it a visible exemplar of the teachings of the medieval Church.

Not even one set of rood screen figures has survived anywhere in

Britain. All of them – probably in excess of 10,000 – were destroyed in the space of perhaps two years or so in around 1547–8. Likewise, as a result of laws and destructions between 1545 and 1547, not a single chantry chapel survived in use. Some were actually destroyed, but the majority were incorporated into the body of the church, as has happened at Childrey. Here, in the early twentieth century, they were restored to something of their former glory, and it is still possible to see how they functioned as separate chapels within the church.

To see the splendour of a chantry chapel that has survived pretty much intact, visit Worcester Cathedral where near the high altar, there is the chapel of Prince Arthur, older brother of Henry VIII, and first husband of Catherine of Aragon. This, due to family loyalty, survived the Reformation and, miraculously, also the civil wars of the seventeenth century. It gives us a glimpse of what has gone.

THE DISSOLUTION OF THE SACRED

The huge abbey of Abingdon, which controlled the life of the church in Childrey and hundreds of other parishes, is no more. Its only remains are a few domestic buildings, such as a sixteenth century long gallery, a hall and the gatehouse. The site of this vast abbey – one of the largest churches in Christendom – is now a park. It was just one victim of one of the most astonishing acts of destruction of the sacred ever undertaken. Between 1536 and 1539 all the monasteries and nunneries in England and Wales were closed. From having more than 3,000 such establishments in 1530, by 1540 England and Wales had none, while in Scotland all the monasteries had been closed by the 1560s. Not a single abbey, monastery or nunnery of the Middle Ages has survived in continuous use to this day. One or two, such as Aylesford in Kent and Caldy Island, off Tenby, Carmarthen Bay, Wales, have been bought back by religious orders in recent years.[4]

The reason given for the dissolution was the corruption of the monastic ideals of chastity and poverty. But the real reason was the desire of the rising bourgeoisie to lay hands upon the Church's wealth and lands and to break the only remaining body of the Church still loyal to Rome. For many of the emerging merchant class, land was the security they most desired. They already had money and goods, but land was at a premium, parcelled up between the Church, the nobility and the King. Henry wanted funds, and the merchants and king found the seizable and saleable land of the monasteries irresistible.

The Reformation resulted in the almost total dismantling of sacred England and Wales. As a result churches, chapels, burial grounds, oratories, shrines, hospitals, schools and gardens were destroyed in a frenzy of iconoclasm and greed. Much of this was organised and directed by specially appointed commissioners of the King and Parliament. These men were responsible for carrying out the theological, social and political decisions of the Court. However, some were more zealous than others and in some cases, local gangs and groups went far beyond what was legally allowed. The official sanction acted as a spur for those who wished to take the law into their own hands.[5]

In the splendidly named village of Whitchurch Canonicorum in Dorset stands a delightful church with a most rare survival. In a side chapel to the north of the nave is the shrine of St Whit, a little-known saint. She is thought to have been a local hermit who lived on Chardown Hill nearby, and is reputed to have been martyred by Vikings in or around 831. It is a simple shrine: a slab of Purbeck stone forms the top, while the base is made of local sandstone. You can see the holes through which pilgrims – thousands a year in its heyday – could touch the tomb and receive blessings. Even on the outside of the church there is a special place to kneel and touch the tomb.

This shrine was once one of over 3,500 in Britain. Pilgrims crossed and crisscrossed the land visiting shrines, seeking blessings, and enjoying each other's company, as Chaucer so splendidly captures in the *Canterbury Tales*. Today, the battered, rather tired-looking shrine of St Whit is one of but a handful of surviving shrines, which include the shrine of Edward the Confessor in Westminster Abbey, superb and numinous in its faded glory, the original shrine tomb of St Thomas of Hereford in Hereford Cathedral, and the worn shrine of St Bertram at Ilam, Derbyshire.

At Great St Mary's, the university church of Cambridge, the loss of physical treasures and religious artefacts is dramatically chronicled. In 1504, the church inventories for 'jewells, goods and chattels' stood at thirteen pages in the churchwardens' accounts. By the reign of Elizabeth I it took up less than half a page.[6]

Another picture of what went on is given in a personal account of

LEFT This magnificent Christ is on the Ruthwell Cross, Dumfries and Galloway. The 7th century cross is one of the masterpieces of Anglo-Saxon Christianity and has carved upon it the 'Dream of the Rood', the greatest Anglo-Saxon religious poem combining the Christ with the Warrior. (*E & E Picture Library*)

RIGHT When the Anglo-Saxon preachers such as Aidan or Dunstan travelled the country, they preached in the open air at sites marked then or later with preaching crosses like this one at Whitby, Yorkshire. (*Martin Palmer/Circa Photo Library*)

LEFT The looming mass of the Norman Clifford's Tower, York is where in 1190 over 150 Jews committed suicide rather than fall into the hands of an anti-Semitic mob. It was the worst of many attacks on Jews in the 12th–13th century ending with their expulsion in 1290. England was the first European country to expel Jews. (*N & K Photography/E & E Picture Library*)

BELOW One of the two 14th century chantry chapels of Childrey Church, Berkshire, restored in the early 20th century. It gives a good idea of the colour and contents of a typical medieval chapel. The brass altar tomb has two figures with traditional Catholic prayers inscribed on the scrolls rising before them. (*Martin Palmer/Circa Photo Library*)

ABOVE Ashbrittle Church, Somerset embodies the layers of the sacred to be found in Britain. The medieval church is on the site of an Anglo-Saxon one. The name indicates a possible Celtic sacral site. The yew tree is believed to be over 3,000 years old and sits on a Bronze Age or even Neolithic burial mound. (*John Smith/Circa Photo Library*)

RIGHT The beautiful but massive weight of the Norman cathedral at Durham embodies the Norman conquerors' attitude to the older sacred landscape of Britain. Where previously modest shrines and churches sufficed, the Normans encased such power centres with their own, more Rome-centred Catholic structures. (*E & E Picture Library*)

LEFT Wells Cathedral, Somerset has the most complete set of medieval (13th century) statues to have survived in Britain. While most churches lost all their statues in the Reformation or 17th century Civil Wars, the 300 statues at Wells were damaged but not totally destroyed. (*E & E Picture Library*)

BELOW RIGHT The only holy well to survive intact in its full 15th century glory is St Winefride's at the appropriately named Holywell, North Wales. The actual well is covered by a chapel with a processional pathway round it, while outside is a bathing pool for pilgrims. (*E & E Picture Library*)

BELOW LEFT Perhaps the most famous example of 'bare ruined choirs' so mourned by Shakespeare is Glastonbury Abbey, Somerset. One of the greatest Celtic, Anglo-Saxon and medieval monasteries, it was destroyed in 1539 after its abbot had resisted the suppression of the monasteries. (*J. Litten/E & E Picture Library*)

Long Melford Church, Suffolk by one of its parishioners, Roger Martyn (c. 1527–1615). He describes in affectionate detail what he remembers seeing in the church before the Reforms. He mentions the Triptych behind the altar, carved 'very artificially' – meaning very well – from one tree and a tabernacle with a great 'fair gilt image of the Holy Trinity, being patron of the church: besides other fair images'. He mentions a crucifix which he now has in his house, and two other tabernacles 'with a fair image of Jesus in the tabernacle' and a 'fair image of Our Blessed Lady having the afflicted body of her dear son, as he was taken down off the cross lying along on her lap'. He recalls the rood screen with affection, as well as the roof of the church which, he says, 'was beautified with fair gilt stars'. By the time he was writing this, it had all gone.[7]

When Henry VIII forbade pilgrimages in 1538, one of the most popular social activities of ordinary people in England and Wales was cast aside overnight. Before that, thousands of people had enjoyed the heady combination of religion and fun; many had taken up pilgrimages almost as a hobby, often forging new routes of their own. But from then on to go on pilgrimage was to risk imprisonment or worse.

In 1541, the shrines which these pilgrims had gone to were forbidden, and thousands were destroyed, leaving only one royal one and a few which seem to have been missed. In some places worshippers hid shrines in church walls, as at Pennett Melangell in mid-Wales, where for hundreds of years the shrine was known by parishioners to exist but was not recovered until the late twentieth century. A similar story can be told about the remains of St Edward the Martyr in the ruins of Shaftesbury Abbey, Dorset, and relics recently discovered in a box in the wall of the church of St Eanswytheat, Folkestone. However, in thousands of churches, the focal point of their significance – a shrine of their local saint, or a shrine holding some relic of a great saint or fragment of the True Cross – was systematically taken apart. Twelve cartloads of gold, jewels, silver and bronze were even stripped from the shrine of St Thomas Becket on Henry VIII's order and brought to the Treasury in London.[8]

The very bones of the saints were ripped out and cast into ditches or burnt. In perhaps one of the strangest cases, the bones of St Frideswide, patron saint of Oxford University from 1434, were taken from their shrine in Christ Church in 1558 and mixed with the bones of a recently deceased ex-nun who had turned reformer and married an ex-monk. The intention was to disparage any attempt to return the bones to veneration, and to mock the very idea of holy relics. Today many churches have marked out where the great shrines once stood, and the tradition of honouring these great saints has returned, though the shrines are only bare outlines compared to their former magnificent glory. My personal favourite is the simple space marked out in Winchester Cathedral, where the shrine of St Swithin, one of the most humble of Anglo-Saxon saints, once stood. The following words, written on a simple framework that reproduces the shape of the old shrine, sum up what was and is best in this tradition:

> Whatever partakes of God is safe in God. All that could perish of St Swithin being enshrined within this place and throughout many ages hallowed by the veneration and honoured by the gifts of the faithful pilgrims from many lands was by a later age destroyed. None could destroy his glory.

In Holywell, North Wales, the devout or the curious can still walk round a magnificent late-fifteenth-century processional route surrounding the holy well of St Winifred. Here the full panoply of the holy well cult can still be seen in its glory, and nuns once more tend this ancient site, renowned since at least the eighth century as a holy place. Only at Holywell can one still sense what visiting a holy well must have been like. The reason that this alone of all such wells has survived has nothing to do with theology but everything to do with Granny. Margaret Beaufort rebuilt the well in 1490. Her son was Henry VII, her grandson was Henry VIII, and her great-grandson was Edward VI. So awesome, threatening, domineering and powerful was this woman that none of her offspring dared offend her, even when she was dead – and therefore no one damaged Granny's favourite holy well. Nowhere else in Britain can you see such a site.

Probably over 10,000 holy wells once marked the land with their special sacredness and their associations of healing and power. Many still survive, but as shadows of their former selves. For example, the holy well at Hope Bagot in Shropshire can still be visited, but it is little more than a stone-lined well, while in Bristol the very ancient and holy well of St Anne at Brislington has been restored, but nothing can restore the chapel and walks which once made this a major pilgrimage site. The holy well on Stapeley Hill in Shropshire survived, minus its medieval chapel (which was pulled down in the late sixteenth century) until the early 1990s, when a local farmer disgracefully destroyed it.[9]

THE CULTURAL REVOLUTION

Let me summarise what these visits to the few remainders of a great past illustrate. They are but a few examples of the fact that between 1536 and 1553 – just seventeen years – England and Wales lost over 3,000 monasteries, 3,500 shrines, and perhaps as many as 10,000 chantry chapels. Stained glass was destroyed in almost every church, almost all holy wells and 98 per cent of all statues were destroyed, and 100 per cent of all wall paintings were whitewashed out. Thousands of annual pilgrimages were banned. An entire way of living and believing was trashed, smashed and ripped out. Only in the Netherlands did anything like this level of destruction take place, and that was fuelled by both religious reform and nationalistic uprisings against the country's Spanish overlords. In the Netherlands, however, the violence of the destruction is openly admitted in their terminology for this period. In both English and Dutch we talk academically of a period of iconoclasm, but in Dutch there is a popular term used to depict the scale of the assault on the churches and on art at that time: 'beeldenstrom', which translates as 'statue storm'. This word has a double meaning. It compares the effect of the destruction to the impact of an actual storm, which overthrows and destroys all in its path. But it also has the meaning of storming a castle – a mass action, intent upon destroying. We, interestingly, have no such term. Our Reformation has to a degree been sanitised, as if we were trying to forget it or ignore its full implications. So it just gets swallowed up into that rather anodyne phrase 'The Dissolution of the Monasteries' or the even more vague term 'The Reformation'. Neither term does full justice to a period in which we did more damage to our past and to our places of worship in twenty years than had been done in the whole of the previous 1,000 years, including all the Viking raids.

The Cultural Revolution of China in the 1960s provides us with, perhaps, the most valid way of understanding the Reformation. During that time 98 per cent of all statues were destroyed and perhaps as many as 70 per cent of all temples and shrines. All pilgrimages were banned, and a complete way of living and believing was trashed, smashed and ripped out.

Like Henry VIII, the ruler of Communist China in 1966 was a man growing older in years and feeling worried about his succession. Mao Tse Tung had forged the Communist Party of China through the 1920s to the 1940s, but by 1966 he felt that the Party had become complacent, bloated, greedy and impure. He decided to appeal directly to the young people in the Red Guards to help him restore the revolutionary fire to the country and to root out all those forces, traditional as well as Communist, which were now holding China down. In 1966 he announced that it was right to overthrow the structures of the past with his cry 'to rebel is justified',[10] and launched what was called the 'Cultural Revolution', designed to root out all that was bad about the past. In reality it very nearly destroyed China itself. The persecution took an unknown number of lives, certainly running into millions. It led to the systematic destruction of much of China's ancient past, ranging from temples to books. It led to anarchy throughout China for nearly two years and then to a system of control through terror for a further seven or eight years.

Like Henry VIII, in pushing open the door to change, Mao was unprepared for the scale of anger and the abuse of this opening which then emerged, leading to a destructive surge, which carried almost everything away. So serious was this that Chou En Lai, the intellectual deputy to Mao, had to use the army to defend great cultural treasures. For example, at Chengdu in Sichuan Province, the People's Liberation Army fought a three-day battle against Red Guards who tried to burn down the great Taoist monastery and library in the city. In the end, the scale of destruction comes close to that which the Reformation caused in Britain. To this day you can see the smashed statues; the ruins of temples and monasteries, and gaps where religious artefacts once stood, just as you can still see the headless statues, the niches where statues once stood and the ruins of the abbeys in Britain.

I think this parallel is important. We are very complacent about the Reformation in Britain. We view it as having been a natural and to some degree orderly thing. But it was not, and we need to face the anger, violence and destruction it released in the same way that China is now trying to face its own Cultural Revoultion. Another useful analogy is the actions of the Taliban in Afghanistan who, in early 2001, destroyed the statues of the Buddha carved by Indo-Greek artists some 1,800 to 2,000 years ago in Afghanistan, which brought, rightly, the condemnation of the world's cultural elite. Yet the scale of that destruction was nothing compared to that which took place in Britain during the Reformation.

As a child I used to wander the ruins of ancient abbeys and monasteries and wonder at the destruction of the Reformation. What on earth could have driven people whose parents and grandparents were often buried in these monastic churches, whose families had built the great monasteries, to strip the lead from the roofs, smash the tombs, pull down the roof and walls and leave the whole exposed to the wind and rain as if nothing sacred had ever been there? I used to look at the fragments of the stained glass, often just a jumble of pieces such as those in the Lady Chapel of Winchester Cathedral, and wonder what savagery drove people to destroy this beauty. I still contemplate all these questions. What was going on? I could never understand why Christians should have inflicted such deliberate and utter devastation on the images, rituals, and buildings of what was, in theory, the same faith as that of those who destroyed them. In China, the Cultural Revolution was led by young Communists who despised religion. In England and Wales, those who smashed the churches, broke up the monasteries, ridiculed the statues of saints and persecuted the old ways of the faith were, at least in theory, members of the same faith.

In 1581, Sir Francis Drake moved into the recently converted abbey of Buckland, in Devon. Fifty years before the house had been a church. Where the High Altar had been they had their bedrooms, where the choir sang was the great hall. On the floors lay the remains of tombs of earlier local gentry. Yet Sir Francis Drake saw nothing strange in living in the remains of such destruction; instead he saw himself as a true Christian gentleman. He spent most of his life fighting against the Church of Rome, and against Catholic powers, especially if they had lots of ships carrying gold. It is unlikely that he saw the Roman Catholic faith as being the same religion as his own Protestant faith. What had happened to the psyche of Britain to produce such a viewpoint?

One can begin to understand the desire for reform, and the wish to sweep away the corruption and indifference of so much of the Church in the late fourteenth and fifteenth centuries. One can understand, too, that the association of the Church with power, authority and control would have created enemies who wanted to humble it and bring it down. Much the same forces created the successive Chinese revolutions of the twentieth century and fuelled the rise of the Communist Party, but it is very doubtful that most people in China wanted their lovely old temples burnt to the ground, the statues thrown out and destroyed, and the precious paintings defaced. It is equally doubtful that the majority of ordinary people wanted the similar destruction that took place in Britain.

In England and Wales it was almost as if the old anti-art tradition had surfaced after millennia underground, as if artistic expressions under the aegis of the Catholic Church had become alien to British sensitivities, causing them to destroy the very works of their own families and ancestors.

Part of the explanation was that religion was changing. Just as in the past social, ecological and economic disasters undermined various faiths in Britain so the Black Death in the fourteenth century, and the changes in social life which flowed from this, had undermined the pact of faith that the people had with the Church. The English Reformation was based on a rejection of the Roman Catholic Church. The Protestants who led it, especially later under Edward VI, saw the Roman Church as the Anti-Christ, and therefore as having no connection with Christianity as it should be. The thirty-nine Articles of the Church of England, printed in the Book of Common Prayer since 1563 and still formally required to be read and assented to by every Church of England priest, are in a quintessentially Anglican way expressions of this sense of repugnance for the 'Church of Rome'. Article 22, for instance, depicts the Catholic Church as a false religion:

> The Romish Doctrine concerning Purgatory, Pardons, Worshipping and Adoration, as well of Images as of Reliques, and also Invocation of Saints, is a fond thing, vainly invented, and grounded upon no warranty of Scripture, but rather repugnant to the Word of God.

I agree with the historian Diarmaid MacCulloch, who has argued that the attack on church tradition and on the icons of that tradition was an attack on what the reformers, especially those who under Edward VI carried the iconoclasm even further than under Henry, saw as the outward manifestations of a 'deceiving history', a false religion. For example, the deliberate destruction of many of the books in Oxford University Library by a man such as Richard Cox, who was the Dean of Christ Church, can only be understood in terms of him perceiving a need to rid the world, or at least England, of the evil of the false religion, to purge it as one used to purge illness through bleeding or medicines. As MacCulloch says: 'Only thus can we fathom the psychology which made people cheerfully reuse the metal from monumental brasses to commemorate their own loved ones, even when the original brasses were memorials to people who had been dead for only a few years.'[11]

My contention is that the Reformation in Britain, especially in England and Wales, expressed more than a rejection of a 'false religion'. It was the manifestation of an extraordinary psychological traumatising of the soul, a wholesale overturning not so much of beliefs, as of the art of beliefs. Some primordial force was unleashed which has only ever been equalled anywhere in the world in the last thousand years by either one faith conquering another, such as the Crusaders taking Jerusalem in 1099, the Muslims overrunning North India and destroying Hindu temples, or by one ideology, such as Communism, seeking to destroy faith. In our history books we tend to skate over the sheer scale and speed of the destruction of the religious and the sacred in our Reformation. This is, in fact the most dramatic aspect of it, the most defining, and perhaps, deep down, the most damaging. For, I would argue, the roots of much of Britain's uncertainty about the spiritual and the religious are rooted in the trauma of that time.

Within twenty years, most of the sacred, and to a certain degree, the intellectual landscape of Britain had gone. In its stead, there gradually emerged a new sense of the sacred within Britain, less linked to geography and place but centred instead in the Word, in the Bible and in the liberty of all, through English Bibles and English Books of Common Prayer, to read and understand for oneself. The art of the sacred was replaced by the sacredness of the Word.

What happened in England and Wales was at one level no different from what happened in Germany, Sweden, Norway and Central Europe. In those countries the churches of the old Catholic Church, with its bishops loyal to the Pope, became reformed national churches whose still-extant bishops were now loyal to the local king. The worst abuses were purged and to a great extent the solid parish work of the local priest and church continued to offer support and succour to those within their care. But in Britain something much deeper and darker happened.

I was made strikingly conscious of this when I visited an old Lutheran church. It was in Bergen in Norway. Here in the wonderful medieval Mariakirken (St Mary's Church) you can see the reforms of the Lutherans. The pulpit takes a central role: preaching the Word of God is vital to Lutheranism. What took me completely by surprise was the number of large, colourful statues of saints all around the church. Some are medieval, but the majority are sixteenth to eighteenth century. I was astonished. Surely these had all been destroyed in the Reformation, and then banned afterwards, as was the case in England, Wales and Scotland? But no. In most Lutheran countries the old artwork remained, and the saints still have much of their power, even if the worship of them is subdued. Nothing like this still exists in Britain. Therein lies the difference between our reformation and virtually all the other reformations in Europe. For some reason we turned not just against the Church, but also our own past, as represented by art.

It is of course entirely possible to explain why the monasteries were closed and their lands and wealth taken. Economic historians explain the economic changes, the rising gentry and middle class, the decline of community and so forth. Ecclesiastical historians point to widespread abuse in the Church that caused dissatisfaction with Catholicism amongst the population – though this has been substantially challenged by Catholic historians such as Eamon Duffy. In Wales, the overthrow of Roman Catholic norms allowed older Church practices to re-emerge, which had often continued, albeit in hidden ways. For example, Glanmor Williams says: 'From the bishops downwards, it was usual for the clergy to take wives, and the practice of clerical marriage remained widespread in Wales right down to the Reformation, when legislation permitted it again.'[12]

None of these theories explains the fury and the systematic way in which the monastic structures and the religious art of Britain were smashed, dismantled and scattered, or the ban on shrines, holy wells and pilgrimages. These events are almost passed over as being a natural outcome of theological reform. However, Bergen and many other Lutheran churches show that they were not inevitable.

Although I have offered some explanations, I find it ultimately very hard to explain what was going on in the collective psyche of Britain during the Reformation. The need to keep exploring, probing, asking, remains. I feel that deep within events of that time there is something of importance that we must try to discern, or it could take us down again.

ELIZABETH I AND SETTLEMENT

When Sir Frances Drake slept in his new house, created from the gutted remains of a great monastery, it was as if he were dwelling in the ruins of a faith that had no significance to him, a religion with no connection to his Protestant Christianity. Indeed, that is how many felt about the old religion. By the 1560s, the relationship between the ordinary people and the remains of the old faith was one of a great distance and discontinuity, even if there were those, such as Shake-speare, who felt a tinge of sadness for their passing:

> That time of year thou mayst in me behold
> when yellow leaves, or none, or few do hang
> upon those boughs which shake against the cold
> bare ruined choirs, where late the sweet birds sang.

The great skill of the Church of England, when Elizabeth I came to the throne in 1558, was that it helped people turn their backs on thirty years of violence, destruction, chaos, religious fervour and persecution, and persuaded them that in the Church of England there was both a continuity with what had been before, and something distinctly new and English. This was a remarkable achievement. The previous thirty years had seen Henry's reforms and their effects, but also much religious persecution. Elizabeth had come to the throne after two brief and dramatic reigns: that of Edward VII, during which hard-line Protestant ideas were imposed upon the people, and Catholics persecuted, and then that of Mary, when the Catholic faith limped back but failed to regain a popular hold.

When Elizabeth came to the throne, there were cries from all sides for revenge. She brushed them all aside, ignoring the thirty years of chaos, and in 1563 made a settlement with the Church, in which freedom of belief was contained within the order of the Church of

England, which was defined by the thirty-nine articles. It was still at this point inconceivable to any one except a few hot heads that there could be more than one Church in a country, but she recognized that the Catholic Church was a reality for many. Francis Bacon observed rightly of her approach to the past and the present that she had 'no liking to make windows into men's hearts and secret thoughts, except the abundance of them did overflow into overt and express acts or affirmations'. In other words, do what you like, believe as you will, but do not do so in any way that troubles the status quo.

The settlement through which order, common sense, decency and control were incorporated into the established Church, was an astonishing achievement and ensured for England and Wales decades – indeed nearly a hundred years – of peace. In the rest of Europe the lack of such a settlement led to decades of persecution, such as the massacre of Protestants in France in 1572 and wars that wrecked Europe, the most horrible of which was the Thirty Years War (1619–49). Elizabeth, through the settlement, held on to that which was best in the old Catholic Church system – parishes, bishops (now purged of much of their wealth and land), the core sacraments of baptism and communion, a sense of being part of a wider, Catholic Church and the use of liturgy and music in worship. What had gone for ever were the monasteries, the key role of the Church as the main provider of education, the power of the priests to control religion, the use of a language for the liturgy and Bible that virtually no one understood and the rites of the medieval Church such as the indulgences of, pilgrimages, shrines and saints, which had so offended the sensitivities of the reformers.

Elizabeth bequeathed a Church that knew it had to be broad; a Church that did not seek to define what you should believe and asked few questions, a Church which fulfilled the rites of passage and sacramentalised life, but left the secular world free of religious constraint. Thus, for example, the old church ban on usury was dropped; it was not the Church's role to enquire how you made your money. The Church of England is often mocked for being too broad. Yet it was this broadness that helped deal with the aftermath of difficulties from the Reformation which elsewhere in Europe cost millions of lives, and it laid the foundations of tolerance, which would eventually enable the Church of England to come to terms with the results of the Civil War.

It is almost as if, after the destruction, upheavals and anxieties of the Reformation years 1535 to 1560, England heaved a sign of relief and went back to being ordinary again.

By the end of the sixteenth century, Britain had changed fundamentally. The loss of the Catholic sacred landscape of Britain under Henry VIII, and in Scotland under the influence of the far more extreme Protestant reformer John Knox, was almost complete, apart from a few areas such as Lancashire and odd parts of Norfolk or Cornwall where, under a thin disguise, the old traditions and the Catholic faith continued almost unbroken. Today you can still join Catholic pilgrimages to pre-Reformation holy sites in those areas, sites which have not ceased since the time of the medieval church. There were not many of them. For the vast majority of people, the only focus of faith left was the parish church and the local cathedral.

As pilgrimage, processions to holy wells, use of holy water and cures from relics were now forbidden, so people turned inwards. I do wonder also whether the rise of 'folk stories' and 'ancient folk traditions' that begins in the sixteenth century is this old faith running into new channels. As Hutton has shown in *The Stations of the Sun* and *The Rise and Fall of Merry England* and writers such as Hobsbawm and Ranger have shown in *The Invention of Tradition*, most of the supposedly ancient traditions of Britain and folk stories are comparatively recent. It would be rather ironic if what many folklorists claimed was evidence of pre-Christian, pagan rituals and beliefs surviving in folk culture turned out on closer examination to actually be fragments of remembered Catholic rituals and beliefs, disguised as 'folk tradition'. The work of historians in this field is just beginning to cut through the romantic nonsense that has accrued around it and a truer picture of the role folklore has played in Britain is beginning to emerge.

While at a very profound level the Reformation brought secularism into play in such force that it left only the inner world to religion, at another level, perhaps the Renaissance and the various reformations across Europe precipitated one of those revolutions which mark not so much technological advance as conceptual and intellectual advance. For millennia, the place and tribe or community you were born in totally determined what you believed. Then the coming of the mission religions offered your community the option of choice. This was still, though, not primarily a personal decision. Your king or leader would decide for you, and that this might then be followed by personal conversion was hoped for, but not that important.

But with religious tolerance and the breakdown of the carefully constructed myth of One Church, the possibility first appeared of making a personal choice of the kind of faith you wanted to have. Historians often speak of the revolution of printing, but printing is just a means. The true revolution was what printing facilitated: the spread of a vast array of ideas, models of faith and teachings. This was the liberation that so many reformers wrote about, and the liberation that many reformers who then became Church leaders, from Geneva to London, sought to control.

One religion had, to all intents and purposes, died. Others were emerging, fudging their connections with the older expressions of faith. This fudging was what was, in part, to create a tradition of dissent which was to be one of the forces that unleashed the Civil Wars of the seventeenth century in Britain.

THE WITCH HUNTS

Before we leave this period for the seventeenth century, we should note one other disturbing feature. When people fear what is happening around them, especially if there is both a physical and metaphysical dimension to this fear, they need scapegoats. The turmoil of the sixteenth century produced just such a scapegoat: witches.

Theories about witches being part of a continued tradition of the so called 'old religion' of Paganism in Europe that existed concurrently with Christianity have been firmly nailed as false in recent years. It is only in the late fifteenth century that the idea of witches really rises up. The first book about them, *Malleus Maleficarum*, was published in 1486, two years after the first Papal Bull to acknowledge witchcraft as 'a fact'. While the forces which led to these two acts had been building up steam for a hundred years or so, it still marked a radical break with the past, when belief in witchcraft was actually considered so silly as to warrant rebuke by the Church. In particular, from the eighth century onwards, the Church had taught that those accused of witchcraft were to be given help to deal with such malicious gossip – hardly a sign that the Church saw such beliefs as real.

Keith Thomas in his study *Religion and the Decline of Magic* has shown that there were virtually no cases involving witches in the medieval period up to 1500:

> But in practice, it seems to have been very rare in England for anything other than a trivial punishment to have been inflicted upon those accused of maleficent magic before 1500. Until the surviving medieval judicial records have been thoroughly sifted it would be wrong to prejudge the issue. But at present, for the whole period between the Norman Conquest and the Reformation, there are not more than half a dozen known cases of supposed witches being executed: and most of these had been involved in plots against the monarch or his friends.[13]

The absence of any such trials – sadly to become part of sixteenth to seventeenth century life – seems to show that as far as the Church authorities were concerned, no such practices existed. If they did, they were certainly not believed to be of any significance.

Thereafter, with the collapse of the security of the Church in the aftermath of the Black Death and the beginnings of the Renaissance and then the Reformation – all of which took away building blocks of certainty from the structure of the faith and Church – there was a rising belief in, and fear of, the existence of witches. It was the historian H.R. Trevor-Roper who first clearly explored the relationship between the rise of the Renaissance and its intellectual achievements and the rise of witch-hunts. As the power of the one Church loosened its hold on society, not only was genuine exploratory thought, inventive individualism and creativity released, but so too, under the guise of free thought, were a lot of very silly and sometimes evil thoughts, often inspired by fear and ignorance fused with pride and nationalism. As Trevor-Roper says:

> And beneath the surface of an ever more sophisticated society what dark passions and inflammable credulities do we find, sometimes accidentally released, sometimes deliberately mobilized! The belief in witches is one such force. In the sixteenth and seventeenth centuries it was not, as the prophets of progress might suppose, a lingering ancient superstition, only waiting to dissolve. It was a new explosive force, constantly and fearfully expanding with the passage of time.[14]

The fragility of the new emerging faith in Britain, and the great uncertainty of the times, inspired a fear and fascination with older sacred spaces and a belief that there might be lingering forces at work. It is only now that we begin to find any record or attempt to understand the stone circles, megalithic monuments and other remains of earlier failed religions. Likewise, the Jesuits became the focus of Anglican fears that the Old Faith of Catholic Christianity might still be lurking in the spaces from which it had been so recently driven.

The witch hunts were the sign of a culture in distress, comparable to the terrible hunts for dissenters and agents of the West by Stalin in 1930s Russia, that Mao continued in the Cultural Revolution and, in a minor way, McCarthy in the USA employed in the hunt for Communists in the 1950s. All are examples of how societies in turmoil create demons, and then attack them as a way of finding solidarity. This is what the witch craze is really about.

The struggle to create a new religion – Protestantism – following the breakdown of the hold of medieval Catholic Christianity is the first example of an older faith surviving a social collapse and effectively reinventing itself. Unlike the ancestor or stone circle religions, Christianity did not die out under the strain of social collapse. As a missionary faith rather than an indigenous one, it was able to carry on if radically altered. As before, aspects of the sacred held dear by the faltering earlier expressions of Christianity were abandoned, discarded or slighted, as part of the process of rejecting what had gone before. Yet none of this quite does justice to the scale of destruction, which remains disturbingly deep in its origins and consequences.

CHAPTER FOURTEEN

CENTURY OF REVOLUTION

THE SEARCH FOR A NEW FAITH

TURNING DOWN A SMALL LANE at Brigflats, Cumbria, just outside the old town of Sedbergh, you come to a quiet corner of England that seems to have remained unchanged for 300 years. To one side is an overgrown Quaker graveyard, full of flowers. A little further on you come to a Quaker Meeting House, which is still in regular use.

Quakers were so called because – hard as it is to imagine today – they would shake with excitement during their meetings; however, the correct name for this Christian community was the Society of Friends. In 1674, members of the Society of Friends bought some land here and built what is considered to be the second oldest Quaker Meeting House in existence. The outside of this delightful building, set in one of the loveliest of gardens, looks like that of a late-fifteenth- or early sixteenth-century parish church, with deep mullioned windows and a porch. Inside, though, the radicalism of this group is manifest. The focus of the room is a reading desk and surrounding it are very simple wooden seats. Here the Word, not art, is paramount. Here what was thought, spontaneously and from the heart, was expressed, and that was sufficient. No priest was here, nor any need for one, and there was no ritual but instead the simplicity of Word and Thought and Book.

The charming mixture of styles – church outside, meeting room inside – captures the dilemma that faced many people in the seventeenth century: were they continuing something that they had known for centuries or starting something new? What exactly were they believing and creating, and what relationship did this have to the old religion of the medieval Church?

THE NEW ESTABLISHMENT

Whereas the faith of the past had created statues and magnificent stone churches, paintings and shrines, the new faith of Protestantism or Anglicanism produced no great art; virtually no new churches were built. Those that were built were poor imitations of earlier medieval styles, such as St James's in Didsbury, Manchester. Instead the sacred manifested itself through words. In fact I would argue that the Reformation in Britain created literature as the new medium for the sacred in a way that it had never been before. Art was replaced throughout the culture by Word and it is no accident that it was Britain which pioneered new literary forms. It is one of the great achievements of the Reformation, but at a loss of more traditional manifestations of the sacred, namely art and architecture.

Between 1580 and 1650 many works explored the idea of faith as an inner journey, such as Jeremy Taylor's *Holy Living* and its natural best-selling sequel, *Holy Dying* (published in 1650 and 1651 respectively). The sense of inner journeying provided by faith is nicely captured in these words from *Holy Living*:

> The Means and Instruments to obtain Faith are, an humble, willing, and docile mind, or desire to be instructed in the way of God: for persuasion enters like a sunbeam, gently, and without violence; and open but the window, and draw the curtain, and the Sun of righteousness will enlighten your darkness.[1]

This shift from the outer journey to the inner journey is perhaps best illustrated by John Bunyan's *Pilgrim's Progress*. This is still the best-selling book other than the Bible of the last 400 years in Britain. It was to be found in more homes in the Victorian era than any other book other than the Bible. What it offered was a literary version of the old pilgrimage; only this time there are no identifiable places as such – no Southwark or Canterbury as in Chaucer's *Canterbury Tales*. Instead there is a psychological journey, a journey through the stages of spiritual growth, of personal distress and troubles, leading, through literature, to a new Promised Land. Nothing illustrates more clearly the replacement of one sacred world with another than that pilgrimages were banned in 1538 and replaced a hundred years later by a metaphysical journey. Modern literature and the modern understanding of ourselves as psychological beings had arrived.

By the start of the seventeenth century the Word, as we have seen, was available to all. Various translations of the Bible culminated in the King James Bible of 1611 (which took at least 50 years to become the popularly accepted version). In many ways the King James Bible exemplifies the Elizabethan Settlement on religion, and the strengths of the Anglican Church. Instigated by the authority of King James as Head of the Church, it drew together the best scholars and writers of its time. Fusing academic excellence with the freedom of good writers, the committee created one of the enduring masterpieces of English, and indeed world literature. Faithful to insights gained by the Renaissance exploration of Greek and Hebrew, it nevertheless produced a translation that was as much interpretation as literal translation.

Over time, and especially following the Restoration of the monarchy and Anglican Church in 1660, it became the best known book in the English language. It is still the preferred Bible of many, a remarkable feat for a translation now 400 years old. Even during the Commonwealth it maintained its favoured status; I have a 1653 edition, produced in slim format to be carried in a soldier's backpack. It lacks the usual dedication to the King, but is still called 'Authorised'. As an instrument for mission, for embedding key metaphors and images from the Bible in popular culture, and for beginning to unify English spelling and grammar, it is without equal. It heralded a period of astonishing literary outpourings and of immense religious speculation.

The sheer burst of energy that the Reformation and printing unleashed in terms of reading, writing and study is almost impossible to imagine today. Everyone had ideas, and almost everybody wanted to get them into print. Books poured out exploring every aspect of the Bible and of Christian faith, ranging from the profound to the absolutely daft.

It did not really matter. People wanted to read, think and discuss. In a world where certainty had gone, the only certainty was that nothing was certain, and everything was possible and believable. Printing meant ideas that previously could only be distributed within a small group were now available to everyone.

The struggle to create a new faith continued not just in words but also in deeds. Elizabeth had been firm: there were to be no separate churches. Everyone had a church – the parish church – and differences were to be discussed and resolved there, within the framework of the established Church. Elizabeth allowed considerable freedom of interpretation but forbade any suggestion that you could form your own church if you were not happy with what was taught at your local church or the Church in general. Despite Elizabeth's strictures, however, there was a struggle for independent churches that drove a horse and carriage through the attempts of the Established Church to retain control of the thoughts, minds and souls of the people in this period. Now people wanted to believe differently and worship differently from each other. Though the sacred was no longer as visible as a feature of the physical landscape, it continued to exist in people's minds and was breaking out of former constraints. Exercising the freedom to believe or not to believe was the last stage in the assault of the secular world on the remnants of the Church as an all-binding, all-powerful force of this country.

THE NEW REBELS

Ironically, many of those who benefited from the forces of secularism and freedom of thought were the ones who most wanted to return to a state where the faith was the determining factor in all things – perhaps as a result of the uncertainty that followed the collapse of the old ways. They wanted a new theocracy – a world ruled by God, only now they wanted to be the ones who determined what it was that God really wanted! The utopian ideas that drove so many to emigrate to North America, led by the Pilgrim Fathers in 1620, were founded on the belief that by returning to a simpler and 'purer' version of Christianity, a complete new way of life could be developed which would create the Kingdom of God on earth. The groups who propounded these ideals, usually vaguely called Puritans, brought all aspects of life under the rule of the Bible as interpreted by them; everything was judged according to the Word of God.[2] The new religious writers often turned back to Anglo-Saxon or the British Church stories, prior to the coming of the 'Norman Yoke', and especially to the Old Testament and figures such as Josiah, who reformed corrupt Judaism in the seventh century BC. They also turned to the 'primitive church' of the New Testament. This is shown in the following quote from John Smyth in 1608. He was one of the founders of the Baptists, a group very much of the opinion that the Church of England was profoundly mistaken, as can be seen:

> wee professe even so much as they object: That wee are inconstant in erroer: that wee wou'd have the truth, though in many particulars wee are ignorant of it: We will never be satisfied in endeavoring to reduce the worship and ministery of the Church, to the primitive Apostolic institute from which as yet it is so farr distant.[3]

The Puritans saw themselves in this mould, believing that it was possible to throw away the abuses, superstitions and errors of 'Popery', and still hold on to the idea of the Church as being the determining guide for everyday life in all its aspects. It was many years before the majority of people finally recognised this as impossible, and even to this day there are some who genuinely believe in the idea of an all-guiding Church.

Perhaps the most dramatic of the groups who challenged the established Church were the Diggers. Founded in 1649, the Diggers were an offshoot of the Levellers, a group who believed that all people were equal, and who agitated for religious freedom and the abolition of the monarchy and aristocracy. The Diggers believed the Bible taught that no one had any right to land that they did not work for the common good. They therefore took over common land and cultivated it, such as at St George's Hill, Oatlands in Surrey, where they established a community of around fifty people.

Unfortunately they were unpopular locally and were constantly harassed, and as a result the community eventually collapsed. However, their principal, Gerald Winstanley, was a powerful advocate of their quasi-communist ideals and his writings have had a significant effect on the radical left both politically and theologically ever since. An example of his libertarian thoughts, which have shaped English radical ideas ever since, can be seen in this quote on freedom:

> All men have stood for freedom ... and those of the richer sort of you that see it are ashamed and afraid to own it, because it comes clothed in a clownish garment ... Freedom is the man that will turn the world upside down, therefore no wonder he hath enemies ... True freedom lies in the community in spirit and community in the earthly treasury, and this is Christ the true manchild spread abroad in the creation, restoring all things unto himself.[4]

While the struggle for understanding faith raged in books, pamphlets, sermons and new churches, the established Church genuinely believed that if there was any split in its midst, order and true faith would be lost. It was therefore essential that the Church as the faithful arm of the State should maintain its control. A sense of this anxiety to keep control is well captured in the Letter of Archbishop Abbot of Canterbury on the topic of Preaching, issued to all clergy in 1622:

> You are therefore to know, that his majesty being much troubled and grieved at heart to hear every day of so many defections from our religion both to Popery and Ana-Baptism [the collective name of groups of radical believers, who believed in the baptism of adults only, not children] or other points of separation in some part of this kingdom, and considering with much admiration what might be the cause thereof, especially in the reign of such a king who doth so constantly profess himself an open adversary to the superstition of the one and the madness of the other, his princely wisdom could fall upon no one greater probability than the lightness, affectedness and unprofitableness of the kind of preaching which hath of late years been too much taken up in court, university, city and country.

CERTAINTIES AND UNCERTAINTIES

The fault-lines of dissent, of varied and various interpretations of the Bible, doctrine and models of what the Church should be, which the reformers introduced in the sixteenth century, began to become significant cracks in the seventeenth century. Despite the best efforts of the established Church, the authority of the Anglican compromise – Catholic but reformed – was challenged more and more. Those who stood in its way ran real risks. A prime example is Archbishop William Laud. In 1633 he became Archbishop of Canterbury and sought to curb Puritanism by firm insistence upon the clergy following the rubrics – orders and procedures – of the Church. He also tried to reintroduce robes and rituals, which to many Puritans – then still mostly within the Church of England rather than outside it – smacked of Rome. Additionally, he attempted to restore respect for the church itself by having the altar properly covered with cloth and venerated.

His enemies began to increase. They saw Laud as the embodiment of the absolutism of Church and crown – for Charles I made it clear he fully supported Laud. Furthermore, Laud was not a very diplomatic person. His intransigence led to the so-called Bishops' Wars in Scotland, 1639–40, when Laud and Charles tried to impose the Episcopal Prayer Book of the Church of England on the Presbyterian Church of Scotland. The wars were a disaster for England and led to Laud being impeached by the Puritan-influenced Long Parliament in 1640. Eventually he was executed in January 1645 as part of the attrition directed against Charles.

Laud is a controversial figure still. He was undiplomatic and often absurdly rigid, but he saw diversity as inevitably meaning division and sought to impose unity for what he believed to be the greater good. He was a hundred years too late. The floodgates of diversity had opened and the Church would be inevitably altered as a result.

When the old faith went, those who benefited most were the rising gentry. The emerging middle class gained monastic and Church land and both money and power. I have already noted that they expressed this by replacing one of the most sacred sites in the parish church, the Easter Sepulchre, with their own monuments known as sepulchral monuments. At Lydiard Tregoze Church in Wiltshire can be seen perhaps the best example of the huge and often frightfully pompous sixteenth- to eighteenth-century monuments to the dead gentry who had risen dramatically, often buying out older leading families in the area. Here can be seen the Golden Cavalier, with curtains held open by devout pages in a classic illustration of the lack of humility that is the hallmark of the gentry of the seventeenth century.

In such gestures the gentry were symbolically placing themselves in the place of the mystery and, to some extent, the authority of the old religion. Whereas in the pre-Reformation tomb carvings the dead lie quietly and devoutly, their hands in prayer, these new tombs often show the dead leaning rather nonchalantly on one elbow, looking rather bored. There was a different spirit abroad. In the seventeenth century there was an emphasis on a personal relationship with God as being something not only possible for everyone, but desirable for everyone. In the medieval period it is rare to encounter the personal prayers of a believer, other than a saint. In the seventeenth century, you cannot avoid them. The sense of the concern of the Creator for you, and your individual relationship with God, is wonderfully captured in one of my favourite prayers, said by Sir Jacob Astley just before he took part in the Battle of Edgehill on 23 October 1642. He prayed: 'O Lord, thou knowest how busy I must be this day. If I forget thee, do not thou forget me'.

There is something fascinating to note here about the rise of the perception of an individual as a person of significance because he or she has a direct line to God, not a relationship with God as part of a wider community mediated by the priest. The growing sense of a personal relationship with God is also reflected in tombstones. You will look in vain for tombstones in churchyards from earlier than the end of the sixteenth century. Indeed, you will find only occasional examples from before that time, for the vast majority of tombstones in churchyards date from the 1660s onwards. Prior to this, the wealthy were entombed inside the church, marked by inscriptions and images, and the rest of the parishioners were buried anonymously in the churchyard. However, with the coming of the idea that everyone, rich or poor, had a personal relationship with God, individual tombstones became the norm. A tombstone at Corsham Church in Wiltshire wonderfully comments upon this. It is not in the churchyard or in the church proper, but somewhat unusually, in the porch. Through this choice of position, William Tasker who died in 1684 and whose tombstone this is, wanted to protest against the hypocrisy of the wealthy who built themselves ostentatious tombs both inside and outside the church.

The marking of burial places of individuals in this way signifies a considerable shift in self-perception by ordinary people as a result of the collapse of the security model of the old religion of the Middle

Ages. Under the medieval Church, you were just part of the community which was held by the Church and given to God at death. It was not really for you to worry about. With the collapse of the old security, there comes the freedom of the personal relationship with God, but also the worry that God might not remember who you are! I am putting this humourously but there is a bit of this lurking in the Protestant relationship with God. I was once in a church where the pastor (it was an evangelical church) prayed to God asking that God would look down on Mrs Jones who had a bad leg and take care of her. Just in case God was wondering which Mrs Jones this might be, the pastor kindly mentioned that it was, 'Mrs Jones at No 45, Cleveland Drive'.

I think that the rise of personal grave markers in the churchyard is a fascinating indication of the new relationship with the sacred. There is a new certainty that is striking in the inscriptions on tombs. Compare for example, this epitaph of 1519, which asks for the prayers of those who read it – as the prayers of a chantry priest would have been sought – with the following epitaph from 1613:

Of yor charite pray for the soules of Gyles Penne gentilman & Isabett his wyff whiche Giles decessed in the yere of our lord god MD and the seid Isabett decessed the xij day of December in the yere of our lord god MDxjx on whose soules Jhu have Mercy Amen.[5]

If Birth or worth, might ad to Rareness life
Or teares in Man, reuiue a Vertuous wife
Lock't in this Cabinet, bereau'd of breath
Here lies ye Pearle inclos'd She wch by Death
Sterne Death subdu'd, slighting Vaine worldly vice
Achiuing Heau'n wth thoughts of Paradise
Shee was he Sexes wonder, great in Bloud
But what is far more Rare, both great & good
Shee was wth all Celestiall Vertues storde
The life of Shaa, & soule of Hungerford.
An Epitaph
Written in memory of ye late right
Noble and Most Truly Vertuous
Mrs Mary Shaa
Daughter of ye Right Hble Walter Lord

Hungerford, Sister & Heyre generall to ye
Right Noble Sr Ed. Hungerford Knit. Deceased
& wife unto Thomas Shaa Esq., leaving
behind Robert Shaa her only sonne,
She departed this life in ye faith
of Christ ye last day of Septembr
Ano Dni 1613.[6]

There is an almost insufferable smugness about the later inscription, with its pious sentiments and sense of personal security, which is totally absent from the earlier inscription. Yet also in this period there is a deeper sense of uncertainty, which is captured in the poems of the metaphysical poets, such as John Donne and Francis Quarles. This sense of the wonders and terrors of a personal relationship with God is expressed in Quarles's poem 'Wherefore hidest thou thy face, and holdest me for thy enemie?' (Job XIII, 24):

> *Why dost thou shade thy lovely face? O why*
> *Does that ecclipsing hand, so long, deny*
> *The Sun-shine of thy soule-enliv'ning eye?*
> *Without that* Light, *what light remaines in me?*
> *Thou art my* Life, *my* Way, *my* Light; *in Thee*
> *I live, I move, and by thy beames I see.*
> *Thou art my* Life; *if thou but turne away,*
> *My life's a thousand deaths: thou art my* Way;
> *Without the, Lord, I travell not, but stray*

THE NEED FOR ORDER

The history of the sacred in the seventeenth century is the search by both Anglicans and dissenters for security, order and for a place within the cosmos, which itself was being radically reinterpreted. The idea that the earth was not the centre of the universe, as expounded principally by Galileo who supported the theories of Copernicus, was deeply subversive to Christian thought. The traditional Christian paradigm had put humanity at the centre of God's purpose. If the earth was not the centre of the universe, but just one planet among many, how did this affect the supreme significance of humanity? This question still remains a pertinent one today. Although we may be intellectually post-Copernicus and Galileo, we are emotionally definitely pre-Copernicus. We still behave, individually and collectively, as if we are the centre of the universe. If we have problems living with our significant insignificance today, imagine the shocks and troubles these ideas caused in the seventeenth century. John Donne, poet and theologian, captures something of their impact in his mocking story *Ignatius His Conclave*, written in 1611, where he describes Copernicus knocking at the gates of hell and being questioned by Satan as to who he is:

> I am he, which pitying thee who wert thrust into the Centre of the world, raysed both thee, and they prison, the Earth up into the Heavens . . . Shall these gates be open to such as have innovated in small matters? And shall they be shut against me, who have turned the whole frame of the world, and am thereby almost a new Creator?[7]

The anxiety and uncertainty of the period, and the consequent search for security and order, are charmingly displayed in many of the gardens of the time. The late-Tudor and early-seventeenth-century formal gardens of the manor houses and converted abbeys illustrate a deep need for order, pattern and significance. Take, for example, the delightful late-sixteenth-century gardens at Little Moreton Hall in Cheshire. Here are knot gardens – exquisite exercises in control and order. Pattern and predictability are the order of the day. There is nothing useful about such a garden. Unlike the functional medieval monastic herb gardens, knot gardens represent power and wealth. The lord of the manor built a small knoll just outside his ordered garden, from where he could view it. He could survey his estate, looking in and appreciating all that had been created for his enjoyment, in a similar way to which he probably hoped God was looking down on the world he had created, and keeping order. Here in one garden is the essence of the late-Tudor gentleman's view of his place, God's place and the importance of order.

While the struggle for understanding faith raged in books, pamphlets, sermons and new churches, the Established Church was desperate to keep control. However, Laud and his successors were fighting a losing battle. Those who had tasted freedom were anxiously pushing the boundaries as far as possible, especially if this broke up the monopoly of the Established Church, which in the eyes of some people had become the Anti-Christ itself. By the end of the seventeenth century, the right to separate from the Established Church and worship elsewhere had been clearly won, as the little Quaker Meeting House at Brigflats so vividly illustrates, but the way to this victory in the cause of searching for the sacred had been hard, long, and at times, extreme.

THE CIVIL WARS

There were many reasons for the Civil Wars that tore Britain apart from 1642 to 1651. We have perhaps romanticised them with the images of the cavalier Cavaliers and the puritanical Roundheads. They were in fact terrible wars which, it is calculated, left at least one in ten of the population dead through warfare, siege, famine, massacre or disruption of ordinary life.

The bare bones of the story are well known. Charles I was not one of our brightest kings, but he had an overwhelming sense of duty, especially towards the Established Church, whose potential fall he saw as meaning the end of royalty as well. Parliament, increasingly filled with radical Puritans, opposed to the Church of England, especially under Archbishop Laud had increasingly been flexing its muscles, for with freedom in religion and thought came the expectation of making your own decisions. There was no longer the old consensus that had meant that Parliaments prior to the Reformation were, with a few notable exceptions, largely rubber stamps for the king's decisions.

Parliament clashed head on with Charles over excess taxes for his wars in Scotland against the Presbyterians, and his abuse of the rights of Parliament. When Charles tried to arrest the five key dissenting MPs he effectively declared war on Parliament, and on 22 August 1642, Charles raised his standard and made this war official.

For five years the wars raged, crossing and recrossing the country. The conflict died down then flared up again in 1648, continuing until the final victory of the Puritan Parliamentarian leader, Oliver Cromwell, in 1651. That so many dissenters staffed the Parliamentary army and many new religious communities arose from the Parliamentary supporters, while the King headed the Established Church, to which he had an overwhelming sense of duty, illustrates the extent to which the Civil Wars were as much wars of religion as wars of secular authority. The religious nature is forcefully expressed in a statement made by a soldier from Cromwell's army who, along with others, burst in on the early evening congregation at St Mary's Church, Walton-on-Thames, Surrey in 1649:

> One of Cromwell's 'godly' soldiers went, as North relates, into the church of Walton-on-Thames with a lantern and five candles, telling the people, that he had a message to them from God, and that they would be damned if they did not listen to him. He put out one light, as a mark of abolition of the Sabbath; the second, as a mark of the abolition of all tithes and church dues; the third as a mark of the abolition of all ministers and magistrates; and then the fifth light he applied to setting fire to a Bible, declaring that that also was abolished. These were pretty pranks to play; but they were the natural, the inevitable consequences of 'Reformation'.[8]

The Church of England could not envisage a land in which there was more than one Church, one pathway to the sacred. The dissenters, on the other hand, seem to have found it hard to imagine why there should be only one Church.

Eventually the King was captured, and tried for crimes against the people. In the victory of the dissenters and the subsequent execution of the King in 1649 we can see the logical end of the belief that there was one Church under one king. This was probably the lowest point of the Church of England.

Milton, too, saw Cromwell's mission as a religious one. In his famous poem in honour of Cromwell 'To the Lord Generall Cromwell May 1652', he says:

> Cromwell, our chief of men, who through a cloud
> Not of war onely, but detractions rude,
> Guided by faith and matchless Fortitude
> To peace and truth thy glorious way hast plough'd,
> And on the neck of crowned Fortune proud
> Hast reard Gods Trophies, and his work pursu'd

The numerous sects, groups and teachings, that emerged from this traumatic time clearly illustrate the extent to which the sacred was unsettled and that no single definition any longer applied.

Cromwell's more repressive side found its strongest and most awful expression in his invasion of Ireland in 1649. Fearing that the Irish Catholics would rise up following the execution of Charles I, he invaded and is held responsible for massacres at Drogheda and Wexford at which apparently virtually no quarter was given. His infamy as a foe of Catholicism was such that until very recently Irish children would be told to behave, otherwise 'Cromwell will get you'.

In Scotland, Cromwell made enemies of the Covenanters, the very force which had brought down Cromwell's antithesis, Archbishop Laud. The Covenanters were so called because they adhered to the National Covenant, a document signed in 1638 by key figures of the Scottish nobility. It was, as John Prebble says 'More than a declaration of faith, it was a political manifesto that challenged the King's prerogative and by implication affirmed that the right to make and change the law rested in Parliament only.'[9]

It was the Presbyterian Covenanters, defenders of Scotland's distinctive form of the Church, who faced down Laud in the Bishop's Wars of 1639–40. It was they who sought to turn the tables and impose Presbyterianism on England at an Assembly of Puritans and allies at Westminster in 1643. They failed largely because Cromwell refused to replace one state church with another; instead he permitted diversity but within staunch anti-Catholic and anti-extremist (e.g. Quakers and Diggers) limits. To many Covenanters, Cromwell had betrayed the true religious nature of the revolution, but they were always a minority in Scotland and their hardline views, despite some clever later media packaging, never actually won great popular acclaim.

Presbyterianism, however, not only survived in Scotland but also flourished. The heart of Presbyterianism is a Calvinistic reading of the Bible whereby 'presbyters' – the Greek word for elders – were to govern the Church in a form of limited democracy. The movement had its origins in Calvin's Geneva, from whence came the Calvinist Scotsman John Knox (1514–72). He opposed all aspects of what he saw as Popery and taught instead the doctrine of Predestination: that each person's eternal fate was sealed by God before the beginning of time. His uncompromising stance sowed the seeds for the Church of Scotland to become the only State Church in Europe which is neither Anglican or Lutheran. While the court tried to make the Church of Scotland an episcopal Catholic but reformed Church, such as the Church of

England, Knox and his successors fought successfully for it to be Presbyterian. To this day, the Queen remains head both of the Catholic episcopal Church of England and the Presbyterian, Calvinist Church of Scotland. The final irony here is that Knox is most famous for his attacks on women in high office. The somewhat forthright title of his most infamous pamphlet, writen in 1558, is fairly unambiguous: *The First Blast of the Trumphet gainst the Monstrous Regiment of Women*. I do hope he is turning in his grave.

The struggle between the Calvinistic Church State vision and the older Catholic and Anglican model lies as a sub-theme behind the Civil Wars and wars between Scotland, England and Ireland of the seventeenth century. It is in a way our equivalent of the terrible wars – such as the Thirty Years War from 1614 to 1648, which pitted Catholic against Protestant across mainland Europe.

AN APOCALYPTIC CLIMATE

There was also at that time a dramatic sense among some that the Second Coming of Christ was imminent. The upheavals of the civil wars were seen as the harbingers of the coming of the Anti-Christ and the Final Battle or alternatively as the first rays of light of the new utopia, the new Jerusalem descending to earth in England. Millennarianism – the belief in the coming 1,000-year reign of Christ – was and continues to be very strong at all times of social unrest in Europe, as Norman Cohn has shown in his masterful study *The Pursuit of the Millennium*. In revolutionary seventeenth-century Britain it was one of the key driving forces, for these were dramatic times. It was such a belief that led James Naylor, an itinerant Quaker preacher, to act out the drama of the Second Coming in 1656 – choosing a somewhat unsuspecting Bristol as his Jerusalem. In the *Annals of Bristol* we read the story of what happened when this poor man went just that little too far:

> On departing Bedminster for Bristol on the 24th [October] a procession was formed on that part of the road reserved for carts, where, says an observant spectator, the mud reached to the knees of the impassioned pedestrians; and Naylor, on horseback, was escorted by his friends into the city amidst singing and screams of rejoicing.[10]

Naylor claimed to be the Messiah and even had followers who could attest that he was. The Annals contain this little comment: 'Naylor [when arrested and examined] repeatedly proclaimed his Messianic character, whilst one of his female adorers positively asserted that two days after her death he has restored her to life.' In a world where all assumptions of what was sacred were open to possibility and exploration, to believe that Bristol was the New Jerusalem and that James Naylor, Quaker, was the Messiah, was no more extraordinary than to execute the King, God's anointed head of the Church and State.

Once again, we are confronted by the aggressive hatred for the forms of organised religion, which were casually abused and destroyed as a result. For during the Civil Wars Cromwell's men and associates destroyed much of what little art had been left by the reformers of the mid-sixteenth century. For example, this sad account of the destruction at Canterbury Cathedral spells out the extent of the wrecking inflicted by the Puritans:

> The windows, famous both for strength and beauty, so generally battered and broken down as they lay exposed to the injury of all weathers; the whole roof with that of the steeples, the chapterhouses and cloister extremely impaired and ruined, both in the timber work and lead ... The communion table [stripped] of the best of her furniture and ornaments. Many of the goodly monuments of the dead shamefully abused, defaced, rifled and plundered of their brasses, iron-gates and bars.

William Dowsing was licensed by Parliament to destroy all 'monuments of idolatry and superstition' in the parish churches of East Anglia, and writes about a day's work in the life of a professional iconoclast:

> Benacre, April 6. There was six superstitious pictures, one crucifix, and the Virgin Mary twice, with Christ in her arms, and Christ lying in the manger, and the Three Kings coming to Christ with their presents, and St Catherine twice pictured ... O Christ govern me by thy Mother's Prayers! And three bishops with their mitres, and the steps to be levelled within six weeks. And 18 Jesus's written in capital letters on the roof, which we gave orders to do out; and the story of Nebuchadnezzar, and *orate pro animabus*, in a glass window.[11]

To the destroyers, the old was associated with the old power structures, and to use Gerald Winstanley's words they were out to 'turn the world upside down'. They succeeded, and what they did was a terrifying thing to behold, especially for those who saw their role in the Established Church as holding together the fragile fabric of the sacred. For example, listen to Bishop Joseph Hall, Bishop of Norwich from 1641 to 1656, on what happened to that jewel of a cathedral. In 1643 a mob descended upon the cathedral and engaged in 'vicious sacrilege' as the bishop put it. He describes how terrible it was for:

> ... the cathedral, now open on all sides, to be filled with musketeers, waiting for the mayor's return, drinking and tobacconing as freely as if it had been turned into an alehouse ... In a kind of sacrilegious and profane procession all the organ pipes, vestments, both copes and surplices, together with the wooden cross which had been newly sawn down from over the Green Yard pulpit, and the service books and singing books that could be had were carried to the fire in the public market place; a lewd wretch walking before the train, in his cope trailing in the dirt, with a service book in his hand, imitating in an impious scorn the tune, and usurping the Words of the litany used formerly in the Church.[12]

The Puritans, and the associated religious sects and groups who gathered around the banner of Parliament, felt no link to the Established Church with its bishops, vestments and rituals. Their iconoclasm was part of a clash between two different belief systems as ideological as the clash of Chinese communists with Chinese Buddhism or Taoism. The old religion of the Establishment was a dying religion, as far as these new groups were concerned, and it was their mission to bury it. That is why soldiers had no compunction in turning cathedrals into stables or smashing stained-glass windows. This was, in essence, one faith fighting for supremacy over another.

It was also a struggle between those who still saw physical beauty of art, liturgy, drama and music as manifestations of the sacred, and those who felt all this was nothing in comparison to the Word. I would argue that from the Reformation to today, Britain has produced masterpieces of literature – the King James Bible, Shakespeare, Milton and onwards, but has failed to produce anything like such masterpieces in the field of the arts. The Reformation replaced the sacred art and landscape of the medieval Church with the language and structure of literature and the supremacy of the Word.

In the end, however, people generally could not accommodate the levels of eccentricity that people like Naylor exhibited and the wilder aspects of the interpretation of the sacred diminished. Soon the outlines of the new non-Establishment, or to use the correct term, Nonconformist, churches began to emerge. The Nonconformists were so called because they refused to conform to the doctrines, polity and discipline of the Church of England. In essence they were versions of the church, but shorn of all that made them look and sound like the Established Church. Thus it was that the wonderfully named Fifth Monarchy Men, the Levellers, the Diggers, the Muggletonians and their like faded into history, while the Baptists, Congregationalists, Unitarians, Presbyterians and Quakers survived to add their places of worship and their inner journeys to the growing tapestry of the sacred in Britain.

THE RESTORATION

The Protectorate, headed by Cromwell and for a brief period by his son Richard, governed Britain for seven years. By 1660, the squabbling, diverse and fascinating, but largely unworkable world of the Commonwealth, with its plethora of sects, fell apart. In a compromise arranged by General Monck, soldier, naval commander and pragmatist, Charles I's exiled son Charles was invited to return to England on condition that certain reforms of previous monarchical abuses should be retained.

To some, the restoration of the monarchy with Charles II's coronation was a welcome return to the old order, as proclaimed on this wonderful inscription on the Royal Coat of Arms plaque in Southwark Cathedral in London:

Fear God. Honour your King.
Meddle not with
Those that are given to change, although you
Are forgiven by an earthly King. Know you that hereafter
You must come to judgement, repent from the evil of

Your ways and sin no more unless worse befall you.
God bless King Charles the 2nd and send him long to reign.
1660.

While many changes effected during the years of the Civil Wars remained, the monarchy and the Established Church took revenge. As well as having Cromwell's body exhumed and publicly hung, the Church ejected those clergy who would not agree to the supremacy of the Church of England. In effect, the Puritan Church lost its place in 1660 and never ever regained anything remotely like its previous power or status. Cathedrals were cleaned up and restored, services were resumed and the parish priests once again acted as if there was only one Church. However, the Church of England could no longer claim to be the only Church in the land. The sacred had broken free, and was never again to be contained in one overarching religious framework. Religious diversity and sacred pluralism had come to stay. The Established Church had to learn to live, usually with very bad grace, side by side with a multitude of other churches.

The origins of the modern understanding of the sacred had arrived, but at what a cost to the old sacred patterns. Confidence in the Church had been shaken so severely that people began to look for other forms of security and the slow development began of the idea that Britain itself was in some special way sacred and chosen, a sentiment found in Milton, for example. As a result of all that had happened in the seventeenth century, the British Church had now to all intents and purposes ceased to identify itself with the faiths of the rest of Europe, be they Catholic, Lutheran or Protestant, and had set about creating distinctly British forms of the faith once again.

Now attention turned to the other landmass where these same views prevailed – the colonies of North America. Since the seventeenth century, Britain has faced either inwards or towards America in its search for religious allies.

The overthrowing of all the norms of the past had also allowed scientific thought to develop to unprecedented heights, and the Protestant world in general was proud of this achievement. We need to remember that the Protestant revolution was also a revolution of thought in which the eighteenth-century Enlightenment was rooted. Much of the energy of the revolution against the religious past was because it was seen to deter science and the opening of people's minds. The first serious stirrings of democracy, science and religious freedom had surfaced, and in those days they were all members of the same family – the family of ideas and values, which had emerged after 'the world had been turned upside down'.

CHAPTER FIFTEEN

RATIONALISM AND ENTHUSIASM

THE PERFECT COUNTRY?

WHEN THE FRENCH PHILOSOPHER Voltaire fled to England in 1726, after an unfortunate incident when he offended a powerful noble, he discovered a country that was as close to paradise as any he thought could exist. In his humorous but biting *Philosophical Letters*, also known as *English Letters*, he compared what he found in London and in England generally with the state of affairs in France. To him England was the home of reason and the Enlightenment. England was moderate, sensible and open, in stark comparison with feudal France, heading towards bloody revolution at the end of the century. The wars of the mid-seventeenth century and the upheavals during which James II tried to reinstate some form of Catholicism in the 1680s had passed. Parliament had essentially won; the Established Church was established but not alone; and dissenters were tolerated, apart from Catholics, and this primarily because they were seen as inherently traitors because of their loyalty to a foreign pope and Catholic powers in Europe, and Unitarians, because they denied the divinity of Christ and thus the doctrine of the Trinity. To Voltaire, it seemed that the people of Britain were more content than those of any other country in Europe.

Voltaire somewhat overemphasises the calm, enlightened spirit of England in order to point out the foibles of his own country, but he has a point. Britain had, to a large extent, worked out its major religious and political traumas. The Glorious Revolution of 1688, where the Catholic King James was replaced with the Protestant William and Mary of Orange, had seemed to settle the question of national religion. Britain, being an island, helped secure this stability. By comparison in mainland Europe proximity to the armies of countries in other religious camps meant neighbouring Protestant and Catholic states were in constant fear of attack and invasion from one another. The one exception was France, where the absolute power of the King, Louis XIV, and the Catholic Church following the expulsion of the Protestant Huguenots in 1685, combined with one of the most fearsome internal intelligence services in the world, seemed unassailable. France was the Catholic Church's favoured daughter and the King saw himself as the embodiment of the godly ruler. Indeed, when things did not go his way, he was wont to be upset with God. After losing the Battle of Malplaquet in 1709 to the British, he complained 'Has God then forgotten what I have done for Him?'[1]

In England, now that new boundaries had been drawn, people were largely content to accept the status quo. The Established Church provided a quiet and relatively attractive service throughout the land, which many attended but few worried themselves about; indeed it was not uncommon for the Prime Minister to hold cabinet meetings on a Sunday morning.

Having survived the Reformation and the Civil Wars, but now shorn of most decorations, the parish church still reflected many of its traditional elements in its layout. The priest stood before the altar as before, proclaiming the mystery of the communion service. The font stood at the west end of the church – even now a sore point with Baptists and other groups which reject the baptism of infants, claiming that such a momentous choice can only be made by adults. I must here tell one of my son's favourite stories. He looked up a fundamentalist website on the King James version of the Bible, viewed by many such folk as being the most authoritative version of the Bible ever produced, personally sanctioned by God. One of the questions conveniently answered by this site was 'Is it true that the King James translators were nothing but a bunch of Episcopalian baby sprinklers?'[2] The voice of dissent is still to be heard and reminds one of the forces with which the Church of England had to contend.

On the lectern was the King James version of the Bible, available for all to read. The pulpit stood in a more prominent place than was usual in medieval churches, emphasising the role of the Word. At the back of the church there would have been various improving but rather dry books and pamphlets. One such proclamation, with only a hint of uncertainty, placed the Church of England at the pinnacle of faith and reason:

> It has been the Wisdom and Happiness of the Church of England, to approve Herself the soundest Part of the Catholic Church, by contributing most to the Support of the Whole, and the Defence of the Common Faith ... And because a farther Confirmation [of the sound teachings of the Church of England] was given in the Marginal Notes from the Authority of the Primitive Fathers, and the true Rules of Criticism, so much of this assistance likewise is taken in, as may secure the Words and Import of the several Articles, either from the Exceptions of ancient Heretics, or from the Cavils of that modern Sect which has refin'd upon all that were infamous in former Ages.[3]

Meanwhile, the dissenters, whilst still suffering under many petty and oppressive laws – for example, they could not attend either Oxford or Cambridge unless they became Anglicans – were on the whole content to care for their own. The world view of the Nonconformists was, in most cases, a peculiarly ordered one, which worked within a highly structured plan of life with an intense awareness of its brevity. Every moment was used to the full, in steady labour, worship, religious instruction, prayer and constant review of your own conduct, with little attention paid to eating, drinking or sleeping, and rarely any moments of relaxation. The Protestant work ethic in fact. This view is nicely captured on a memorial to an eighteenth century Nonconformist minister at the Ainsworth Presbyterian Chapel, Lancashire:

In
Memory of the
Rev'd Joshua Dobson,

Pastor of this Church 35 years.
Reader
expect not from this plain stone
a flattering memorial of his virtues.
They are recorded
by the faithful witness
in
the BOOK OF GOD
from thence
it shall one day be proclaimed,
with what candour and humility:
with what diligence in acquiring,
and pleasure in communicating knowledge
and with what peculiar patience
under peculiar and long afflictions,
he preached and lived
the GOSPEL OF CHRIST.
in the mean time,
from hence
he being dead, yet speaketh:
and silently yet forcibly admonisheth
his once beloved people,
to remember his solemn counsels,
and to meet him at the great tribunal.

What everyone feared and despised, whether Anglicans or Non-conformists, were 'Enthusiasts' – those who went beyond the pale, breaking the unwritten laws of convention and coexistence and, to some extent, reawakening memories of the excesses of the Civil Wars period. Indeed, the tombstone of one eighteenth-century Anglican clergyman in Gloucestershire has the following, presumably admiring epitaph: 'Here lies the Revd Thomas Jackson, Rector of this parish for 49 years without Enthusiasm.' Equally revealing is this memorial in Exeter Cathedral of 1762:

A instructive, animated and convincing Preacher,
A determined Enemy of Idolatory and Persecution,
A successful Exposer of Pretence and Enthusiasm.

METHODISM

The enthusiasm to which the Established Church objected was to find its most expressive form in the Methodist movement of the eighteenth century. Just as the bitterness generated by the Act of Uniformity of 1662 and other such actions by the Establishment had diminished and the Established Church thought it had a *modus vivendi* with the Nonconformists, a new destabilising force appeared. The Act of Uniformity in 1662 was designed to root out the Puritan/Presbyterian ministers in the churches of the newly restored Episcopal Church of England. Resistance to the Act led to 961 ministers being deposed. A large number of them were in Lancashire, always a home to dissenters. You can still see in Manchester's Albert Square a building dedicated in honour of the 200th anniversary in 1862 to the honour of the 300 plus who were deposed in Lancashire. In some areas, such as Cheshire and Leicestershire, three-quarters of the clergy changed during this period, as illustrated by the lists of incumbents displayed in most churches.

The key figure of the Methodist movement was John Wesley, though he was one amongst an extraordinary group of men who included George Whitefield and the Welshman Howel Harris. They all experienced salvation, which changed their lives and set them preaching. While Whitefield and Harris came to be seen as founders of Methodism, alongside Wesley, in reality they were equally successful Enthusiasts and evangelicals who brought their own traditions and followings into the camp of the later Methodists.

John Wesley was born in 1703 to an Anglican clergyman and his passionately Christian wife Susannah. He had had a disastrous experience as a missionary to the Native Americans in North America, and had returned to London, dispirited. On 24 May 1738 he had an experience that gave him to a passionate understanding of salvation and drove him out into the world again. He describes what happened:

> In the evening I went very unwillingly to a society in Aldersgate Street, where one was reading Luther's preface to the Epistle to the Romans. About a quarter before nine, while he was describing the change which God works in the heart through faith in Christ, I felt my heart strangely warmed. I felt I did trust in Christ, Christ alone, for salvation; and an assurance was

given me that he had taken away my sins, even mine, and saved me from the law of sin and death.[4]

After this dramatic moment, Wesley felt called and he took to the roads, preaching to the most outcast of peoples. He started near Bristol, in those days an early industrial city with coal mining, glass making, pottery works and ports. He went especially to the miners at Kingswood, with whom the Church had virtually no relationship. Preaching in the open air, he overcame opposition and cynicism from the tough miners and their families and touched them with his genuine concern for their spiritual and material welfare. His view of the world and of the role of the poor in the salvation of Christ is captured in one of the most famous of the hymns written by his brother Charles:

> *Where shall my wondering soul begin?*
> *How shall I all to heaven aspire?*
> *A slave redeemed from death and sin,*
> *A brand plucked from eternal fire,*
> *How shall I equal triumphs raise,*
> *Or sing my great Deliverer's praise?*
> *Outcasts of men, to you I call,*
> *Harlots, and publicans, and thieves!*
> *He spreads his arms to embrace you all:*
> *Sinners alone His grace receives:*
> *No need of Him the righteous have;*
> *He came the lost to seek and save.*

By the early 1740s, inspired by the astonishing preaching powers of John Wesley, George Whitefield and Howel Harris, people were falling down 'slain in the Spirit' at meetings all over Britain and America. Wesley rode roughly 8,000 miles every year on his preaching rounds. Soon the people inspired by him wanted to have their own organisation. Wesley never wished to leave the Anglican Church but wanted to reform it rather than establish a new church. However, he found his experience of salvation unwelcome in the somewhat self-satisfied Church of England. Slowly, and against the wishes of Wesley himself, a new church was formed. The people of this church were called Methodists. Originally the name was a mocking term used by their opponents against their 'methodical' approach to faith, but the Methodist faithful turned it into a proud statement of their independence.

Theologically the differences between most Methodists and Anglicans were largely a matter of emphasis. Methodists (except for the Welsh Calvinist Methodists and the Primitive Methodists) were generally a little more evangelical and earnest than their Anglican counterparts. It was the Primitive Methodists, formed in 1811, who turned their backs on the usual style of church-centred life and promoted instead the evangelical rally and what would later be termed house-churches: meetings in homes for worship and study. The Calvinists' theology differed significantly and they were the most opposed to the more relaxed theology of the Church of England.

It was the personal aspect of Methodism that contrasted to Anglicanism. Methodists cared for and reached out to the most downtrodden and outcast. This is well captured in the introduction to the autobiography of one such convert:

> Moses Welsby was born and brought up in a public-house, his early surroundings and habits were rough and wicked, and he literally ran an evil course. He was a noted dog-runner and pigeon-flyer, the racecourse knew him well, and in gambling and drink he spent most of his hardly-earned wages as a coal miner. Till his thirty-sixth year he lived without God, in a land of Bibles and Christian influences.[5]

By 1791, when Wesley died, there were 294 preachers and 71,668 members of the new church in Britain, 19 missionaries and 5,300 members of mission stations, mostly in the Caribbean, and 198 preachers and 43,265 members in North America.

This huge achievement rocked the Established Church and the Nonconformist churches. Suddenly religion, which had been neatly labelled and packed away following the disturbances of the seventeenth century, was breaking out again. It also alarmed the late-eighteenth-century Establishment, which was concerned to control the unrest of the poor, especially the rapidly growing urban poor, the offspring of the Industrial Revolution. The Methodists took to the poor and dispossessed the essence of the sacred, the possibility for change and redemption;

they taught people to read – for example, the Methodist-influenced circulating schools educated nearly half the population of Wales between 1734 and 1771 – and they formed the earliest trades union movements. All this, the Establishment feared, would foster rebellion among ordinary people. In the event, however, the Establishment was wrong.

It is much debated by historians as to whether Methodism actually stopped revolution from breaking out in the late eighteenth or early nineteenth centuries by giving self-respect to ordinary people. Some historians appear to regret that the poor and dispossessed did not rise up, as happened in 1789 in France. Personally, I feel that the social conscience and vigour that Methodism brought to British culture far outweighed any possible benefits of any revolution. I think that some historians have had a rather romantic view of revolution. The scale of misery, death, destruction and eventual corruption that the French Revolution led to makes me grateful that Britain did not follow suit, but instead evolved more slowly towards a system which tries to do its best for the majority. I would also argue that the educative role of Method-ism did more than most revolutions to equip ordinary people to argue and campaign for their rights.

Ultimately Methodism became one of the pillars of British life, though it never lost touch with its more working-class roots. In a sense, it raised its working-class members to lower- or middle-class status through thrift, teetotalism and a ban on gambling. It also provided a strong sense of civic duty and its members came to be valued as upright if independently minded citizens.

SCIENCE AND CLASSICISM

Outside the emerging revival movement, the sacred was also being explored in remarkable new ways by science, though these explorations barely touched the lives of ordinary people for much of the century. Through most of the eighteenth century, science walked hand in hand with the sacred. The most famous example of this was Isaac Newton, the most respected scientist in Europe, who died in 1727. For him scientific discoveries revealed more about God. He maintained a dynamic tension between his discoveries and his theology, as did virtually all the scientists of the time. The poet and wit Alexander Pope summed up the general attitude towards Newton and his findings in his epitaph:

Nature and Nature's laws lay hid in night:
God said 'Let Newton be!' and all was light.

The new force of change both threatening and revitalising traditional religion was now the new model of the universe being established through scientific thought. It threatened because it continued the collapse of the medieval cosmological world view; it revitalised because the medieval model was associated with Catholicism, and the Protestant mind liked to see that world discredited and enjoyed the challenge of creating new world views, ones which could be as 'reformed' as the faith itself. Most early scientists were clergy, partially because the universities required ordination as a condition of becoming a Fellow, but also because they were conscious of holding a tension between eternal truths and new ways of understanding. This was what the Reformation had been all about. Science was but part of that same movement of intellectual freedom and enquiry.

In many ways, however, the earlier religious upheavals had already prepared the way for the new scientific paradigms. The breakdown of a monolithic model of the sacred, which was one of the most significant outcomes of the Reformation and Renaissance, had established a harmony within which a degree of difference and pluralism were now accepted as inevitable, even positive. This viewpoint helped open the mind to the understanding that other established orders, such as Aristotelian science and classical Galenic medicine, might not be as incontrovertible as they seemed. It is no accident that the emergence of religious pluralism came at the same time as the emergence of intellectual pluralism, which opened the way for scientific exploration.

In an age when science and religion came to be considered equally valid ways of exploring the universe and were often applied together, it seemed as if science was proving what the Church of England embodied: that order, rules, law and symmetry framed the universe and did so according to wisdom revealed in Scripture and in Nature. This was explicitly stated by the first historian of the Royal Society, Thomas Sprat, who wrote in 1667:

That the *Church of England* will not only be safe amidst the consequences of a *Rational Age*, but amidst all the improvements of *Knowledge*, and the subversion of old *Opinions* about *Nature*, and introduction of new ways of Reasoning thereon. This will be evident, when we behold the agreement that is between the present *Design* of the *Royal Society*, and that of our *Church* in its beginning. They both may lay equal claim to the Word *Reformation*; the one having compassed it in *Religion*, the other purposing it in *Philosophy*. They both have taken a like course to bring this about; each of them passing by the *corrupt Copies*, and referring themselves to the *perfect Originals* for their instruction; the one to the Scripture, the other to the large Volume of the *Creatures* . . . The *Church of England* therefore may justly be styl'd the *Mother* of this sort of *Knowledge*; and so the care of its *nourishment* and prosperity peculiarly lyes upon it.[6]

To see this joint order of religion and science clearly, and to see the beginnings of a counter-movement as well, we need to go to Bath in Somerset. I pointed out earlier that Bath shows us, layer upon layer, the notions of the sacred that have shaped our minds and our land. In the redesigning of this holy city in the eighteenth century are writ large two understandings of the sacred which shaped and formed the sacred of the eighteenth century and are still powerfully at work today.

The classical and geometric redesigning of Georgian Bath began in earnest in 1725. Three architects, Beau Nash, Ralph Allen and John Wood, gradually demolished and replaced virtually all of the old Bath. For inspiration, they turned to classical Rome. John Wood's revolutionary plan for the city designed three areas to be known as 'the Royal Forum of Bath', another no less magnificent area for the 'Exhibition of Sports', to be called the 'Grand Circus', and a third area for the 'Practice of Medicinal Exercises', to be called the 'Imperial Gymnasium'.

The classical lines of symmetry and order in these new buildings reflected a romantic notion of what Rome had once looked like, but more importantly they also embodied in architecture insights into order that Newton had discovered. For Georgian architecture believed it built according to a divinely revealed order, and the mystical nature of numbers and order was a crucial part of the overall mystique of these new buildings in Bath. Newton had revealed a world of order and balance; a world that God had created in such a way that all humans really needed to do was maintain His divine pattern and symmetry, one that science was now exploring and explaining to an increasingly fascinated audience. In particular, the notion of a perfectly balanced watch or clock captured the sense of order that science was revealing and theology was confirming as being the very nature of God. Following the anarchy of the Civil Wars, and conscious of the continuing chaos and disturbances on the continent due to religious rivalry, British theologians saw the absence of emotion, and the elevation of a more dispassionate God who ordered the universe for humanity to work within, as a great potential strength.

This order was seen to have been most perfectly developed in Greek and then Roman architecture. The symmetry of design and the use of mathematical principles and balance were perceived as embodiments of ancient and divine wisdom. In contrast, the more flamboyant and extravagant architecture of the Gothic period was seen as indicative of a loss of this sense of order.

Remember that prior to the rebuilding of Bath, architecture had been somewhat haphazard. Even London after the fire of 1666 had mostly reverted to its old disorderly and irregular street plans despite the best efforts of the architect, Christopher Wren, to make it more orderly. The rebuilding of Bath was the first time since Norman rule that any systematic British urban planning had occurred, and it was subsequently copied in other parts of the country.

In Georgian Bath, the new cosmology – of a God of order revealed by science and articulated in architecture – is dominant. It is interesting to note that the three men hardly built a single church in their new estates. To see what the Georgians created in this respect you need to visit nearby Bristol, where the Friends Meeting House of 1747 is an early example of ecclesiastical classical architecture, followed by the Congregational Church in Penn Street of 1753, and the Unitarian Chapel in Lewins Mead of 1787. It is curious that here it was the Nonconformists who went for the new classical style. Indeed, few Anglican churches were built in the classical style. Of those that were, the best examples are St Martin's-in-the-Field in Trafalgar Square or Derby Cathedral, both built in the 1720s by James Gibb. They show how the Established Church made use of the classical model but was also constrained by it, which was very different from the spreading ambience of medieval architecture.

Classical architecture fitted exactly within the gentle certainties of eighteenth-century Deism, a new, rather bland way of considering the nature of God. Deism grew out of the thinking expressed by Thomas Sprat of the Royal Society about the Church of England. It was assumed by much of the religious establishment, shorn as it was now of passion, enthusiasm and ardour by the horrors of the struggles of the seventeenth century. That there was a God was generally agreed. That He did anything other than establish the order of the world by setting the clockwork of nature in motion was generally not accepted, and indeed was seen as a little retrogressive, indeed even primitive. Miracles were out; science and cool detachment were in. While for many, Deism was a respectable form of Christianity for an enlightened denizen of eighteenth-century Britain, for others it actually became an alternative to conventional Christianity. It is, however, often hard to tell what it represented for the majority of eighteenth-century writers and thinkers. The ordered, symmetrical, precise, calm and hierarchical rebuilding of Bath resembling a romantic vision of classical Rome, shorn of its brutalities but also of any outward manifestation of Christianity, embodies the Deist world view. Bath is the Deist mind given urban form.

This was recognised at the time. Wesley was a fierce critic of Wood, having accused him of being an elitist and effectively a pagan. Wesley had actually denounced Wood in one of his sermons as an immoral force. One day they came face to face in Bath walking in opposite directions along the pavement. Wood the embodiment of the dispassionate precise Deity who never got involved, Wesley the Enthusiast whose faith was based upon intense personal experience of God; Wood the elitist and servant of the wealthy and Wesley the friend and advocate of the working classes. Walking towards each other, Wood saw his opportunity, and he blocked the pavement saying, 'I never give way to fools.' Wesley rose to the occasion and promptly stepped off the pavement, bowed deeply and said, 'However Mr. Wood, I do!'

THE RETURN OF THE WILD

At the same time, however, that the Georgian architects were remodelling Bath in the image of the Deist cosmos, elsewhere this same world view was being subtly undermined, for example at one of the greatest gardens in Britain: Stourhead in Wiltshire. Here, at the height of the classical Georgian period, Henry Hoare built a magnificent classical house and a marvellous set of gardens to complement it. In doing so he fused two worlds, which were emerging side by side in Georgian thought, for in these gardens classical statues and classical temples are dotted around amidst a 'wild' and 'natural' setting. Included too were medieval elements, such as the old High Cross from Bristol and a mock medieval bridge, and pagan creations such as temples to Diana and other classical deities. All this was eventually topped by a weird hybrid building of 1772 called Alfred's Tower, set up where tradition says Alfred the Great summoned the men of Wessex to drive out the Norse invaders. The classical Deist vision expressed in the statues and temples is challenged by the other elements in the garden, such as the wilderness and naturalism of the overall design and the introduction of medieval artefacts, for they invoke forces associated with the raw energy of the sacred, and the celebration of Nature as essentially untameable.

To understand this we need to look at the plans of the garden for the Palace of Versailles outside Paris, began in 1662 by the Sun King Louis XIV. Here order, rigid lines, due process, mechanical waterfalls and straight-lined lakes are the visible expression of what was to become the later core of Deist belief. All is order, all has its place, all can be controlled. Compare it with the 'natural order' of Stourhead with its winding lakes, bending streams, flowing undulating landscapes, wild clumps of trees and half-hidden temples. How different it is, and how little it expresses Deist belief.

The search for the wild was beginning at the same time as the quest for the classical was reaching its peak. Alexander Pope's garden in London is usually taken to be the first attempt to return to the wild. He explains it in his Epistle to Lord Burlington of 1731:

> *To build, to plant, whatever you intend,*
> *To rear the Column, or the Arch to bend,*
> *To swell the Terra, or to sink the Grot;*
> *In all, let Nature never be forgot.*
> *But treat the Goddess like a modest fair,*
> *Nor over-dress, nor leave her wholly bare.*
> *Consult the genius of the Place in all;*
> *That tells the Waters or to rise or fall.*

This romantic vision of Nature and of the sacred was to grow alongside the classical-order model until they parted company with the emergence of the Romantic movement in the late eighteenth century.

The gentility and order of the eighteenth century can be likened to the yearning for peace, order and stability that marked the twenty years after the Second World War and the rise of suburbia and 'suburban' values. It was the children of those who sought respectability and stability in the suburbs who led the hippy and political revolutions of the 1960s. The constraints that seemed so vital to their parents were seen as restrictive and oppressive, and they inspired a search for a counterculture. In a much more gentle way, this is what happened to the sacred in the eighteenth century. It broke out of the neat order of the Deists and escaped in a number of ways. The eighteenth century saw a tremendous burst of interest and speculation about the remains of the old sacred places. Wood, the architect of Bath, for instance, was not just a builder and classical designer, but also a great enthusiast for Britain's 'ancient monumental past'. This picked up on a more specifically Christian vision of Britain as sacred, which had emerged in the Civil Wars – most clearly articulated by Milton.

The first manifestation of this was the great evangelical awakening that tore through Britain from the 1740s onwards. It is no accident that this happened at exactly the time that Britain, the first industrialised nation, was ripping into its natural environment and creating huge industrial cities, such as Manchester. The Industrial Revolution destroyed so much so fast that it provoked a sense of shock and horror compounded by a sense that those in control lay outside the older Establishment. A new idea of the sacred was also being born in the power of creating new things, new inventions and opening the world to exploitation and development. To become co-creators with God was the vision underlying the development of new ideas and techniques for some, particularly the Quakers and Unitarians. The Industrial Revolution also broke families and communities apart and drew people from the land towards the mushrooming cities. Ecological, social and psychological damage was done by forces that no one seemed to know how to control and which were largely ignored by those in charge of the country. As it increasingly affected more ordinary people there was an urgent search for a new sense of the sacred.

These factors explain the success of the evangelical movement, as large numbers of people found the sacred in a sense of being saved and brought into a new, caring community, primarily the Methodists. For people who had lost any control over their external surroundings, these groups supplied the opportunity to focus upon their inner spiritual world. One of the greatest achievements of the Methodists and later groups, such as the Baptists and Salvation Army, was that strengthening the poor's sense of inner worth led many to tackle the problems of the external environment.

The search for a romantic sacred past, untainted by the reviled and rejected Catholic medieval past, was one of the great eighteenth-century quests. To begin with, as in the case of the greatest of the early investigators of the stone circles, William Stukeley, these explorations were for a native religion, which could be seen as a part of the overall divine revelation by God to the world. From the start of the seventeenth century the Jesuits in China had been putting forward theories that the Chinese had, at the same time as the Children of Israel, been given a divine revelation, but over time this had become obscured and lost in a haze of superstition. The Jesuit mission in China, which lasted from 1598 to 1771 and had many successes, was largely directed towards helping the Chinese rediscover their supposedly 'lost' faith in one God and in the ethics and laws of the Old Testament. In Britain, Stukeley and others tried to do the same with their own 'ancient' culture. They tried to show that at the same time that China and Israel were receiving their divine revelations so were the ancient Britons.

Stukeley was particularly fascinated by Avebury and Stonehenge in Wiltshire and spent months charting and drawing them. He, almost accidentally, began the popular idea that these sites were connected with the Druids, because he encouraged people to call him a modern-day Druid – indeed, he recorded in 1723 that he took some delight in describing himself as 'the Druid as they called me'. He certainly seems to have toyed with the rising Deist fascination in the Druids, which was emerging both from the study of classical writers and as a response to the discovery of the 'noble savage' of North America.

The significance of the discovery of the native 'Indians' of North America on the concept of the sacred was that they provided a model of religious life apparently free of dogma, buildings and priests. The romantic concept of the noble savage, untainted by the cynicism, hierarchies, structures and even clothing of civilisation, was deliberately developed as a counter ideal to both the stuffiness of religion, especially Puritan religion, and the demands of civilisation as defined by Europe.

People were searching for 'pure religion' untainted by dogma and belief. Some believed that they found just such a Deist vision in the classical writers' accounts of the Druids. The Druids were a particular favourite of John Toland, whose book *Christianity Not Mysterious*, published in 1696, was the first popular book to present Deism as an enlightened version of Christianity. Toland developed his ideas of the Druids as an earlier and more perfect form of Deism.

Stukeley toyed with these ideas, but then in 1726 he changed his views radically and was ordained as a clergyman in the Church of England, after which he became one of the most determined opponents of Deism within the Church. He claimed that Druid religion was 'of Abraham's religion entirely' and though 'we cannot say that Jehovah appeared personally to them' they had 'a knowledge of the plurality of persons in the Deity' with a religion 'so extremely like Christianity, that in effect it differ'd from it only in this; they believed in a Messiah who was to come into this world, as we believe in him that is come'.[7] In other words, Stukeley viewed the Druids as being in exactly the same state as the ancient Israelites.

To Stukeley in his search for a native religion his studies of Stonehenge were a key that would unlock the meaning of being British. Others, however, had different perceptions of the ancient sites. Wood is thought to have based his design of the Circus in Bath on pictures of Stonehenge drawn by Inigo Jones in his book *Stone-Heng*, published in 1655, and from Wood's own book on Stonehenge, called *Choir Gawre, vulgarly known as Stonehenge* and published in 1747, in which many of the wilder fantasies of many contemporary Stonehenge enthusiasts are first to be found. It is clear that Wood thought by copying Stonehenge he was building a pagan site. Thus, far from bolstering Christianity as a revealed religion, as Stukeley had hoped, the ancient sites were becoming foci for the growing desire for a sacred untouched or tainted by Christianity to which the nostalgic and romantic could turn. In a sense, the sites also prompted a reinvention of a kind of new Brutus myth, as we explored in Chapter 12. It was claimed that the British were descendants of some ancient and wise people, the priests of Atlantis or the magicians of the Phoenicians, who had sought refuge here, building Stonehenge and Avebury to keep alive their ancient wisdom and carry on their astrological and magical practices. Ignoring the by now increasingly discredited Brutus storyline, sacred historians sought to find a new significance for the special role of Britain and the British.

The rise of Freemasonry is an example of the quasi-pagan, mystical view of a special people and the role of Deist symmetry. Descended from Scottish guilds, Freemasonry tried to fuse Stukeley's view of a revelation to the earliest peoples, combined with somewhat implausible theories about ancient secrets of the builders of the pyramids, Stonehenge and the Temple in Jerusalem, to produce a secret society of men who believed that they alone understood how the world worked and what God had intended. The quasi-religious rituals and 'mystery' of the Freemasons were an attempt to mimic elements of secret mystical cults culled from classical Greek and Roman writers. Free-masonry is in effect Deist theology fused with romantic lost-masters mythology all wrapped up in pseudo-Enlightenment 'science' and brotherhood.

The remythologising of Britain had commenced. Thereafter the study of ancient sites from Stonehenge and Avebury to Glastonbury and the Uffington White Horse would frequently disappear into a quagmire of fabulous nonsense designed not to shed light on history but to explain, elevate and make special the English or British as something divinely ordained, or to elevate a new kind of sacred nature to the position once occupied by God alone. The wide-ranging ideas produced confirm the wise and prophetic words of Thomas Tanner who, in 1695, wrote of Stonehenge and the various theories already floating around that: 'Tis of its self so singular, and receives so little light from history, that almost every one has advance'd a new notion.'[8]

Neo-paganism and Deism were primarily the concerns of the gentry, of intellectuals and the influential. The concerns of ordinary people were different. For many the parish church offered a structure and security that sufficed. For others, their involvement in Nonconformist churches offered solidarity against the Establishment. But for many, both within the churches and without, religion had become dry, for some of no significance whatsoever. Even the Quakers had stopped quaking. It is perhaps important to stress that earlier groups such as the Baptists, Congregationalists and Presbyterians were already Christians who created new versions of their own particular Church in order to deal with the existentialist and pragmatic crisis of the Reformation. The

Methodists, however, essentially converted the unchurched, the heathens of Britain. Those people, such as the miners of Bristol, lived an almost unbelievably savage and degraded existence and had no links with the Church whatsoever.

What Wesley and Methodism did was to give many people pride in themselves and a vision of belonging to a religion that transcended colour, age, class and country. In so doing one could say that he freed the British Churches from their insularity and reminded them that they were part of the conceptual revolution of the mission faiths: that what they believed was true for all people and all times, and that they had a responsibility to convert others to their views and practices.

Wesley unleashed a missionary spirit that was to take Christians of all denominations from Britain to every corner of the world in the next 100 years. Their missionary work coincided with the expansion of the British Empire and it is too easy to associate Christianity with the Empire. However, the rulers of the Empire were often very intolerant of the missionaries and vice versa. Wesley would have had no truck with the idea which lay behind imperialist visions of the British being a special people descended from ancient pagans, hence his hostility to Wood. Nevertheless both missionaries and imperialists were to some extent enthused by the same vision, and in the next century, the sacred in Britain began to be exported, as it had never been before.

CHAPTER SIXTEEN

DOUBT AND MISSION – THE VICTORIANS

HYMNS OF FAITH

The sea is calm tonight.
The tide is full, the moon lies fair
Upon the straits; on the French coast the light
Gleams and is gone; the cliffs of England stand,
Glimmering and vast, out in the tranquil bay.
Come to the window, sweet is the night air!
Only, from the long line of spray
Where the sea meets the moon-blanched land,
Listen! You hear the grating roar
Of pebbles which the waves draw back, and fling,
At their return, up the high strand,
Begin, and cease, and then again begin,
With tremulous cadence slow, and bring
The eternal note of sadness in.
Sophocles long ago
Heard it on the Aegean, and it brought
Into his mind the turbid ebb and flow
Of human misery; we
Find also in the sound a thought,

Hearing it by this distant northern sea.
The Sea of Faith
Was once, too, at the full, and round earth's shore
Lay like the folds of a bright girdle furled.
But now I only hear
Its melancholy, long, withdrawing roar,
Retreating, to the breath
Of the night-wind, down the vast edges drear
And naked shingles of the world.
Ah, love, let us be true
To one another! for the world, which seems
To lie before us like a land of dreams,
So various, so beautiful, so new,
Hath really neither joy, nor love, nor light,
Nor certitude, nor peace, nor help for pain;
And we are here as on a darkling plain
Swept with confused alarms of struggle and flight,
Where ignorant armies clash by night.
'Dover Beach' by Matthew Arnold, published 1867.

The Victorian poet Matthew Arnold was rather like the official mourner at a funeral. According to his poetry and criticism, everything around him was in decline and decaying. He was the son of the famous Rugby school headmaster, Thomas Arnold, who stressed that the role of schools was to produce Christian gentlemen who represented a proper fusion of the scientific and the theological, religion and order in their public lives.

Matthew Arnold seems to have felt that this was impossible, spending much of his life as an inspector of schools and for ten years (1857–67) as Professor of Poetry at Oxford, bemoaning the terrible state of most things around him. In the sighing and moaning of the beach and waves in 'Dover Beach', published in 1867, he saw a reflection of his deep worry: the dying of religion – or to be more accurate, the dying of religion amongst intellectuals and his peer group.

When Matthew Arnold wrote the poem he perceived religion to be on the wane because science had broken away from its embrace with the sacred which had sustained both through much of the eighteenth century. Now science saw itself as opposing religion or, at the very least, as raising profound questions as to its significance. It seemed to embody the belief that the world was improving and therefore the things of the past were no longer sufficient or appropriate for the present. Christianity, long revered for its antiquity, now seemed outmoded and obscure. A new light was shining, and it was called science, and it was based on facts. Or so it seemed.

Matthew Arnold stands at one end of the spectrum of the Victorian relationship to the sacred: the end of those who believed that its day was essentially over. At the other end was Reginald Heber. An intellectual and a poet, he is commemorated in a splendid stained-glass window over the high altar in his home church of Malpas, Cheshire. The window is very striking, not least for the fact that he is most definitely not in Malpas, nor, indeed, anywhere in England, for there are some very un-Cheshire looking characters in the window. Heber is perhaps one of the most famous of the Anglican missionary bishops appointed Bishop of Calcutta in 1823. He was a great educationalist, and schools founded by him can still be found in India. To any one familiar with Anglican missionary history, Heber is well known. He is also known for his hymns, such as 'Brightest and best of the sons of the morning'. Nothing could be further from the pessimism of Arnold's poem than the first verse of that hymn:

> Brightest and best of the sons of the morning,
> Dawn on our darkness and lend us thine aid;
> Star of the East, the horizon adorning,
> Guide where our infant Redeemer is laid.

Heber is perhaps best known for his poem/hymn 'From Greenland's icy mountains', one of the great missionary hymns of the nineteenth century. The hymn expresses a vision of a world begging to be given the Gospel – a vision that assumes that God is seated somewhere very near to England and sends out His favoured people, the English, to bring hope to the hopeless. He talks of 'each remotest nation' being given the Gospel by 'we, whose souls are lighted, by wisdom from on high'.

In 'Dover Beach' and 'From Greenland's icy mountains', we have two very different views: one poet bemoaning the death of religion and another extolling that the world is about to become as sacred and as holy as England. The difference between these views illustrates the challenges to and problems of the sacred in Britain in the nineteenth century and much of the twentieth as well.

What exactly was going on in this century of such hopes and fears? During this time secularism arose as a particular theory, first explicitly expounded by the social reformer George Holyoake, imprisoned in 1842 – the last person to be imprisoned for atheism in Britain. Holyoake argued for a system of interpretation and order based solely on principles from this world, without reference or recourse to any belief in God, gods or an afterlife. Science challenged faith, and for the first time it was acceptable, even almost obligatory, to dismiss faith. Yet more churches were built, more people were brought by a powerful personal conversion to Christianity, and more religious organisations were founded in this century than in virtually the whole of the previous 300 years. While faith was being doubted at home, it was being exported to Africa, India, China and the Americas in such a scale and intensity that the map of world religions was redrawn; indeed, Kenneth Scott Latourette said in the volume on the nineteenth century in his series on the history of Christianity: 'In the nineteenth century the geographical stream of Christianity so broadened that we have been compelled to allot as much space to its expansion as we did to its course in all the preceding 18 centuries.'[1]

The missionary societies were essentially late-eighteenth and early-nineteenth-century creations. Although the Church of England had created a missionary society in 1698, the Society for Promoting Christian Knowledge, aimed at Nonconformists, Quakers and Native Americans, it was the evangelical revival of the eighteenth century that spawned the major missionary societies. These, such as the London Missionary Society, founded in 1795 by a mixed group of evangelical Congregationalists, Anglicans, Presbyterians and Methodists, saw the whole newly explored and 'discovered' world as needing salvation. Often from working-class backgrounds, converts made by the evangelical movements and churches in Britain offered themselves to go to 'the ends of the earth'. For many it was a disaster, as they were ill-prepared to face the diverse cultures they encountered. Yet many laid the foundation for the conversion of whole areas – especially Africa and the Pacific – and helped establish Christianity as the largest religion in the world today.

RECOVERY OF THE SACRED

At one level, religion was never as visible as it was during the Victorian era. There was the continued effort of the missionary movement, and in many households the impact of Methodism could be seen in the practice of morning and evening prayers. There were subsequent revivals, such as the great Welsh revivals of the early nineteenth century and the emergence of the American Revivalist meetings of Dwight Moody and Ira Sankey, whose missions in the 1860s to 1890s in the UK were hugely popular to the extent that their hymn-book became the staple of evangelical churches for the next 100 years. It was the time of the founding of the Salvation Army, and a plethora of Methodist splinter churches, new denominations and chapels, especially in working-class areas.

The Salvation Army arose directly from the vision and mission of Methodism. Its two founders, the remarkable married couple William and Catherine Booth, were both Methodist converts and evangelicals who disagreed with the Methodist hierarchy for being too aggressive in their preaching style. In 1865 they founded the Movement, which in 1878 retitled itself as the Salvation Army. Seeing the struggle against sin and evil as a war, they deliberately adopted a military style – uniforms, marching band, and military titles – as well as the language of warfare, such as their magazine *The War Cry*.

The Salvation Army took up the challenge of reaching the poorest and most oppressed sections of the working class – going where 100 years previously Wesley had gone. The Methodist Churches had by and large become too respectable to go into such places. From 1880 onwards the powerful evangelical dimension of their 'war' was complemented by the social action and projects for which they are justly famous world-wide: hostels for the homeless, detoxification programmes, housing projects and feeding the down-and-outs. The extraordinary success of the Salvation Army was acknowledged by the fact that the Church of England created in 1882 its own somewhat paler version called the Church Army.

Today the classic inner-city landscape is dotted with Gothic Revival churches from this period, raising their spires to heaven from amongst the grime of the industrial estates. These churches are so called because architects such as Pugin and Scott felt that the Gothic style could bring grace and wonder to the slums of Britain, and to a great degree they were right. For example, the gems of St Francis's in Gorton, and Holy Trinity in Platt, both areas of Manchester, grace and improve an otherwise rather poor environment. Holy Trinity, designed by Edmund Sharpe and built in 1845, is a graceful, inspiring and beautifully coloured church, which faces two ways – literally and metaphorically. On its south side lie the former gardens and park of Platt Hall, which was once one of the ancient estates of rural Lancashire but was swallowed up by the urban growth of south Manchester between 1850 and 1870. The south side of the church, viewed through the trees and across the lake and parkland of the old estate – now a public park – looks like a country church. The north side, however, looks on a different landscape. Here serried rows of terrace houses stretch out towards the centre of Manchester, embracing some of the most troubled areas of the inner city. Viewed from that side, the church rises up as a vision of another world and time, a symbol of what humanity can create in the midst of often ugly ordinariness, yet it is also the parish church for these rows of huddled houses. It was built here because the nineteenth-century inhabitants needed a church, a priest and a place of the sacred in their urbanised and polluted environment. This notion of the need for beauty in the midst of squalor was well expressed by the architect J.P. Seddon in 1872 at the Church Congress:

> If our church doors were not shut out of service time, what valuable aids to education might not their walls be made? We blame the poor for dullness of apprehension, but do little to enlighten them. Our own houses are closed to them, and the art provided for their cottages are but pot dogs and bad lithographs.[2]

There is an important aspect of the sacred in this slightly patronising view – an aspect that enthused many Church leaders in inner-city areas. This was the sense of the sacred as an uplifting beauty, which could enlighten and revive those who saw it. A supreme example of this, now surrounded by university buildings, but originally set in a poor slum area, is the Roman Catholic Holy Name Church on Oxford Road, Manchester. It is still a glorious blaze of colour and design for the weary city dweller, even today.

THE SACRED AS SOCIAL CONSCIENCE

It was through evangelism that in this century Christianity became a major engine for social reform. The anti-slavery movement emerged, essentially, out of the evangelical conscience, which was intimately aware of the Bible's injunction that 'all men were brothers'. Most of the members of the Anti-Slavery Society, the main force behind the abolition of the slave trade in the British colonies (slavery was banned in Britain in 1807) were devout – and generally politically conservative – evangelical Christians. After slavery was banned in Britain the fight against the slave trade in other parts of the world was continued by the missionaries and the Royal Navy, who were the equivalent of the human rights' activists and peacekeeping organisations of today but with greater success. The Navy regularly captured and successfully prosecuted slave traders, freeing slaves and giving them land in British colonies. The great dream of the slaves of the American South was to make it to British soil in Canada, and therefore to freedom.

Lord Shaftesbury's labour reforms, too, sprang directly from his evangelical, even eschatological beliefs. He was not uncommon in being inspired to work for the betterment of all by his religious convictions, but his inspiration was his evangelical belief in the absolute authority of the Bible, which meant that he took its message profoundly seriously. He describes his basic beliefs about Christianity and the Bible:

> The Bible is God's word written from the very first syllable down to the very last and from the last back to the first ... Nothing but Scripture can interpret Scripture. I should reject it if announced to me by man. I accept it, believe it, bless it, as announced in Holy Writ ... and like the Israelites, I bow and worship.[3]

He believed what the Bible stated: that he was his brother's keeper – especially of the poorest and most vulnerable. He took as absolute truth the Gospel teachings to love the poor, imprisoned, homeless and oppressed. In Matthew 25: 31–46, Jesus says that anyone who failed to feed the poor, visit the prisoner, clothe the naked and tend the sick has failed to do as He commands. In Shaftesbury's actions, we see this command carried out not just faithfully, but lovingly. It was Shaftesbury who forced Parliament to enact the Ten Hours Bill (1847: limiting the working hours of women and those below eighteen to ten hours a day Monday to Friday, and eight hours on Saturday, with no work on Sunday), the Mines Act (1842: banning women and children under ten from working in mines), the Lunacy Act (1845: recognising mental ill-health as an issue requiring care, not condemnation, and providing for treatment by the State), and many others which brought dignity, decent wages and legal protection to the most downtrodden and oppressed. He also pushed through the Lodging House Act, reforming the slum dwellings in which so many of the poor lived, and described by Dickens as 'the finest piece of legislation ever enacted in England'.

Shaftesbury did all these things in order to prepare the way for the Second Coming of Jesus, making the world a fit place for Him to return to. This religion-inspired vision of creating a better world, a more sacred world, is one of the strongest forces running through Britain at this time and as such was a manifestation of the sacred. It motivated the Sunday schools, the charities and the social societies. It flowed into politics, through the involvement of religion in the emerging trades union movement, virtually all of whose founders were either lay preachers in the Methodist tradition or had been given the skills to read and write through Sunday schools and chapels. Religion under-pinned the Chartist Movement, which sought to expand the franchise and to reform the Houses of Parliament. C.R. Fay nicely summed up the levels of religious and social interaction on these areas by saying:

> In the Ten Hour Movement and the Anti Corn Law League, the workers learned in the company of their middle and upper class champions how to campaign. In the Chartist movement they learned how to act alone: the Chartists having no friends higher than the ranks of the Baptists and Primitive Methodists.

THE ESTABLISHMENT

Such manifestations of Christian social conscience often stood in stark contrast to the more *laissez-faire* attitude of much of the Established Church. The sense that the Church was just part of the Establishment is well captured in a picture of this time. Proudly displayed upon the walls of Bangor Museum in North Wales is a pub sign of 1850, known as The Four Alls. It depicts four figures in a row. On the left is Queen Victoria and beneath her are the words, 'I Govern All'; next comes an Anglican clergyman in full robes and with prayer book with the words underneath, 'I Pray for All'; this figure is followed by a soldier in full dress uniform, and inscribed underneath are the words, 'I Fight for All'; finally there is a working man with beneath him the phrase, 'I Pay for All'.

A powerful if eccentric critic of the Established Church was William Cobbett, who died in 1836. He adored the countryside and loathed the rise of the industrial cities and the poverty, exploitation and misery they had created for so many. Writing in the first three decades of the nineteenth century, it was he who coined the phrase 'the great wen', meaning tumour or swelling, to describe London. Iconoclastic, bombastic, and highly opinionated, he never feared to strike out at what he saw as hypocrisy and nonsense. One of his funniest, but also angriest, pieces is on the abuse of livings in the Church of England, whereby people were appointed to a number of parish livings, took the accrued monies and then lived off them in Bath, London or other fashionable areas, rather than in the actual parish which was generally in the middle of the countryside. Readers of Trollope will enjoy the following tirade by Cobbett:

> If the late Bishop of Winchester had lived in Catholic times, he could not have had a wife, and that he could not have had a wife's sister, to marry Mr Edmund Poulter, in which case, I may be allowed to think it possible, that Mr Poulter would not have quitted the bar for the pulpit, and that he would not have had the two livings of Meon Stoke and Soberton and a Prebend besides; that his son Brownlow Poulter, would not have had the two livings of Buriton and Petersfield; that his son, Charles Poulter, would not have had the three livings of Alton, Binstead, and Kingsley; that his son-in-law Ogle would not have had the living of Bishop's Waltham; and that his son-in-law Haygarth would not have had the two livings of Upham and Durley.[4]

And so it goes on.

Things were changing, though, and by the end of the nineteenth century no such polemic against the abuse of episcopal power in this way could have been fairly written.

In particular, the Church of England was profoundly affected by the Oxford Movement (1833–45). Centred upon a group of High Church dons at Oxford, led by John Keble and John Henry Newman, they were concerned about the general laxity of the Church and dismayed at the decline in its role and significance, as reflected later by Arnold in 'Dover Beach', but were determined to halt it. They opposed the liberalism and incipient Deism of much of the Church and sought to restore it to a more Catholic stance. The revival of liturgy, vestments and architecture of a more medieval Church style began with this movement, as well as the tradition of the High Church becoming somewhat anti-liberal. For example, the fact that most Anglican churches today have a choir, organist and robes to wear is a direct result of this movement. Through a series of 'Tracts for the Times' (hence the movement's other name of Tractarians) the movement, spearheaded by influential intellectuals such as Edward Pusey, aroused fierce debate within the Church of England as to the Church's true nature and role.

In the end, many in the movement converted to Roman Catholicism, led by Newman. He even became a cardinal. But the questions raised by the movement led the Church of England to seek to reform its structures throughout the nineteenth century, essentially creating a professional clergy, properly trained and funded, instead of a clergy consisting principally of cast-off third sons of the upper classes.

THE RELIGION OF SOCIALISM AND SCIENCE

To the surprise of many, the sacred was experiencing something of a revival through evangelism, social action and internal ecclesiastical reform. By contrast secularism was confronting certain crises of what to do in a society which in part was increasingly distancing itself from religion, even becoming antagonistic towards it, but which also needed new myths, new 'traditions' to live within.

In particular, there was a serious struggle taking place for the right to be the voice of the voiceless. Karl Marx, writing in the British Library, had created a vision of a new socialist understanding of history, philosophy, religion and the future – socialist in that it saw social forces rather than individualistic forces at work in society. He recognised the power of religion to articulate the case of the dispossessed, but in common with many secular reformers he ultimately saw the Church and religion in general as part of the old order that had to be over-thrown. In continental Europe, this led to polarisation, with the Church becoming a pillar of the conservative Establishment and opposed to socialism. In Britain, such hard-and-fast demarcation lines did not work. Many of the leaders of the trades unions, of social reform and political change were Christians and were involved precisely because of their faith. This caused British secular socialists to compete with religion by creating their own notions and models of the sacred; indeed, many such movements modelled themselves on successful Christian evangelical and missionary programmes.

Robert Owen was the main missionary with a religious approach to socialism without the need to have churches. He founded, among many other things, Halls of Science, which sprang up in all the major cities of Britain, teaching popular science. In these he encouraged the preaching – literally – of socialism, and the creation of Sunday schools for socialism. In 1838 he even appointed 'social missionaries' to go out and convert people. The Halls of Science created their own festivals, loosely based on Christian ones, and their own rituals. Every Sunday evening they held their main sessions, competing directly with the churches. Despite hostility to these rivals who were poaching their flocks, the churches had to acknowledge that the emphasis on temperance, self-improvement and reflection greatly enhanced the behaviour of the working classes. They were possibly also successful because the evangelical revivals had inspired a longing for new religious movements. Indeed, the churches even had their own socialists, known as Christian Socialists and active in the 1840s and 1850s.

Though these Halls of Science were tremendously popular during the nineteenth century, today you can find virtually no trace of them. However there is one interesting building that reflects the somewhat unexpected results of the interaction between religion and socialism. Upper Brook Street in Manchester is a typical inner-city main road. Cars rush along it, in and out of the city centre, passing flyovers, university buildings, car salerooms, cheaply built offices, car parks and the edges of council estates. In this setting the old Free Chapel stands out. This is partly because the former minister's house and Sunday school room is now the Islamic Institute, but it is mostly the building itself which is so striking. Despite being empty and neglected for at least the last twenty-five years, it has a grace and beauty that seems to challenge the ordinary ugliness of virtually everything else around it. Thin lancet windows soar up from the ground, while delicate butt-resses hold it upright, like pallbearers at a funeral. Overgrown, half propped up with bits of scaffolding, and its windows broken, this is one of the more astonishing manifestations of the sacred in Britain. Here, the first Labour Church was formed by John Trevor in 1891.

Trevor was a minister of the Free Church, an offshoot of Unitarian-ism. Deeply committed to socialism, he created a church here dedicated to its principles, but which saw socialism as a religious movement. Trevor preached that God was behind the Labour movement in general, and socialism in particular. He created a network of Labour Churches, of which there were thirty by 1907. However, as they grew they shed their Christianity and began to teach socialism as a religion.

> By 1912, all references to God had been dropped; the purpose of the Labour Church was described as that of giving expression to the religious and general principles of socialism – it was definitely said not to be theological.[5]

While all this was going on amongst the working classes, faith was slipping at a more Establishment level. Matthew Arnold was right to see the Sea of Faith in retreat. What he did not foresee or notice was that some very interesting new seas were also being created.

The intellectual world of the Victorian era was one of the most questioning and at the same time most certain that there has ever been. It questioned everything by creating so much that was new and which broke old traditions and assumptions. A delightful insight into this is offered by J.G. Farrell's splendid book *The Siege of Krishnapur*, which, although a novel, is so well researched and imagined that it might as well be true. In it, the central figure is the Collector, the most senior representative of the old East India Company, which ruled large sections of India. He was involved with the Great Exhibition of 1851, and never ceased to marvel at the new machines, new technologies and new possibilities that the Exhibition promoted. For him they are har-bingers of progress, which will sweep away ignorance and make the world a better place. He sees the Great Exhibition as a fusion 'between the spiritual and the practical. It is the one that imbues the other with

The layers of Sacred Britain are most visible at Bath, Somerset. Beneath the Roman baths pictured here are the remains of the Iron Age sacred site. The Roman baths were themselves sacred, while above them stands Bath Abbey, an Anglo-Saxon foundation. Beyond the Abbey, the 18th century Georgian crescents and streets of Bath were modelled on Greece, Rome and Stonehenge. (*Dallas and John Heaton/Corbis*)

The Royal Crescent, Bath. In the geometric designs of Georgian Bath Deist theology, romantic notions of Greece, Rome and Ancient Britain met. The main architect, John Wood, saw himself as creating an essentially pagan sacred landscape. (*John Wyand/English Heritage Photo Library*)

BELOW In St. Michael's Church, Kirby Le Soken, this 19th century stained glass of St. Aidan captures another side of Victorian Christianity. The quiet, meditative posture combined with the full High Church vestments speaks of a content English Church, apparently at ease with itself. (*Anson/E & E Picture Library*)

ABOVE This pious 19th century stained glass window from St. Nicholas' Church, Blakeney, Norfolk shows St. Columba. However it actually tells us more about 19th century Anglicanism than about the 6th century saint. His visionary stance, his 'whiteness' and the ritualistic pose embody the missionary movement: the Empire and the impact of the High Church Oxford Movement. (*Ken Murrell/E & E Picture Library*)

purpose', and, as the actual official text of the Catalogues of the Great Exhibition said, 'The progress of the human race, resulting from the labour of all men, ought to be the final object of the exertion of each individual.'[6]

This progress generated both optimism and fear, as illustrated by the story of the thirty miles-an-hour limit. By the 1840s when the railways had developed to make travel possible for just about everyone – indeed creating a desire to travel which had not been seen since the ending of pilgrimage in the 1530s – they caused great concern. In many early evangelical tracts, the railway station was used as an image of the temptations of the Broad Way which leads to perdition – the way of sin, travel, enjoyment and fun. But they also inspired a quasi-scientific fear, as it was claimed that the human body would disintegrate if a railway coach travelled at more than thirty miles an hour. There were earnest debates about this issue and calls for legislation. Many saw this claim as a way of controlling the potential of the railways for swift and easy access to all parts of the land. To the engineers, however, it was a challenge that spurred them to experiment until they could build faster engines to prove that it was a false claim.

The rise of science as a quasi-religion in its own right created considerable confusion for the Establishment. For example, the theory of evolution had developed in the latter half of the nineteenth century into a philosophy of superiority and determinism through the belief that, for instance, Australian Aboriginals or Africans were more primitive forms of human beings. Much effort was expended in measuring skulls to show, scientifically of course, that Caucasians were more intellectually developed because their skulls and brains were larger. Determinism meant you could create a philosophy of guiltless action. If you had been programmed by nature to act selfishly – 'nature, red in tooth and claw' – then morality, especially Christian morality, was an irrelevance.

At one level the development of science and technology was taken as a sign of the superiority of Christianity, particularly British Christianity, with so much science and so many inventions exported from Britain impacting upon the entire world. This was certainly the view held by much of the rest of the world. It is still a view expounded by extreme Christian evangelicals today, as well as one held by, for example, certain extreme Muslim groups who see videos, computers, televisions and so forth as symbols of Christian imperialism. At another level, this self-same force was destroying or ignoring the very religion and culture from which it emerged.

SCIENCE VERSUS RELIGION

The achievements of Matthew Arnold's father capture something of the problems created by the dichotomy of this age. In 1828, the thirty-three-year-old Thomas Arnold, a clergyman in the Church of England, became headmaster of Rugby School. As one of his biographers put it, he had the great tact to make himself both loved and feared. The public schools of that time were little more than unruly hothouses for the over-wealthy and over-privileged sons of the aristocracy and rising middle classes, with only a passing resemblance to places of learning.

Arnold changed all that. He saw schools as training places for real Christians, strong in body through physical exercise; in mind through proper education in the sciences as well as the classics; in soul through a proper regime of chapel services and religious education; and in spirit, through the creation of a school ethos that would underpin all that the pupils did at school and in later life. This ethos is perhaps best summed up by one of Arnold's main disciples, John Percival, the first headmaster of Clifton School, Bristol. He described the purpose of Clifton as 'a nursery or seed-plot for high-minded men, devoted to the highest service of the country, a new Christian chivalry of patriotic service'.[7] Although much mocked later, this ethos spread through the public school system to create a generation or more of well-educated, compassionate and public-spirited young men as well as women later in the century, for example at Cheltenham Ladies' College founded in the 1880s.

Yet the focus on proper education as well as upon manly Christianity was a problem. The dichotomy was that for many, lessons in chapel were subtly undermined by what they discovered later in the sciences or studied in the classics. From science they saw a very different world from the one traditionally depicted by the Church or in the Bible. For example, geology was forcing the abandonment of the biblical account and timing of creation. In the classics, especially in the works of Homer and Caesar, they saw vigorous empire builders and warriors whose beliefs and achievements owed nothing to Christianity.

For these young men and women Christianity was found to be lacking. The nineteenth century is therefore in part a search by these people who were trained for a mission. They went out to rule the Empire, to govern Britain, to become captains of industry and to staff the universities for the sacred. They went with a sense of sacred duty and history to satisfy a desire to feel part of something greater than themselves – a desire not always satisfied by Christianity.

IMPERIAL DESTINY

Into this vacuum came a host of new expressions and explorations of the sacred, of which possibly the strongest was that which America called Manifest Destiny, but which Britain called Imperial Duty or Destiny. In its crudest form, it was expressed by jingoistic Imperial nationalism and religion as, for example, in the words of General Sir Garnet Wolseley who said: 'A nation without glory, is like a man without courage, a woman without virtue. Those who in youth learn to value it as a holy possession are, as life goes on, inspired by its influence. It becomes, eventually, a sort of national religion.'[8]

Some went further, linking free trade with the will of God as yet another example of God at work through the Empire or the West. For example, Rutherford Alcock, one of the British consuls appointed to the Chinese ports, forcibly opened to foreign trade in the 1842 Treaty of Nanking following the first Opium War between Britain and China said: 'commerce is the true herald of civilisation . . . the human agency appointed under a Divine dispensation to work out man's emancipation from the thraldom and evils of a savage existence.'[9]

The concept of Imperial Duty is perhaps most startlingly expressed by one who might not have been expected to hold such views, but who was a product of the forces of the times that I have described: John Ruskin. He was brought up in a loving and very Bible-centred evangelical home and never lost his feel for that tradition, but his first visit to the Continent revealed to him the artistic and cultural riches of Catholicism. This discovery broke the mould of certainty that his upbringing had given him. He remained faithful, however, to his background and despite being attracted by Catholicism, did not convert. In the 1850s his faith suffered from the ideas about evolution that were developing at the time and in particular from the discoveries of the geologists about the age of the planet. He described how distressing he found these, all those geologists and 'their dreadful hammers'. In this he reflected the ambiguity of many Victorians to evolution. They liked its social determinism, which put white people at the top of the evolutionary tree, but they feared the loss of a more comforting cosmology and purpose which Christianity embodied in the Creation story, but which was singularly missing from evolution.

Ruskin was also deeply attracted to and involved in socialism. He was also one of the founders of the Working Men's College – now known as Ruskin College – and lectured at Working Men's Institutes up and down the land. His religious views were never quite clear, for he oscillated between old-fashioned evangelical biblicism and a sort of mystical religion of beauty, inspired but not directed by Catholicism. He was attracted to spiritualism – a movement dating from 1848, which by 1882 had developed into the Society for Psychical Research. It sympathetically explored trances, spirit possession and mediums – and he toyed with all sorts of somewhat odd theories such as phrenology and séances. He was a deeply committed man, with the highest principles, who used learning to free others from ignorance and oppression. He taught many to love beauty, to build creatively and to rise above their own expectations. He was to some extent a man looking for a reason for his energies and commitments. The Church never quite gave him that. It is in this context, shared by many intellectuals of his time, that the following statement needs to be seen and understood. Ruskin wrote:

> There is a destiny now possible to us, the highest ever set before a nation to be accepted or refused ... Will you youths of England make your country again a royal throne of kings, a sceptred isle, for all the world a source of light, a centre of peace; a mistress of learning and of the Arts, faithful guardians of time-honoured principles?[10]

The idea that it was destiny, a force greater than just history or opportunism, that had given Britain the greatest empire in history, was to underpin much of what happened in the last half of the nineteenth century. Referring to this destiny, Kipling famously described its responsibilities:

Take up the White Man's burden-
And reap his old reward:
The blame of those ye better.
The hate of those ye guard.

Combined with this sense of destiny was the concept of an essentially sacred Empire. This was an extraordinary transformation. For the first half of the nineteenth century the growth of the Empire had been considered dubious at best. India only became a responsibility of the Crown when it was necessary to take over from the corrupt and moribund East India Company. Many opposed the taking of lands in foreign parts and asked why we should do so. The Cambridge historian J.R. Seeley looked back in 1883 and wistfully commented, 'We seem, as it were, to have conquered and peopled half the world in a fit of absence of mind.' Prime ministers resisted the idea – Gladstone spent much of his political life fighting against the growth of the Empire, and Palmerston saw the taking of other people's lands as none of our business. He famously rejected the attempts to make war on China, but when it happened against his express wishes, he denounced the taking of Hong Kong.

Yet by the end of the nineteenth century Britain ruled nearly a quarter of the globe, from Canada to Australia, from vast chunks of Africa to India, and her rule was seen in mystical terms. Ruskin set the tone, but perhaps the clearest expression is found in that most peculiar of hymns, 'I vow to thee my country' by Sir Cecil Spring-Rice. The first verse seems to have completely dethroned God and replaced Him with Britain:

I vow to thee, my country, all earthly things above,
Entire and whole and perfect, the service of my love:
The love that asks no question, the love that stands the test,
That lays upon the altar the dearest and the best;
The love that never falters, the love that pays the price,
The love that makes undaunted the final sacrifice.

This nonsense fed a generation or more of those in search of the sacred, for whom the Empire filled a void. This vision of Empire was also fed by a tremendous sense of superiority, which manifested itself in seeing

Britain in particular, and Christian Europe in general, as the highest evolution possible of thought and belief, practice and intellect. For example, the frontispiece of the Revd J.G. Wood's *The Natural History of Man*, published in 1870, is very illuminating. It shows a white man, calmly seated, with a Bible propped up on his knee, expounding to a range of docile and decorated savages, who are offering him goods. Behind him, standing in rapt attention are Chinese, Siamese and Arabian people. Behind them are more figures, becoming more barbaric and savage the further away you get from the white man with his Bible, until they can be seen fighting. Likewise, the series *The Faiths of the World* (undated but from *c.* 1880), compiled by the Revd James Gardiner, opens with this ringing affirmation:

> The Religion of God is one, but the Religions of man are many. The one God-derived religion, Christianity, stands separate and apart as it were from all the others. It not only is, but on comparison with others is seen to be infinitely superior to them, and is shown thereby to be alone the product of Divine inspiration.[11]

The linking of Christian evangelism to trade and Empire was not universally considered to be a good thing. Throughout its history the East India Company (1600–1857) had Anglican chaplains in such places as India, Indonesia and the China coast. But with the odd exception, none of these clergy felt it incumbent upon them to try to preach 'to the natives'. Indeed, the Company, as good Anglicans, expressly forbade such action, considering it impertinent. It was only from 1833 onwards when India was, by Parliamentary decree, opened to missionaries, that the situation changed. Missionaries poured in and the old balance of tolerance changed, sometimes for the good, for example *suttee* (the burning of widows) was banned in India, and sometimes for the bad, for example aggressive missionary activity was one of the triggers of the 1857 Indian Mutiny.

The missionary societies often faced strong opposition from the mainstream churches – especially the Church of England. Many felt that if a people had a faith, they should be left alone with it. However, the dramatic stories of Livingstone's missionary adventures in Africa fired the imaginations of many and gained the missionary movement respectability.

The Empire also embodied that other great belief of the Victorian era: progress. The great historian Lord Macaulay put this notion into respectable intellectual clothes in his *The History of England*, published in 1848 – a sort of secular version of the old sacred histories of Gildas, Bede and even a hint of Geoffrey of Monmouth – though Macaulay would have hated that thought. In his preface, Macaulay wrote:

> Yet, unless I greatly deceived myself, the general effect of this chequered narrative will be to excite thankfulness in all religious minds, and hope in the breasts of all patriots. For the history of our country during the last 160 years is eminently the history of physical, of moral, and of intellectual improvement. Those who compare the age on which their lot has fallen with a golden age which exists only in their imagination may talk of degeneracy and decay: but no man who is correctly informed as to the past will be disposed to take a morose or desponding view of the present.[12]

The desire for a belief that the world was getting better created its own deity: Manifest Destiny/Imperial Duty. It was the destiny and duty of the whites to rule the blacks because evolutionarily they were clearly – to Victorian scientists at least – the most advanced. This belief is crisply expressed by the Revd J.G. Wood in his monumental *The Natural History of Man*, where in the volume *An Account of the manners and customs of the uncivilised races of men*, covering Australia, New Zealand, Polynesia, America, Asia and 'ancient Europe', he says, 'Following up the principle of taking the least civilised races in succession, we naturally pass to the great continent of Australia and its adjacent islands.'[13]

It was destiny that of all the white nations, Britain, with its 'traditions of freedom', should be the most advanced of the white nations. It was destiny that being the most advanced people in the world – in a sense a new chosen people – Britain should have the best scientists, army, inventors, intellectuals, writers and democratic system in the world. Indeed, some did actually believe that Britain was the chosen land of the chosen people. The British Israelite movement traces its origins to Richard Brothers, who in 1793 launched a new religion: the Anglo-Israelites. From this came the British Israelite Movement which taught – indeed still teaches – that the Israelites of the Bible and the Jews of today are two different people. British Israelites claim that the true Israelites are the British and that therefore the chosen race is none other than the Anglo-Saxons, who now should take their rightful place as the centre of world history. At the end of the nineteenth century this theory attracted a number of wealthy and influential people of the Establishment, fusing as it did the anglocentric vision, the Empire, religion, bits of Christianity and a sense of chosen purpose in history.

The Empire, Britain and Queen Victoria herself became part of a new mythology of sacred Britain, charged with a sacred mission to improve the world. Historian Jan Morris puts this well:

> This was a novel kind of religion for the English. Not since the days of Elizabeth I had they revered a monarch so, or responded with such devotion to the spirit of kingship, and it was especially in the imperial context that Victoria achieved this charisma. The Empire gave her the eponym Great White Queen, endowing her with a legendary force not unlike Moby Dick's, and it was the Empire which made of her an unorthodox Earth-Mother, ample, experienced, kindly, wise, to whose serge skirts the heathen or ignorant might cling in sanctuary, and beneath whose stern admonishment tyrants and rebels alike might reform themselves.[14]

As the unofficial national anthem of this period put it:

> *When Britain first, at Heaven's Command,*
> *Arose from out the azure main,*
> *This was the charter of the land,*
> *And guardian angels sung the strain,*
> *'Rule Britannia, rule the waves;*
> *Britons never will be slaves'.*

The Empire also had its place within another strand of thought which was quietly undermining the old sacred visions and role of the Church. The belief in Progress.

Evolution meant many things to many people. Contrary to popular imagination, it did not really rock the religious world as science as such. What really disturbed people was the concept of progress, of improvement. For if things were getting better, if we were becoming more civilised and more learned, more inventive and so forth, then what role did the past have in all this? Why should the writings of Jews of the past – be that Old Testament or New – be of significance to a British Empire which had invented electric lights and the telegraph? Were not religion in general and Christianity in particular simply too old, too non-British and too out of date to be relevant? This strand was to run for decades under the fabric of supposedly Christian Britain. It was one of the reasons some Army Officers gave for leaving Christianity and adopting Islam – a more recent faith!

Progress, duty, honour, might, Empire and knowledge were the creed of some. Struggle, labour rights, humane treatment and socialism were the concerns of others. Both had their religious dimension, and both their sacred role.

EASTERN WISDOM

During the Victorian period many were able to have previously unimaginable contact with other religions and faith traditions and to learn about them. In 1875, Max Muller, Professor of Comparative Philology in Oxford, launched the *Sacred Books of the East* series, a massive academic effort that brought to the reading public's attention some of the most profound non-Christian religious texts in the world. These texts had almost without exception never been translated into English before. Suddenly it was possible to read the Words of the Buddha, study Confucius, enter the mythological world of the Zoroastrians and voyage through faith on the songs of the *Rig Veda*. Some of the books became bestsellers overnight, especially the Chinese and Hindu volumes. Others were not quite so popular. The introduction to one of the books must count as the best put-down of a text by a translator ever:

> The translator of the Satapatha-brahmana can be under no illusion as to the reception his production is likely to meet with at the hand of the general reader. In the whole range of literature few works are probably less calculated to excite the interest of any outside the very limited number of specialists than the ancient theological writings of the Hindus, known by the name of Brahmanas. For wearisome prolixity of exposition, characterised by dogmatic assertion and a flimsy symbolism rather than by serious reasoning, these works are perhaps not equalled anywhere.[15]

Generally, however, in the search for faith by Victorian Britons, these books played a crucial role. Not so much because of what they actually said, because few read them thoroughly or with any real understanding, but because they made 'sacred books', especially those with an Eastern tinge, very popular. From this popularity arose a number of new religious movements, which claimed to bring together the wisdom of the East and the West. Often these movements claimed to have received direct teachings from 'Masters' whose habitat ranged from 'the Mountains of Tibet', through to 'Native American Teachers' or 'Masters on another star'. Such movements played upon the sense of loss, insecurity and desire for the sacred, which for many was not fulfilled by conventional religion.

General Younghusband, who as a stout evangelical and Imperialist had served the Empire from South Africa through India to China, had a mystical experience after leading the British march into Tibet in 1904. It came at a time when he had been questioning whether Christianity was adequate for the new world that was appearing. In 1912 he wrote a book called *Within*, in the last paragraph of which he says:

> Then, generations hence . . . when we have given up the habit of incessantly looking without rather than within . . . then, may be, a pure God-Child will arise, more perfect even than Jesus. Intuitively he – or perhaps she – will see into the innermost core of things ... With the hot glow of Love this divinely-human Being will transfigure all the sordidness of life: make life's beauty shine forth in untarnished radiance; and send a note of poignant sweetness singing through the souls of men.[16]

Younghusband went on to become one of the great religious experimenters of his age, creating the World Congress of Faiths, the first real interfaith movement, in 1936. He also thought that he was destined to create a new Christ through a relationship with one of his followers. His abilities and confusion are typical, if somewhat dramatic, of their time.

The journey of Annie Besant is characteristic of many who participated in the new religious movements. Born in 1847, she had a conventional religious upbringing and married a clergyman when she was twenty. In 1873 they separated, because she had fallen for the teachings and probably for the person of Charles Bradlaugh, an atheist and the main prophet of secularism. Upon being elected MP in 1880 he refused to take the oath on the Bible. He was barred from the House, which prompted a major debate, lasting several months, on whether an atheist could be an MP. Eventually the ardent Christian Gladstone won the debate for Bradlaugh and he took his place. To Bradlaugh and Besant at the time, religion was the curse of the enlightened, progressive world. In 1889, however, Besant abandoned secularism and turned instead to the mystical teachings of Madam Blavatsky and the Theosophists, becoming a high priestess in 1891. Theosophical principles were drawn from sources that included ancient Egypt, Tibetan 'Masters', Hindu mythology, and the legends of Atlantis. The movement had a sizeable following and continued for decades. Its core was a mixture of beliefs, but included transmigration of souls, belief in a new master who would reveal the Truth to this age, and a powerful emphasis on the equality of all.

Although in earlier ages there were people whose imaginations were fired like this, such as James Naylor, the seventeenth-century Messiah of Bristol, never before had people had access to so many new religious ideas, texts, myths and personalities with which to feed their imagination. And, unlike in earlier ages, no one in the Victorian era was persecuted for having such beliefs. The tolerance of the previous century, seen by so many Enlightenment scholars and writers of the time as the death knell of religion and fanaticism, in fact paved the way for the rise of a plethora of religious ideas in the nineteenth century.

Secularism, even Deism, helped create a tolerance and even an indifference to faith, which meant nobody was too worried what you believed as long as it was not too socially embarrassing. In such a culture, the influence of other sacred traditions from the East fused with a mystical sense of science as revelation and with the notion of Destiny to create an ambience within which diversity, pluralism and eccentricity could flourish, an ideal situation for the sacred and religious ideals to grow.

THE SACRED IN CITY DESIGN

The humanly created environment tellingly illustrates some of the many ideas of the sacred in Victorian Britain. Most medieval cities and towns were either laid out with a basic Christian cosmology underlying them (thus, for example, the sacred area being in the east – as with Norwich, or the city laid out like a cross – as with Bristol) or the positions and dedications of churches wove a sacred mythology and geography around them. In the gardens and country houses of the Tudors, the breakdown of the old religious order and the rise of control and power were themes made explicit in places such as the garden of Little Moreton Hall. In the eighteenth century, the Order and Reason of the Deist deity were manifest in the architecture of Bath and the other great Georgian centres.

Yet, somewhat ironically for this age of mission and evangelism, no such sacred geography underlies Victorian urban planning. The Victorians built masses of churches, but they were in opposition to what else was built around them and the sacred was present purely in their artistic beauty – as we have seen in the Gothic Revival churches – not as part of a grander statement. Victorian building brought no inherent sacredness to an area: the great estates and suburbs the Victorians built at that time were relentlessly secular and devoid of any sense of something grander. Only occasionally does the religion of Empire appear in a cluster of street names, indicating that they were built when a new colony was founded or the Crimean War was being fought. To see the sacred in Victorian design you need to look elsewhere.

It is the public parks, a totally new concept first developed in the 1840s, that express the sacred in the Victorian landscape. Here the ordinary working person could escape the dirt, noise and fervour of the bustling industrial cities and find nature. The wandering paths, little hills and valleys, clumps of trees and undulating grasslands of the usual civic park embody a notion that nature is wild and free and that humanity needs to connect with this once in a while. Birchfields Park in Manchester is a good example. Opened in 1887, the park had to be fought for against the rapacious designs of the speculative builders who were developing the area. It was the City Council who decreed it should be built, and it is a delightful place of open space, streams, tree-lined avenues, dells and groves.

Such parks are sacred places, in the sense that they were the first manifestation of the cult or faith in nature *per se* which was to give rise to the National Trust and the environmental movement in the next 100 to 150 years. It was a faith that linked humanity to nature rather than

God. It built upon the Romantic movement, but whereas the Romantic movement had no specific plans or models for putting its beliefs and values into practice, the urban planners did. In creating urban parks they built upon the ideals of nature that Blake, amongst so many other poets, had explored. Wordsworth, for instance, laments humanity's separation from nature in his poem:

> *The world is too much with us; late and soon,*
> *Getting and spending, we lay waste our powers:*
> *Little we see in Nature that is ours;*
> *We have given our hearts away, a sordid boon!*
> *This Sea that bares her bosom to the moon;*
> *The winds that will be howling at all hours,*
> *And are up-gathered now like sleeping flowers;*
> *For this, for everything, we are out of tune;*
> *It moves us not – Great God! I'd rather be*
> *A Pagan suckled in a creed outworn;*
> *So might I, standing on this pleasant lea,*
> *Have glimpses that would make me less forlorn;*
> *Have sight of Proteus rising from the sea;*
> *Or hear old Triton blow his wreathed horn.*

John Davidson, in his poem 'London', captures the linking of the old sacred, St Paul's, with the reverence, and almost veneration of nature as equally sacred, especially when set against the smog and crowds of urban London:

> *Athwart the sky a lowly sigh*
> *From west to east the sweet wind carried*
> *The sun stood still on Primrose Hill;*
> *His light in all the city tarried:*
> *The clouds on viewless columns bloomed*
> *Like smouldering lilies unconsumed.*
> *'Oh sweetheart, see! how shadowy,*
> *Of some occult magician's rearing,*
> *Or swung in space of heaven's grace*
> *Dissolving, dimly reappearing,*
> *Afloat upon the ethereal tides*

St Paul's above the city rides!'
A rumour broke through the thin smoke
Enwreathing abbey, tower, and palace,
The parks, the squares, the thoroughfares,
The million-peopled lanes and alleys,
An ever-muttering prisoned storm,
The heart of London beating warm.

The second place to look for the sacred in Victorian cities is in part underground. The careful construction of sewers and waterworks expresses the Victorian quest to clean the cities. This included the defeat of cholera, which killed hundreds of thousands in the 1830s to 1850s, and the building of decent housing. In this environmental work one can find the spirit of service and of 'the good of all' which arose from both the evangelical religious impulse and from the secular, scientific impulse, and became, in a sense, a sacred mission.

This mission is passionately expressed in a book called *In Darkest England and the Way Out*, written by General Booth, the founder of the Salvation Army. His title deliberately picks up on the missionary movement's desire to 'save' 'darkest Africa'. He sees the living conditions of the poor in 'darkest England' as worse than those of the Africans. He writes:

If, after full and exhaustive consideration, we come to the deliberate conclusion that nothing can be done, and that it is the inevitable and inexorable destiny of thousands of Englishmen to be brutalized into worse than beasts by the condition of their environment, so be it. But if, on the contrary, we are unable to believe that this awful slough, which engulfs the manhood and womanhood of generation after generation, is incapable of removal; and if the heart and intellect of mankind alike revolt against the fatalism of despair, then, indeed, it is time, and high time, that the question were faced in no mere dilettante spirit, but with a resolute determination to make an end of the crying scandal of our age.[17]

By the early years of the twentieth century, a wide range of sacred ideas, groups, notions, hopes and fears was circulating in Britain. It was a land that saw itself as sacred, and sacred for the good of the world, a land where duty and honour had risen to religious levels of intensity, but where service to the poor and the struggle for equality and justice were also part of the sacred vision. It was a land where, on the whole, people expected the world to get better and better. It was with great confidence that the Victorians entered the twentieth century. Within less than twenty years, virtually all that confidence was gone, blown to pieces on the Western Front.

CHAPTER SEVENTEEN

SHOCK OF THE
UNTHINKABLE – THE
PAST 100 YEARS

I AM TEMPTED WHEN ADDRESSING THE TASK of commenting on the
sacred history of the last 100 years to echo the words of the twentieth-
century Chinese Marxist, Chou En Lai, who, when asked what he
thought of the French Revolution, replied, 'It is too early to tell.' At one
level we are too close to the events; indeed, we are still part of the events.
It was, after all, only when the Iron Curtain fell in 1989 that the Second
World War really came to an end. The advent of information technology
may be significant or it may just be another way of sending letters and
making telephone calls, and about as revolutionary. Terrorism may be
the new universal threat, or more likely, the struggle for access to drinking
water will be the cause of future wars. We are too close to tell.

What is clear, however, is that the sacred has been through difficult
times in the last 100 years, but is still much more powerful than many
would have us believe. It has weathered and survived Marxism, fascism
and even the advent of Freudian psychoanalysis. We have heard that
religion is a tool for class oppression, the weak morality of a decadent
society, and a father-centred illusion, but it still survives. It has just
about survived two world wars and the creation of nuclear weapons,

which have endowed humanity with apocalyptic powers earlier cultures ascribed solely to God. Worldwide, there has been more persecution of believers from more world faiths than at any time in history. From the Soviet Union through China to the genocides of the Armenians, Holocaust and Cambodians to name but a few, Christians, Muslims, Buddhists, Taoists, Jews and indigenous traditions have been persecuted by ideologies and by sheer brutality.

THE MYTH OF PROGRESS

Yet the twentieth century began with such hopes. The Darwinian idea of evolution and progress – that the world was getting better just as evolution produced 'better' species – had shaped the British Imperial dream, and it had shaped the Americans notion of their own Manifest Destiny. The phrase was first used in 1845 by the journalist John L. O'Sullivan as justification for the USA spreading across the whole of North America, absorbing states such as Texas, California and Oregon. It was later extended to cover the worldwide role of the USA – a kind of anti-imperialist counter culture that then became imperialistic when it seized the lands of the old Spanish Empire in Cuba and the Philippines.

In what was perceived as a struggle for the Soul of the world, for many, it was clear that either humanistic ideologies, such as Marxism, socialism and the triumph of free trade, or religious forces, such as Christianity, were destined by history and evolution to rule the world. In 1911, one of the first Labour MPs and the future first Labour Prime Minister, James Ramsay MacDonald could write the following as his final piece of text in a book on socialism:

> But as these changes in organization, these fluctuations between individualism and sociality, serve the end of human liberty and progress, so the motive force behind socialism is not merely mechanical perfection and social economy, but life itself. Hence around it are ranged the living impulses of religion, of ethics, of art, of literature those creative impulses which fill man's heart from an inexhaustible store of hope and aspiration, and which make him find not only his greatest happiness but also the very reason for life itself, in pursuing the pilgrim road which mounting up over the hills and beyond the horizon, winds towards the ideal.[1]

No clearer illustration is needed that for some the sacred had joined hands with the social and were seen by many as part and parcel of each other – a peculiarly British tradition within the Labour, socialist and even the communist parties (one of the founders of the British Communist Party was the Vicar of Thaxted).

Equally, the watchword of the Protestant missionary movement, at its greatest extent in terms of funds and personnel at the turn of the century, was 'The Evangelisation of the world in this Generation'. And they genuinely thought it was possible. This sense of optimism, of history moving inexorably towards a better future and the triumph of a world view – in this case Christianity – is well captured in this late-nineteenth-century hymn:

God is working his purpose out as year succeeds to year,
God is working his purpose out and the time is drawing near;
nearer and nearer draws the time, the time that shall surely be,
when the earth shall be filled with the glory of God as the waters cover the seas.
A.C. Ainger

For fourteen years into the twentieth century, this hope fed and sustained many in Britain. It also fed the various new religious movements. These included the theosophists, whose optimism for the future was founded on a mixture of hopes for a new master teacher suited to the more enlightened beings that they believed we were becoming. Theosophy also manifested itself in practical work, such as for the freedom of India. They also included the Baha'is, whose prophets writing in the late nineteenth century foresaw a world of people living as one family and believed that humanity was growing wiser and more mature; and the Hermetic Order of the Golden Dawn, who believed that because humanity was getting better and wiser the mysteries of the past were being reintroduced and secret masters were guiding humanity towards a world of perfect peace and happiness. All was going to be wonderful, happy, equal and joyful.

Meanwhile, as the then Archbishop of Canterbury, Randall Davidson, scurried around London seeing his friendship with the Prime Minister and the Cabinet as a sign that the Church was being taken seriously by the State, Lenin was working away in London as well, but was perhaps more in touch with reality than the Archbishop – or equally deluded. For some of his time he was in London planning the most radical challenge to all authority since the French Revolution, a challenge that was to shake religions around the world. He too believed that through his work a better world would emerge and that this, once again, was inevitable because history was moving inexorably towards such a communist world. In 1913 Lenin could write:

> The Marxist doctrine is omnipotent because it is true. It is comprehensive and harmonious, and provides men with an integral world outlook irreconcilable with any form of superstition, reaction, or defence of bourgeois oppression. It is the legitimate successor to the best that man produced in the nineteenth century, as represented by German philosophy, English political economy, and French socialism ... The proletariat is becoming enlightened and educated by waging its class struggle; it is ridding itself of the prejudices of bourgeois society; it is rallying its ranks ever more closely and is learning to gauge the measure of its successes; it is steeling its forces and is growing irresistibly.[2]

It was a heady time for utopians, dreamers, the hopeful and those who saw the future in terms of great ideals and aspirations. Science was improving the world and making everyone more rational, sensible and wise. What could possibly go wrong?

In 1914 the dreams collapsed. The psychological impact of the First World War on every aspect of society is almost impossible to imagine today. The greatest 'civilised' nations of the world, the heartlands of Christianity that were set to spiritually conquer the world, revealed themselves as tribal, brutal, inhuman and irrational as any imagined 'primitive' tribe in Africa. The so-called civilised nations destroyed each other with a violence and hatred that shocked the whole of the world. The moral, spiritual and social standing of Europe, and especially the British Empire, fell from its pedestal and was never to be re-erected. Lenin's belief, expressed above, that the workers would no longer follow the jingoistic lead of the bourgeois crumbled into dust as the International, the international meeting of socialist and communist groups, fell apart and split along the lines of the war itself.

As the scale of destruction and social collapse became clear, the belief in the inexorable progress of humanity towards greater maturity and a better future was shattered. Today, with only really the exception of the Baha'is, who still believe in the myth of inexorable progress, no religious or social movement would express their hopes in such determinist and optimistic ways. The dream of utopia was smashed by the First World War and then usurped by the twin evils of communism as a state system of control and terror, and by the rise of fascism. The utopian vision of the early twentieth century has been challenged continually by: the Holocaust in the 1940s; Stalin's outrages; the excesses of the Cultural Revolution in China in the 1960s and 1970s; subsequent genocides such as Cambodia in the 1970s and Rwanda in the 1990s; and the extremism of countries such as Afghanistan.

What did all this do to the sacred in Britain? To answer that, let us look at Sacred Trinity Church in Salford, Greater Manchester. This old parish church stands in the thick of industrial Salford; only the River Irwell separates Salford from the city centre of Manchester.

It was to this church that Engels came in the 1850s to write up his notes, which eventually became the Marxist classic *The Condition of the Working Class in England*. He graphically describes the experience of visiting Salford and especially the area around Sacred Trinity:

> The narrow side lanes and courts of Chapel Street, Greengate, and Gravel Lane have certainly never been cleansed since they were built . . . and if any one takes the trouble to pass through these lanes, and glance through the open doors and windows into the houses and cellars, he can convince himself afresh with every step that the workers of Salford live in dwellings in which cleanliness and comfort are impossible.[3]

This is still one of the poorest areas in Britain today, and in 1914 it was a parish of staggering poverty and deprivation. Then the war came and Salford men signed up by the thousands. Many thousands more would have signed up had they been fit enough, but poverty, pollution and ill-health meant that a considerable number of men from the parish of Sacred Trinity were turned down. There were so many in fact that the Government was shocked into looking into the reasons why. It was one of the factors that lead eventually to the creation of the welfare state and the National Heath Service.

The Salford soldiers marched past the church on their way to the stations that were to take them to the south and across the sea to France. Then the telegrams started coming home, hundreds upon hundreds of them, each bringing its dread message of the death of a loved one in the trenches. Inside Sacred Trinity a war memorial hangs upon the wall. Upon it are written the names of 400 Salford men who died. Such a number would be shocking enough if they were the list of those lost from a parish in the four years of the First World War, but these 400 died on just one day: 1 July 1916 at the Battle of Thiepval.

There are some 18,000 Anglican parishes in England. Of these only the 'lucky 28', such as the tiny hamlet parish of Middleton-on-the-Hill, Herefordshire, did not lose at least one man killed in the First World War. The sheer scale of human loss, suffering and misery and the resulting disruption and dislocation of human lives that resulted has dimmed with time. One only needs to read a war poet or a biography of the period to appreciate the sheer numbing awfulness of this war.

The Church and indeed virtually all the religious structures of the day were chaff in the wind before such purposeless suffering. Most within the Churches saw the war initially as a holy war and as worthy of Christian chivalry. Indeed, God was seen by many as clearly being on the British side. This is explicitly stated in a fascinating pamphlet called *How God Won the War* first published in 1935. It tells how 'A Day of Trouble' had come upon the British because the Germans had broken through in late August 1914 to the area around Mons:

> It was realised that a 'Day of Trouble' had arrived, and that God alone could help us. Churches were crowded with the whole of the British Nation at prayer.
>
> Then occurred the event afterwards known as the appearance of the 'Angels of Mons', in answer to National Prayer . . . While a detachment of British soldiers was retiring through Mons under very heavy German artillery . . . they knelt behind a hastily-erected barricade . . . Suddenly firing on both sides STOPPED DEAD and a sudden silence fell.
>
> Looking over their barrier, the astonished British saw four or five wonderful BEINGS much bigger than men, between themselves and the halted Germans. They were white-robed and bareheaded, and seemed rather to float than stand . . . Next thing the British knew was that the Germans were retreating in great disorder.[4]

Nonsense such as this might have helped if the war had been over by Christmas 1914. It was not and for every vision of an angel, millions died terrible, meaningless deaths. As the true horror of the war began to emerge, most found it unbearable and retreated into moral crusades. The poet and army officer Siegfried Sassoon told the story of arriving back in England shattered by the war through wounds and psychological trauma. As he was carried off the train at Waterloo, a clergyman approached him and thrust a leaflet into his hand condemning sexual laxity and the spread of venereal diseases. Nothing captures more starkly the degree to which the religious could not handle the war. This failure, so graphically depicted in the names of the dead of one day in Sacred Trinity, Salford, or in the story told by Sassoon, was a massive failure of the sacred at a time when it was most needed.

Not only had the myth of the perfection and increasing maturity of the human race been lost on the fields of France and in the trenches, but also there was nothing much to put in its place. Into this gap came the spiritualists, offering an opportunity for last words to the dead via mediums and séances, a chance for grieving parents, siblings and lovers to say farewell. Sir Arthur Conan Doyle and Rudyard Kipling were amongst the many who found solace through this strangely British form of spiritual contact with the dead. Virtually all other forms of the sacred had failed, as in the end did spiritualism itself, discredited and spent as a force long before the next wave of horror, the Second World War, erupted.

In other countries, revolution followed the First World War. Russia, Hungary, Germany, Austria, bits of the old Austro-Hungarian Empire and China, all suffered revolts of one kind or another. Britain avoided a revolution for the simple reason that the disillusionment of the war, the collapse of an all-embracing utopian vision, was taken seriously and deeply by the British. Many had drawn comfort from seeing themselves as the chosen instruments of God, of Manifest Destiny and Imperial Duty, and these had failed, mythologies and ideologies gone bad. There was no way we were going to commit ourselves again to some grandiose scheme, communist or fascist, by which we felt we could determine the future. For the British, the shattering of the myths of the white man's superiority and of the inevitability of progress was the shattering of all such great myths. In that sense, the British were unwittingly post-modern, sceptical of mega-narratives long before anyone else. This distrust of grand schemes, and a cynicism and wariness of idealism, still marks British thinking.

The social and political history of Britain between the wars is a strange one. It was a nation that no longer trusted the forces of conservatism, yet could not give itself to the vision of socialism which MacDonald espoused in 1911, in part in fear of communism and Russia, and in part in fear of utopian ideals. Indeed, MacDonald himself was to find the struggle for the vision of a socialist Britain too much in the late 1920s and early 1930s. He found himself in a time of economic crisis in 1931 creating a largely conservative National Government, which lead to him being derided by his own party.

Germany's militarisation, with a clear sense of purpose, attracted many within Germany and many within Britain, from both the Catholic and Protestant Churches, from the newer religious movements looking for new masters and teachers and, perhaps more notoriously, from the aristocracy and even royal family. Here was a nation that seemed to have found a purpose. Fortunately, the distrust of grand schemes held most sections of British society back from seeking a similar sense of purpose here. Towards the end of the 1930s the main concern was to avoid war – which given that all the main leaders and most of the people at the time had seen the awfulness of the First World War, was entirely understandable.

Throughout this time, the Empire was held together with determination, but was increasingly being challenged by figures such as Gandhi. Although the Empire did not begin to fold until after the Second World War, the writing was on the wall. In India, the jewel in the imperial crown, Gandhi and others were making it ever clearer from the 1920s onwards that the British were going to have to leave. In the Middle East, the British attempts failed to establish the Empire through the lands mandated under the auspices of the League of Nations after the First World War. Palestine was a problem from the outset and it was clear that British rule was only going to be transient.

As a large part of the rest of the world began to ask the British to go home, so they needed to find some meaning in the developments and their new place in the world. To a great extent it was the romancing of Britain that helped. In the 1920s Britain was beginning to be seen by some as a strangely holy place. For the first time since the great British sacred myths of Geoffrey of Monmouth and *Le Morte d'Arthur* that had so influenced the Tudors, Britain was searching for a new mythological understanding of itself. For example ley lines – supposedly showing how ancient Britons had known about forces of power in the landscape – were first invented by Alfred Watkins in his book *The Old Straight Track*. I say invented because unfortunately they have no substance in either history or geography, other than the remarkable fact that one can draw a straight line between any two sites and probably hit three or four others by chance on the way.

In the 1920s and 1930s the writer and academic Margaret Murray, claiming to detect an unbroken line of paganism in British folklore, created a sense of Britain as a mystical old land in touch with ancient truths through her books such as *The Witch Cult in Western Europe* (1921) and *The God of the Witches* (1931). This eventually prepared the ground for the rise from the 1960s onwards of the increased interest in pagan religion in Britain. Drawing upon an astonishingly wide range of sources from around the world, writers within this genre have manufactured what has been described as the only religion ever given to the world by the British. It is rooted in both a genuine desire to find a greater, deeper and more significant spirituality and in a romantic notion of the past, deeply involved in a British nationalism and romanticism, as captured in this quote from Vivianne Crowley:

> It is the task of Paganism today to give to those who seek its ways the inner knowledge, light, energy and peace with which to live our lives in harmony with one another and with all living creation and to answer the eternal questions of humankind: 'Who am I? What must I do to live well and honourably? What is the meaning of the mystery of life and of the divine?
>
> Through the dark ages of the past millennia, the truth of Paganism has been hidden from us – buried beneath the rubble of our desolate temples, hidden beneath the churches of another and alien faith. Now the call has rung out from the Rainbow bridge of Bifrost between the Worlds. Let us rise to answer its summons.[5]

Wicca, and the collection of beliefs that might best be described as neo-paganism, is another quintessentially British invention. It is not of itself an actual continuation of some surviving paganism, as has been amply shown by writers from Ronald Hutton to Keith Thomas. However, it claims places of great British antiquity for its own and weaves around them the most wonderful series of ideas, stories and notions. Take Glastonbury Tor, for example. In the exotic and always fascinatingly irrelevant shops of New Age Glastonbury, you will find any number of books on the Goddess and Glastonbury; on the priestesses and the Tor; on the chalice as the female image; on Wicca and the spirals of the Tor – and so on and so on. Very little if any of it is actually historically accurate, but it is very comforting.

Wicca and the other romancing of British traditions, such as the surge in Arthurian novels, stories and 'histories' which emerged in the 1920s, represent the retreat of the sacred of Britain from being assumed to be the norm for the whole of the world to being something which helped the British re-establish their own identity at home. It also served to reconcile the British to the horrors and angst caused by the First World War, overcome the loss of faith in the Empire and find some sort of new meaning. To a certain extent, the crisis of the loss of faith in Empire, the collapse of belief in progress and of science as being invincible, can be compared to the experience of the British at the collapse of the Roman Empire and the subsequent Anglo-Saxon invasions.

On both occasions we have needed to reinterpret ourselves and the circumstances affecting our lives. Each time a larger world in which we had felt we had a place and were secure fell apart we had to contend with loss of land, scale and grandeur. It is noticeable that the pagan movement bears a resemblance to the British Church that Bede so criticised. It is essentially a very British movement and while some of the more thoughtful members of the various movements see links to other peoples and lands, it is a nationalistic movement, with perhaps more in common with the extreme views of the far right than it would like to think. To describe Christianity as an 'alien faith', as Crowley does above, is a nonsense and is rooted in a somewhat disturbing notion of what is truly British. It was T.S. Eliot who put his finger on what drives people into mythic pasts and fantasies. Following Hiroshima, he said 'Human kind cannot bear very much reality'.

By the time the Second World War came, Britain was a very different place from the imperialistic nation of 1914. It had remoulded itself as a heroic ancient culture, which had passed on its wisdom to others around the world and which now wished to live quietly, almost in retirement. The sacred was no longer something the British were exporting. Instead it was something we were recovering and also something we were receiving from other cultures and faiths. Flowing beneath this was a strong strand of nationalism, of patriotism, the inevitable consequence of the sense of being forced back from the forefront of the wider world stage due to the rise of Germany, the power of the USSR and the surges of nationalism in China and India, together with the loss of confidence in ourselves which was such a hallmark of the 1930s. Churchill summed this up in Parliament on 12 November 1936: 'So they [the Government] go on in strange paradox, decided only to be undecided, resolved to be irresolute, adamant for drift, solid for fluidity, all-powerful for impotence.'

It was also Churchill who best summed up where the British now found themselves when the Second World War was at its worst. On 4 June 1940, when the German air force was within sight of defeating the RAF, and troops were poised on the other side of the Channel, Churchill made this famous speech: 'We shall defend our island, whatever the cost may be, we shall fight on the beaches, we shall fight on the landing grounds, we shall fight in the fields and in the streets, we shall fight in the hills; we shall never surrender.'

His vision was of the British defending their island, and these powerful words echoed the sense of Britain standing alone and in doing so standing for all that was best. It was a very different mentality from the 'go and get them' approach of the First World War.

The Second World War saw Britain fighting not really specifically for the defence of others or for the sake of the Jews but for survival against forces that were now greater than she was. The fight for survival led to the question of the relevance of the Empire and ultimately forced the British to reflect upon themselves as an embattled island people whose own land was sacred to the cause of freedom. It prepared the way for many to feel deep sympathy with the similar aspirations, visions and beliefs of those who sought to remove us from their own 'sacred' lands: India, Burma, Africa and so forth. The war also focused attention on our needs at home for labour and skills. Thus the Empire ceased to be somewhere we sent our young men and women to serve after the war, and became instead a pool of cheap, compliant labour that could be brought to Britain to help maintain a standard of living we had developed.

The war once again taught us to distrust grand schemes and omnipotent/powerful leaders. Nazis, communists and fascists were not for us. Instead the war gave many people the sense that our role was to challenge such powers and it is significant that, to the astonishment of our allies such as America and the USSR, the 1945 General Election did not vote Churchill and the Tories back in, but instead elected the most radical political party Britain has ever had: the Labour Government of Prime Minister Clem Attlee. This Government nationalised key industries such as coal, the railways and water, and granted independence to India in 1947 and Burma in 1948. It was the clearest statement possible that Britain now saw itself as a very different place from the Empire-builders of the past. From now onwards the common good and the rights of other peoples were to be held as of such fundamental importance that no subsequent Conservative Government could turn the tide, nor tried to do so. Britain had discovered a new sense of her own importance and with many fits and starts this was to shape politics from 1945 onwards.

Mythologically we reinvented the reasons for the Second World War. It had begun in confusion due to obligations towards Poland and against the expressed wishes of the then Prime Minister in 1939. However, following the fall of the Nazis and in particular with the discovery of the concentration camps, it was recast as a moral crusade. What had become a struggle to survive when it looked as if Britain alone against the Nazis might fall in the dark days of 1940 subsequently became a struggle to uphold democracy and freedom against tyranny. Upon this basis Britain was unable to gainsay the independence movements which were surging through the Empire at exactly the same time.

The British emerged from the Second World War with a profound sense of their own moral importance. It was to some extent also a sacred sense in that it saw the principles of Christian virtue, fused with a vague sense of British values such as fair play, democracy and freedom as its source, which made them feel special once again, but for very different reasons, as they had felt under the spell of the Empire. However there was now a force abroad that more profoundly challenged the basic assumptions of our place, role, significance and understanding of the sacred than anything since the collapse of the Roman Empire or since the failure of the stone circles religion.

The advent of nuclear power with its capacity to destroy life on earth was as cataclysmic an event as any invasion or plague of the past. Indeed, more so, for in the past destruction had been limited. Now we had the power for total or virtually total destruction. What did this mean for the sacred if we now had the power to end time and history – a power formally only ascribable to God?

There is a wonderfully moving story of one of the greatest philosophers Britain produced in the twentieth century. Professor Donald MacKinnon was an eccentric Cambridge genius whose wit and wisdom were like rapiers, even if he resembled a mammoth on the outside. He realised, within days, the significance of dropping bombs on Japan, and when the Bishop of Oxford at that time stood up at a public dinner and praised the invention of the bombs and their use, MacKinnon crawled along behind the High Table and bit the Bishop on the ankle.

MacKinnon saw that the unleashing of the knowledge of the atom and the creation of nuclear weapons heralded a new stage in the sacred worldwide. He realised that for the first time we had the power to act as God and bring time, history and human existence on this planet to an end. We could enact the Apocalypse. Arthur Koestler, who as a writer worked with mythologies and within science fiction, comes down to earth with a bump when he says:

> If I were asked to name the most important date in the history of the human race, I would answer without hesitation 6 August 1945. From the dawn of consciousness until 6 August 1945, man had to live with the prospect of his death as an individual; since the day when the first atomic bomb outshone the sun over Hiroshima, he has had to live with the prospect of his extinction as a species.

MacKinnon had immediately grasped the significance. The world was no longer a safe place. Where once God or the gods decided when the world would end, now we could enact it thoughtlessly. Death could rain down on us at any time, and at times the Cold War made this seem very likely. I recall clearly the Cuban missile crisis of 1962, and the terrors it evoked. My parents, along with most of the adult world, feared nuclear warfare was about to break out and we would all perish. Growing up in the era of nuclear fear was a frightening experience in which the sacred and timeless seemed insignificant against the seemingly imminent all-destroying powers of the bomb.

The response to this was twofold from a sacred perspective. Firstly, for many, a fear of the bomb led them to wish to run away. It was all too frightening, and the Cold War struggle between the West and the USSR caused many to despair of the world and to seek retreat. It is no accident that there was a rapid rise of retreat centres, places dedicated to reflective weekends or weeks, after the Second World War, as people sought to find peace and tranquillity as well as to deepen their spiritual quest. The rise of alternative movements in the 1950s and 1960s owes a great deal to the desire to want to do as the musical song said, 'Stop the world I want to get off'. A great many of the 'alternative' movements, including alternative religion or, as it prefers to describe itself, spirituality, arose from this desire to opt out and to be left alone.

The second way in which the sacred reacted to the new situation was to try to break the very forces of oppression, fear and violence that were likely to be the triggers that would launch the nuclear holocaust so many thought was imminent. The search for justice and equality which was so firmly rooted in the sacred of the late eighteenth century and the nineteenth century reached its climax after the Second World War with the creation of the welfare state and the National Health Service, and in the foundation of movements such as Oxfam, Christian Aid and, at a more personal level, the Samaritans.

For many, these were the fulfilment of Judeo-Christian ideals, and visions of the sacred right of all to health, education and security. Many Christians claimed the creation of the welfare state and the National Health Service as the two most Christian actions Britain had ever undertaken and the sacred nature of both should never be forgotten. Of all the many religious books written during the twentieth century, one of the most important and effective was a thin booklet written by the Archbishop of Canterbury, William Temple, in 1942. *Christianity and the Social Order* was the Church's contribution to a growing movement to enshrine basic human needs as sacred rights within Britain. It paralleled the Beveridge Report, which laid the foundations for the National Health Service and the welfare state. In it he said:

> The worst evil afflicting the working-class in England is insecurity; they live under the terrible menace of unemployment . . . Unemployment is a corrosive poison. It saps both physical and moral strength . . . Now it is no part of the duty of a Christian as such to draw plans of a reformed society. But it is part of his duty to know and proclaim Christian principles, to denounce as evil what contravenes them, and to insist that these evils should be remedied.[6]

The sacred duty of protecting the poor, defenceless and needy was at last being fulfilled. Today the social sacred world and the spiritual sacred world hardly ever come into contact. Those involved in the social sacred world of Christian Aid, Muslim Aid or the Catholic Fund for Overseas Development dismiss much of the alternative spiritual world and the newer religious movements as irredeemably self-centred, selfish, self-obsessed and thus of little real use or significance to the needs of ordinary people. There is some truth in this, but only some, for there can be no doubt that there are new religious expressions, new experiences and understandings of the sacred emerging in Britain today that can take their place alongside any of the great religious traditions of the past. As in the past, to a very great degree these are being spurred on by environmental concerns and the stresses and strains placed upon contemporary society by issues such as pollution, genetic engineering, climate change, disappearing habitats and so forth.

But there is a new dimension, one that has never before played such a significant role in the transformations of the sacred in Britain. Pluralism is now the norm. Everywhere, from the small market town to the cities, from school textbooks to the bookshops, from radio to television and films, the worlds of diverse beliefs are available as never before. It is as easy to buy a Tao Te Ching or the Koran as it is to buy the Bible. There are mosques, Sikh temples, Buddhist shrines, synagogues and sundry other religious places across the length and breadth of Britain. There are new pilgrimage paths for devout Buddhists, Muslims, Hindus and many others. This has become a sacred land for many faiths and cultures. It will shape the history, the sacred history and sacred landscape of Britain in the future as surely as the great faiths that have risen and fallen in the past. But none of these will become the dominant force, as there is now a real sense in which there is no dominant sacred myth or vision in Britain.

At the beginning of the third Christian millennium, what is the state of the sacred in Britain today? I would argue that it is complex and fluid, and that we have been here before.

Though we pride ourselves on being rational people, we still have to live mythologically. Everyone does, for as Jung put it so well, without a mythology of creation and purpose for ourselves in the midst of the universe 'we would be crushed by the sheer awe-ful-ness of the Universe'. Our problem is that we no longer inhabit just one or two major myths. In the nineteenth century, you basically had a choice between belief in the myth of science and progress, or the myth of evangelical salvation, for both of which the Empire could be understood as a consequence.

Today we lack what post-modernists call a mega-narrative, an overriding story that guides our lives. The basic Christian myth still trickles away under much of our culture, such as the stories from the Bible, liturgy, prayer and other such manifestations of belief, which have little or no place in the lives of the vast majority of people. Against this, science, once thought to be a serious contender for the place of new religion, has also failed.

It also runs as an undercurrent beneath our culture – evolution and psychological terminology. There is an abiding hope that science can perhaps solve crises such as the pollution of the environment. But as with Christianity, few place their hopes openly and completely in science compared with the late nineteenth century.

Even cynicism has its problems. One of my favourite bits of graffiti takes the existentialist angst of which the German philosopher Frederich Nietzsche was the most powerful exponent with his radical teaching that 'God was dead' as an idea and turns it upside down, ending with a splendidly British appraisal. The graffiti was in three different hands and represented a dialogue of sorts:

'God is dead – Nietzsche'
Underneath which was written:
'Nietzsche is dead – God'
Beneath which was scrawled:
'And I'm not feeling very well either – John'

I think that final line could act as the motto of our time. We are not feeling very well. We are not that much at ease with our world, for we have polluted and destroyed so much of it. We may be sitting on the edge of another ecological collapse which as we have seen from at least 5,000 years of our history always leads to massive changes in what we believe and do. We have learnt to voyage within through psychology and its attendant furies – psychoanalysis and psychotherapy – yet this has done little to make us better able to understand our world or even ourselves. We no longer live in a sacred world that owes its identity to just one faith tradition. Even the regular attendant at church, mosque or synagogue will have a world view shaped as much by secular forces and by models of the sacred derived from, say, yoga or alternative medicine as from Christianity or Islam. This produces extreme reactions from fundamentalists, as was clear in the bombing of the World Trade Center on 11 September 2001. But the future does not lie with them, certainly not within Britain, where the wariness of utopian ideologies still runs deep.

If I look back over the sacred history we have travelled through in this book, I think that our current state of mind, the current state of the sacred in Britain has very powerful similarities to at least three other eras. At its most gentle, it is similar to the collapse of the ancestor religion c. 3000 BC when the old stories ceased to make sense of the new realities. As a result, the ancestors were neatly packed away, for they were no longer relevant. Yet when the first stone circles began to be built, nostalgia resulted in the creation of mock tombs in the centre of the circles.

Maybe we are heading into or are already in a repeat of that most astonishing of eras, the period of apparent agnosticism from the fall of the stone circles to the coming of the Celtic influence – c. 1000–400 BC. This might seem rather extreme, for we still have our churches, temples, mosques and Buddhist centres unlike the fallen stones of the circles. But perhaps we are coasting on the remains of devotion and the initial upsurge of enthusiasm for newer faiths. Today, perhaps that coasting is coming to an end for we no longer have within much of our culture a familiarity with the conventions of religion – be that Christianity, Judaism, Islam or Buddhism. All these traditions are ceasing to function effectively, and what is taking their place is relatively piecemeal and haphazard.

Perhaps there is one final era from our past that gives us a hint of where we are now and what we can expect. After the Black Death, old certainties died but the structures continued and then either reinvented themselves or were replaced by Reformation Christianity – to all intents and purposes a new religion. The period from the mid-fourteenth to mid-seventeenth century was one of turmoil, diversity, protest, experimentation, false leads and dead ends. Slowly a new way of believing emerged which had to make sense of the continuity, albeit in a much reduced and altered form, of the older version of Christianity and of the rise of rationalism through the Renaissance and then Enlightenment. Pluralism has been a reality of the sacred in Britain since the mid-seventeenth century. It is this pluralism that perhaps more than anything will be the determining force of the sacred for the coming 100 years or so. Whether it will then produce something more all encompassing or whether it will create a new pluralist form of the sacred is one of the great questions confronting us.

I suspect that it will be many years before a new story comes to hold centre stage and it will do so only out of a crisis beyond our imagination. I am not being apocalyptic, just looking back at the way our sense of the sacred has always been fatally challenged and then changed by environmental and concomitant social forces of crisis. I have no idea what will eventually emerge, though I suspect it will contain strong elements of the mission faiths – Christianity, Islam, Buddhism – simply because they have the inherent ability to reinterpret themselves and make themselves relevant to the outside world as well as the inner world in ways that indigenous traditions – amongst which I would now include Wicca and neo-paganism – do not.

Meanwhile, the sacred continues to shape us even when we least expect it. It flows through the best of the social actions and concerns of our society. It moulds our understanding of our potential, and ourselves, yet it also reminds us of sin, foolishness and failure – unpopular ideas in a world of hype. The sacred will always surprise us, for just when we think we know what it is, it emerges in new forms or its influence upon us subconsciously manifests itself in ways we could never have expected.

The sacred in Britain is never going to die. Like the yew tree which, when the environmental conditions are not conducive to growth, can hibernate for up to 400 years until the conditions are right again, perhaps the sacred in Britain and indeed in much of the world is about to enter just such a phase. It will be hard for those who have to live through such times. For many there will not be a sense of loss because they do not have a sense of belonging to the sacred at present. For those to whom this matters, there will always be the faiths that we have, but their hold and relevance will never return to what they once were. Religion lives because it changes and the dynamism of that change is the ever-changing nature of our relationship with the sacred.

END NOTES

Chapter 2

1 Hutton dates this as 25,000 BC (*The Pagan Religions of the Ancient British Isles*, Blackwells, Oxford 1991: 2), and in correspondence with the author says that this is now generally accepted.

2 See, for example, Jean-Marie Chauvet, Eliette Brunel Deschamps and Christian Hilliare, *Chauvet Cave*, Thames and Hudson, London 1996.

3 On the Chinese literary sources, see *Shi Jing* (The Book of Songs), which has poems dating from the tenth century BC and the later *Chu Ci* (Songs of Chu) dating from *c.* 400 BC; both contain poems deriving from Shamanic chants that refer to the bear cult. In particular, see the translation of *Chu Ci* entitled *The Songs of the South*, by David Hawkes, Penguin, London 1985; on p. 129, this contains an account of the transformation of the great shaman Gun into a brown bear by other shamans. More generally on the bear cult see, for example, imaginative reconstructions in Jean Auel's *Clan of the Cave Bear* or the role-playing supplement *GURPS Ice Age*.

4 See, for example, G.R. Levy, *The Gate of Horn*, Faber, London 1963: 22–3, 43; or Anne Baring and Jules Cashford, *The Myth of the Goddess*, Arkana, London 1993.

5 Dr. Michael Rappenglueck of the University of Munich claims to have found a map of the Pleiades cluster in the shaft known as the 'Dead Man' in the Lascaux Caves in France. However, the jury is still out on this, and even if the Pleiades are mapped, this is a standout case both in the poverty of the actual artwork and in the fact that no sun or moon, let alone graphic depiction of a star, has yet been found.

6 Margaret Anderson, in personal correspondence with the author, refers to her grandmother (1874–1965), who claimed this was the case.

7 Aubrey Burl, *Rites of the Gods*, J.M. Dent & Sons, London 1981: 47; Hutton 1991: 21.

8 Nigel Saul (general editor), *Historical Atlas of Britain – Prehistoric and Medieval*, Alan Sutton Publishing, London 1994: 7. See also Clive Ponting, *A Green History of the World*, Sinclair-Stevenson Ltd., London 1991.
9 Ponting 1991: 69.
10 Robert Bewley, *Prehistoric Settlements*, B.T. Batsford, London 1994: 30.

Chapter 3

1 Hutton 1991: 14.
2 Aubrey Burl, *A Guide to the Stone Circles of Britain, Ireland and Brittany*, Yale University Press, New Haven 1995: 74.
3 On Greece, see H.D.F. Kitto, *The Greeks*, Penguin, London 1991: 76–7. For China, see Martin Palmer, Jay Ramsay and Zhao Xiaomin, *I Ching*, Thorsons, London 1995: 7–8.
4 Most of the information given here is derived from Christopher Chippendale, *Stonehenge Complete*, Thames and Hudson, London 1994, and Burl 1995 and Hutton 1991.
5 Hutton 1991: 138.

Chapter 4

1 Wendy O'Flaherty (translator), *Rig Veda*, Penguin, London 1981: 150–1, 161.
2 I am grateful to Gordon McClennan for pointing this out in correspondence.
3 For the 'invasion' of Celtic peoples into Britain, see Frank Delaney, *The Celts*, Hodder & Stoughton/BBC, Routledge, London 1996, or Prudence Jones and Nigel Pennick, *A History of Pagan Europe*, London 1995. Against such an 'invasion', see the very succinct summary of views in Barry Cunliffe, *Iron Age British History*, B.T. Batsford, London 1995: 19–24, or John Cannon (editor), *Celts* in *The Oxford Companion to British History*, Oxford University Press, Oxford 1997: 181–2.
4 Hilary Sumner-Boyd and John Freely, *Strolling Through Istanbul*, KPI Paperbacks, London 1987: 125–6.
5 Tacitus, *Annals* xiv. 30, translated by Michael Grant, Penguin, London 1971.
6 Comment made at a public meeting in July 2000 and amplified in correspondence with the author.
7 For example, the present-day Holywood near Dumfries, which may recall the great sacred forest in that region known as the Medionemeton, the name Derry, which seems to indicate an oak grove, or Druid's Grove at Newlands Corner, Surrey. See Martin and Nigel Palmer, *Sacred Britain*, Piatkus, London 1997: 27, 98, and also Andrew M. Currie, *Dictionary of British Place Names*, Tiger Books, London 1994.
8 Lucan, *De Bello Civilis*, iii. 399–400, 411–12 in James Rattue, *The Living Stream*, Boydell Press, Suffolk 1995: quoted on p. 23.

Chapter 5

1 Kenneth Cameron, 'Eccles in English Place-Names', in M.W. Barley and R.P.C. Hanson (editors), *Christianity in Britain: 300–700 AD*, Leicester University Press, Leicester 1968.

2 Robert Young, *Analytical Concordance to the Holy Bible*, Lutterworth Press, London 1973: 171.
3 Richard Morris, *Churches in the Landscape*, Phoenix, London 1997: 20–5, 30–5.
4 Ronald Hutton's essay, in Philip Carr-Gomm (editor), *The Druid Renaissance*, Thorsons, London 1996: 28–9.
5 Martin Palmer, *The Jesus Sutras*, Piatkus, London 2001.
6 B.R. Rees, *Pelagius – A Reluctant Heretic*, The Boydell Press, Woodbridge 1988: especially p. xii.
7 Bede, *A History of the English Church and People*, translated by Leo Sherley-Rice, revised by R.E. Latham, Penguin, London 1968: 49–50.
8 Bede 1968: 58.
9 Bede 1968: 59.
10 Bede 1968: 59–60.
11 I am grateful to the staff of the Whithorn Museum and their splendid talks and displays for much of the information in this section. See also Andrew Patterson, *A Way to Whithorn*, St Andrew's Press, Edinburgh 1933, for further details. My thanks to Andrew for the many days of walking and talking that inform this section.
12 Sister Joan Chittister OSB, 'Monasticism: an ancient answer to modern problems', in Martin Palmer and Elizabeth Brueilly (editors), *Christianity and Ecology*, Cassells, London 1992.
13 Eric S. Wood, *Collins Field Guide to Archaeology in Britain*, Collins, London 1979: 118. See also *The Ordinance Survey: Ancient Britain*, 1990.
14 Hutton 1991: 257–64. For a somewhat more critical summary of the end of paganism and the role of Christianity in Britain, see Christina Oakley's article in Philip Carr-Gomm 1996: 260.
15 In particular, the somewhat eccentric theories of Margaret Murray, which claimed that witchcraft was a surviving popular pagan religion, have been discredited. For this and other claims of pagan survival, see Hutton 1991: Chapter 8; Hugh Trevor-Roper (a former believer in Murray's thesis), *The European Witch Craze of the Sixteenth and Seventeenth Centuries*, Penguin, London 1990, first published in 1970: 11–14; Keith Thomas, *Religion and the Decline of Magic*, Penguin, London 1991; Karen Louise Jolly, *Popular Religion in Late Saxon England*, The University of North Carolina Press, Chapel Hill 1996.
16 Jolly 1996: 173–4.
17 H.T. Timmins, *Nooks and Corners of Shropshire*, Lapridge Publications, Hereford 1993, original version 1899: 216.
18 Geoffrey of Monmouth, *The History of the Kings of Britain*, translated by Lewis Thorpe, Penguin, London 1966: 187–8.
19 Bede 1968: 57.

Chapter 6

1 John Julius Norwich, *Byzantium – The Early Centuries*, Penguin, London 1990: 233.
2 Bede 1968: 54.
3 Llandaff Charters: 75.
4 I am indebted to G.H. Doble's *Lives of the Welsh Saints*, edited by D. Simon Evans, University of Wales Press, Cardiff 1971, for much of the basic information in this section.

5 See Thomas Cahill, *How the Irish Saved Civilization*, Anchor Books, New York 1955, for a wider discussion of this.
6 Robert van de Weyer, *Celtic Fire*, Dartman, Longman and Todd, London 1990.
7 Doble 1971: 42.
8 See Malcolm Seaborne, *Celtic Crosses*, Shire Publications, Aylesbury 1994, and J. Romily Allen, *Celtic Crosses of Wales*, J.M.F. Bookbinding Services, Llanerch 1989, first published in 1899.
9 Patterson 1933: 54.
10 For details on Iona, see Peter W. Millar, *Iona*, Canterbury Press, Norwich 1997.
11 Adomnan of Iona, *Life of St. Columba*, translated by Richard Sharpe, Penguin, London 1995: 104–5.
12 Adomnan of Iona 1995: 105–6.
13 For instance, in the sixteenth-century *Life of St. Columba*, by Manus O'Donnell.
14 Adomnan of Iona 1995: 224.

Chapter 7

1 Gale R. Owen, *Rites and Religions of the Anglo-Saxons*, Barnes and Noble, New York 1996, first published in 1981: 8–9, 23–4; Peter Hunter Blair, *An Introduction to Anglo-Saxon England*, Cambridge University Press, Cambridge 1970, first published in 1956: 238–9.
2 Webb, J.F. (translator), D.H. Farmer (editor), *The Age of Bede*, Penguin, London 1983: 51–2. See also Martin and Nigel Palmer, *Sacred Britain*, Piatkus, London 1997: 152–3.
3 Kenneth Hurlestone Jackson, *A Celtic Miscellany*, Penguin, London 1951: 279–80.
4 Webb and Farmer 1983: 66.
5 Bede 1968: 66.
6 Bede 1968: 102.
7 Bede 1968: 103.
8 Bede 1968: 186.
9 Bede 1968: 192.
10 John Prebble, *The Lion in the North*, Penguin, London 1972, first published in 1971: 35, 49.

Chapter 8

1 Owen 1996: 43–6.
2 Bede 1968: 127.
3 Author's own translation.
4 For discussion of this see Paul Cavill, *Anglo-Saxon Christianity*, Fount, London 1999: 133–43, and Owen 1996: 11.
5 Bede 1968: 332.
6 Eric John, *Reassessing Anglo-Saxon England*, Manchester University Press, Manchester 1996: 23.
7 *The Anglo-Saxon Chronicle*, translated and edited by Michael Swanton, J.M. Dent, London 1996: 55, 57.
8 For this section, see John Marsden, *The Fury of the Northmen*, Kyle Cathie, London 1994.

9 *Alfred the Great – Asser's Life of Alfred the Great and Other Contemporary Sources*, translated and introduced by Simon Keynes and Michael Lapidge, Penguin, London 1983: 211–12.
10 *Asser* 1983: 103.
11 *The Anglo-Saxon Chronicle* 1996: 114–15.
12 Donald Atwater, *A Dictionary of Saints*, Penguin, London 1965: 108.
13 Owen 1996: 176.

Chapter 9

1 James Bruce Ross and Mary Martin McLaughlin (editors), *The Portable Medieval Reader*, Penguin, New York 1977, first published in 1949: William of Malmsebury quote on pp. 407–8.
2 *Alfred the Great*, translated by Simon Keynes and Michael Lapidge, Penguin, London 1983: 174.
3 Ross and McLaughlin 1977: 233–4.
4 Ross and McLaughlin 1977: 408.
5 Ross and McLaughlin 1977: 409.
6 *The Anglo-Saxon Chronicle* 1996: 220–1.
7 I am indebted to John Davies, *A History of Wales*, Penguin, London 1994, first published in Welsh as *Hanes Cymru* in 1990, for much of the information in this section.
8 Doble 1971: 207–9.

Chapter 10

1 Quoted in Elizabeth Hallam (editor), *The Plantagenet Chronicles*, Tiger Books, London 1995: 112.
2 Ross and McLaughlin 1977: 360.
3 Ross and McLaughlin 1977: 249.
4 Eamon Duffy, *The Stripping of the Altars*, Yale University Press, New Haven 1992: 279.
5 Ronald C. Finucane, *Miracles and Pilgrims – Popular Beliefs in Medieval England*, St. Martin's Press, New York 1995, first published in 1977: 163.
6 Robin R. Mundill, *England's Jewish Solution*, Cambridge University Press, Cambridge 1998: 16–17.
7 For the Crusades, see Stephen Runciman, *A History of the Crusades*, 3 vols, Penguin, London 1951, and Donald E. Quellet and Thomas F. Madden, *The Fourth Crusade*, University of Pennsylvania Press, Philadelphia 1997.
8 Colin Platt, *The Abbeys and Priories of Medieval England*, Chancellor Press, London 1995, first published in 1984: 62.

Chapter 11

1 Philip Ziegler, *The Black Death*, Penguin, London 1998, first published in 1969: quoted on p. 192.

2 Ziegler 1998: 139.
3 Ross and McLaughlin 1977: quoted on p. 218.
4 Ross and McLaughlin 1977: 219.
5 William Langland, *Piers Plowman*, translated by A.V.C. Schmidt, Oxford University Press, Oxford 1992: 96.
6 Philippe Aries, *The Hour of Our Death*, Barnes and Noble, New York 2000, first published in 1981: 124.
7 Eamon Duffy, *The Stripping of the Altars*, Yale University Press, New Haven 1992: 101.
8 Geoffrey Chaucer, *The Canterbury Tales*, rendered into modern English by Nevill Coghill, Penguin, London 1978, first published in 1951: 197, 200.
9 Keith Thomas, *Religion and the Decline of Magic*, Penguin, London 1991, first published in 1971: quoted on p. 58.
10 From Wycliffe's translation of the Bible, *c.* 1380, in *The English Hexapla*, published by Samuel Bagster and Sons, London 1845.

Chapter 12

1 Gerald of Wales, *The Journey through Wales/The Description of Wales*, translated by Lewis Thorpe, Penguin, London 1978: 117–18.
2 Geoffrey of Monmouth, *The History of the Kings of Britain*, translated by Lewis Thorpe, Penguin, London 1966: 171.
3 I am indebted to David Rees and his fascinating book, *The Son of Prophecy: Henry Tudor's Road to Bosworth*, John Jones, Ruthin 1993, for much of the information in this section.
4 Rees 1993: 23.
5 For example, Michael Baigent, Henry Lincoln and Richard Leigh, *Holy Blood, Holy Grail*, Dell, New York 1983, and Michael Bradley, *Holy Grail Across the Atlantic*, Hounslow 1999.

Chapter 13

1 See, for example, Eamon Duffy, *The Stripping of the Altars*, Part I, Yale University Press, New Haven 1992.
2 J.J. Scarisbrick, *Henry VIII*, Methuen, London 1976: 152–61.
3 Diarmaid MacCulloch, *Tudor Church Militant*, Penguin, London 1999: Chapter 1; W.J. Sheild, 'Reformed Religion in England', in Sheridan Gilley and W.J. Sheild (editors), *A History of Religion in Britain*, Blackwell, Oxford 1994.
4 Colin Platt, *The Abbeys and Priories of Medieval England*, Chancellor Press, London 1995: Chapter 8. For particular accounts, see W.F. Mumford, *Wenlock in the Middle Ages*, Mumford, Harlescot 1977: Chapter 6; and Peter Bishop, *The Sacred and Profane History of Bury St. Edmunds*, Unicorn Press, 1998: Chapter 4.
5 Duffy 1992: 478–503.
6 John Binns and Peter Meadows (editors), *Great St. Mary's: Cambridge's University Church*, Cambridge 2000: 25.
7 Duffy 1992: 37–40.
8 See, for example, Peter Mullen, *Shrines of Our Lady*, Piatkus, London 1998: 47–68.

9 See, for example, Francis Jones, *The Holy Wells of Wales*, University of Wales Press, Cardiff 1992, first published in 1954: Chapter 4.
10 Jonathan Spence, *Mao*, Weidenfeld and Nicholson, London 1999: 177.
11 MacCulloch 1999: 134–5.
12 Gilley and Sheils 1994: 79.
13 Thomas 1991: 540.
14 H.R. Trevor-Roper, *The European Witch Craze of the Sixteenth and Seventeenth Centuries*, Penguin, London 1990, first published in 1970: 11–12.

Chapter 14

1 Jeremy Taylor, *The Rules and Exercises of Holy Living*, Griffith, Farran, Okeden & Welsh, London, first published in 1650: 167.
2 Martin E. Marty, *Pilgrims in Their Own Land*, Penguin, New York 1985: Chapter 6.
3 W. Clark Gilpin, *The Millenarian Piety of Roger Williams*, University of Chicago Press, Chicago 1979: quoted on p. 50.
4 Christopher Hill, *Puritanism and Revolution*, Panther, London 1968, first published in 1958: Chapter 3; and Christopher Hill, *The World Turned Upside Down*, Pelican, London 1975: Chapter 7.
5 From Yeovil Parish Church, Somerset, A.B. Connor, *Monumental Brasses of Somerset*, Kingsmead Reprints, Bath 1970: quoted on p. 78.
6 Connor 1970: 331–2.
7 T.S. Healy (editor), *Ignatius His Conclave*, Oxford University Press, Oxford 1969: 15.
8 Hill 1975: 110–11.
9 Prebble 1972: 242.
10 John Latimer (editor), *Annals of Bristol*, William George, Bristol 1900: 269–70.
11 David Cressy and Lori Anne Ferrell (editors), *Religion and Society in Early Modern England*, Routledge, London 1996: 185.
12 Rena Gardiner, *The Story of Norwich Cathedral*, Workshop Press, Blandford Forum 1987.

Chapter 15

1 J.M. Cohen and M.J. Cohen, *The New Penguin Dictionary of Quotations*, Penguin, London 1993: 258.
2 This can be found in all its bizarre glory at http://www.chick.com/reading/books/1581/158cont.asp.
3 B. Kennett and W. Borham, *A Brief Exposition of the Apostles Creed According to Bishop Pearson*, John Knapton, London 1726: iii, iv.
4 Rupert E. Davies, *Methodism*, Penguin, London 1963: 58.
5 Owd Mo, *From Coal-pit to Joyful News Mission*, Thomas Champness, London, n.d.: 7.
6 A. R. Peacock, *Creation and the World of Science*, Clarendon Press, Oxford 1979: quoted on p. 5.
7 Stuart Piggott, *Ancient Britons and the Antiquarian Imagination*, Thames and Hudson, London 1989: 145.
8 Piggott 1989: 115.

Chapter 16

1 *A History of the Expansion of Christianity – The Great Century*, Harper and Brothers, New York 1944: 440.

2 Morris 1995: 439.

3 From 'Life and Works of the Seventh Earl Shaftesbury', London 1889, in Barbara W. Tuchman, *Bible and Sword*, Macmillan, London 1982, first published in 1952: quoted on p. 177.

4 Anthony Burton, *William Cobbett: Englishman*, Aurum Press, London 1997: quoted on p. 213.

5 From 'The Christian Socialist Movement in England', by Gilbert Clive Binyon, in Stephen Mayor, *The Churches and the Labour Movement*, Independent Press, London 1967: quoted on p. 67.

6 J.G. Farrell, *The Siege of Krishnapur*, Fontana, London 1985.

7 Patrick French, *Younghusband*, Flamingo, London 1995: quoted on p. 8. This is a splendid book, which casts many a light upon this extraordinary period.

8 James Morris, *Heaven's Command*, Penguin, London 1995: quoted on p. 39. The title of this book itself illustrates the point I am making.

9 John Keay, *Last Post – the End of Empire in the Far East*, John Murray, London 1997: quoted on p. 69.

10 Ruskin's Inaugural Lecture as Slade Professor of Fine Art at Oxford, 1870.

11 Revd James Gardner, *The Faiths of the World*, Division 1, A. Fullerton, London, n.d.

12 Lord Macauley, *The History of England*, Penguin, London 1986, first published in 1848.

13 Revd J.G. Woods, *The Natural History of Man*, vol. 1, George Routledge and Sons, London 1870: 1.

14 Morris 1995: 329.

15 *Sacred Books of the East*, vol. xii, translated by Julius Eggeling, Clarendon Press, Oxford 1882.

16 French 1995: quoted on p. 284.

17 General Booth, *In Darkest England and the Way Out*, Salvation Army, London 1890: 16.

Chapter 17

1 J. Ramsay Macdonald M.P., *The Socialist Movement*, William and Norgate, London 1912: 248.

2 V. I. Lenin, *What Is To Be Done?*, USSR, 1968: quoted on p. 5.

3 Frederick Engels, *The Condition of the Working Class in England*, Panther, London 1969, first published in 1892: 95.

4 Cecil Wightwick Haywood, *How God Won the War*, R.S. Hart Publisher, Farnham 1935: 10.

5 Vivianne Crowley, *Phoenix from the Flame*, Aquarian, London 1994: 255.

6 William Temple, *Christianity and the Social Order*, Penguin, London 1942.

INDEX